Among Murderers

Among Murderers

Life after Prison

SABINE HEINLEIN

UNIVERSITY OF CALIFORNIA PRESS

Berkeley Los Angeles London

University of California Press, one of the most
distinguished university presses in the United
States, enriches lives around the world by advancing
scholarship in the humanities, social sciences, and
natural sciences. Its activities are supported by the
UC Press Foundation and by philanthropic contributions from individuals and institutions. For more
information, visit www.ucpress.edu.

University of California Press
Berkeley and Los Angeles, California

University of California Press, Ltd.
London, England

Library of Congress Cataloging-in-Publication Data

Heinlein, Sabine 1973-.
    Among murderers : life after prison / Sabine Heinlein.
        p.   cm.
    Includes bibliographical references.
    ISBN 978-0-520-27285-9 (cloth : alk. paper)
    1. Criminals—Rehabilitation—United States—Case
studies.   I. Title.
    HV9304.H45   2013
    364.80973—dc23   2012025825

Manufactured in the United States of America

22   21   20   19   18   17   16   15   14   13
10   9   8   7   6   5   4   3   2   1

In keeping with a commitment to support environmentally responsible and sustainable printing
practices, UC Press has printed this book on Natures
Natural, a fiber that contains 30% post-consumer
waste and meets the minimum requirements of
ANSI/NISO Z39.48-1992 (R 1997) (*Permanence of
Paper*).

To Giovanni García-Fenech

CONTENTS

ACKNOWLEDGMENTS

Angel, Adam, and Bruce: I am indebted to you for your openness, your honesty, your courage, and the endless hours you spent with me. Thank you!

Thanks also to the Fortune Society, its clients and staff, for opening your doors: Barry Campbell, JoAnne Page, David Rothenberg, Rene Sing, and "Rich Stone," as well as the many others who were willing to share your experiences and expertise.

I am grateful to Mae Dick and all the Quakers in Rochester and at the Attica Correctional Facility, particularly Richard Robles, whose frequent letters provided crucial insight from behind bars.

When you begin your career as a writer, you are often warned of the loneliness it requires. You rarely hear of the many friends and colleagues who are there to help. A million thanks to Robert Boynton, in whose class the seeds of this project were planted and who has been an avid supporter from beginning to end. David Samuels, thanks for helping me hear my own voice—and for never mincing words. Erin Soros, thank you so much for inviting me to read from my manuscript at the University of East Anglia. I am grateful to Ted Hamm from the *Brooklyn Rail* for publishing my first stories about society's outcasts and to Karol Nielsen and Willard Cook from *Epiphany* for publishing an early excerpt from this book. Thanks also to Ted Conover, who gave instrumental advice after reading an early draft.

I am grateful to Roxana Robinson for her support and to Sam Swope for taking the time to review with me each chapter of this book for several hours in the very (!) early morning.

The evenings of food, drinks, and laughter with Carrie Villines, Rachel Stevens, and Leslie Hutchings helped me to get up the next day and continue my work. Franziska Lamprecht, please never stop visiting me when I least expect it. I so very much appreciated Josh Weinstein's afternoon visits, which invariably turned into hours of inspiring conversation. Thank you to Melissa Dunn for helping me think when I couldn't think anymore and to Deborah Lutz for being an excellent reader and much-appreciated supporter. I am grateful to Karl Monger for valuable editorial input on an early draft and to Alexandra Zendrian for her help with transcriptions. I am indebted to Bill Dineen, whose "life should be good" made all the difference in the world, and to Simon Eskow, who listened and cheered me on and up when I most needed it.

I am also grateful to Glenn Martin, Ronald Mincy, Devah Pager, Gabriel Torres-Rivera, Jeremy Travis, and—most of all—Edward Latessa, each of whom took time out from their busy schedules to discuss the challenges of reentry and rehabilitation with me. Many important thoughts were formed as a result of these conversations.

Many thanks to the Corporation of Yaddo, the MacDowell Colony, the New York Foundation for the Arts, and the Margolis Award for understanding my work and providing me with financial support, time, and space.

Thanks are also due to Rachel Berchten, Stacy Eisenstark, Chris Lura, Alison Mudditt, and Naomi Schneider of UC Press for guiding the book through its various production stages. Joe Abbott did a magnificent copyediting job, saving me many embarrassments.

And finally, if I had to name one person whose intelligence, love, enthusiasm, support, humor, and ideas made the writing of this book possible, it would be my husband, Giovanni García-Fenech. Thank you for never saying no when asked to read the same section for the one hundredth time and for believing in me like no one had ever believed in me before.

Acknowledgments

By talking and hanging out with murderers, child molesters, burglars, drug dealers, and robbers, I entered a parallel world unfamiliar to most of us. Although these former criminals are among us, our lives rarely intersect. What is life like for those who have spent several decades in prison and are released into a world in which people and places they once knew have ceased to exist? What is it like to start over from nothing? And did prison succeed in making them see the error of their ways?

I was still working on my master's degree at New York University's Carter Journalism Institute when I set out to learn how New York's growing net of reentry organizations helps former prisoners ease back into freedom. The goal of these agencies is to rehabilitate their clients—to restore their livelihoods and prevent them from going back to prison. After spending large parts of their lives locked up, these men and women need a roof over their heads, medical care, and a job—any job, really.

In 2007 I began to attend reentry events where advocates, ex-cons, and their family members discussed the challenges of life after prison. I talked to the clients and staff of reentry organizations with Pollyanna-ish names like STRIVE (Support and Training Results in Valuable Employees), CEO (Center for Employment Opportunities), and the Fortune Society. Most clients of the Fortune Society, STRIVE, and CEO were people with extensive rap sheets—and most were out of luck. Few had ever learned to strive for anything, and it is safe to assume that they will never become CEOs. What they needed most was individual attention and love.

One man I spoke to had forgotten how to turn on a faucet after living in a prison cell for twenty years. When I accompanied another recently released man on his walk through the city, he almost got run over when crossing the street, not once but five times in half an hour. His sense of public space had atrophied so completely that whenever he managed to avoid the traffic, he bumped into other pedestrians. I once tried to show yet another ex-offender how to turn on a PC, go online, and check his emails. It would have been easier to teach a child how to drive a car. Freedom was a relief, surely, but it was also a challenge. It wasn't something that could simply be embraced. The men had to painstakingly learn how to master this freedom. I noticed that no one had ever addressed those seemingly minor obstacles of prisoner rehabilitation and reintegration; this is how the idea for this book came into being.

A growing number of reentry organizations backed by public and private funds have tried to smooth the individual's return to society. In the last decade reentry has become a hot-button topic. Reentry resource centers, reentry round tables, reentry institutes, and reentry initiatives have popped up across the country. The work of advocates and legislators has yielded impressive results: The Second Chance Act was signed into law in 2008. Aimed at improving the lives of ex-offenders, it authorizes federal grants to government agencies and nonprofit organizations for employment assistance, substance-abuse treatment, housing, family programs, mentoring, victims' support, and other services that may help reduce recidivism. In 2009 New York's tough drug laws, which had been signed into law by Governor Nelson Rockefeller in 1973, were revised to remove mandatory minimum sentences.

But despite the reentry movement's recent successes, the term *reentry* sounds like wishful thinking. At the reentry meetings I listened to advocates endlessly introduce services, strategies, and legislative goals. At the end of these lectures a man or woman of color would usually stand up, trying to share his or her sad life story. "I just came home after serving fifteen [or twenty or thirty] years," the person would begin before spiraling into a rambling tale of alienation. Eventually someone from the panel would cut off the speaker, leaving the rest of the story unheard.

Naturally, the phenomenon of ex-prisoners attempting to become part of our society begged for a name, but "reentry" seemed hopelessly removed from what it really meant to be released from prison. There was nothing guided or measured about becoming part of mainstream society. Besides, did these men and women really succeed in "reentering" our world?

In 2009 almost 730,000 people were released from U.S. prisons.[1] Many ex-prisoners return to the same crime-ridden and impoverished neighborhoods that raised them, and a very select few find permanent employment. Two-thirds of them land back in prison.[2]

Incarceration affects a disproportionate number of men of color. More than half of all incarcerated men are African Americans, and greater than 20 percent are Hispanics.[3]

These harrowing statistics and my own personal experiences with ex-prisoners and reentry organizations made me wonder: How can we rehabilitate these disenfranchised masses? How do contemporary institutions approach rehabilitation, and what role does the general public play in this process? Few of us consider the individual who bears the brunt of this burden. What attempts at rehabilitation does the ex-prisoner himself (or herself) make? How do ex-prisoners learn to navigate their freedom? What resources can they count on, and what obstacles do they encounter? While society may be comfortable talking about racial and social disparities in the abstract (or in public policy terms), in this book I talk about these issues by looking at real human beings who have faced the challenges of reentry.

Besides the commonly cited objective of reducing recidivism, no one discusses what constitutes successful rehabilitation. Is it simply a matter of keeping an individual out of prison and of finding him or her a job? We will see that this issue encompasses a number of mundane aspects, as well as several significant moral ones. The life stories of the three men of color, men who spent several decades in prison for murder and were released into the hands of the Fortune Society in 2007, illuminate these complex questions.[4]

CONNECTING

I must have interviewed at least fifty former prisoners before I finally found a subject: Angel Ramos. Angel's horrific crimes and his extraordinary journey to freedom, his willingness to let me accompany him to his programs and to share with me even the most mundane details of his life, made him a perfect subject for this book.

Angel was released in March 2007 after having served twenty-nine years in prison. At eighteen years old he had taken one life and nearly two others. After he was caught, he tried to escape from New York's Rikers Island. Considering his journey, he was remarkably upbeat and optimistic. Most important, maybe, wherever he went, people seemed to like him. A short, sturdy man, Angel was of Puerto Rican descent and had grown up in East Harlem, the neighborhood where he committed his most heinous crime. He had smooth brown skin; a mustache; and short, curly hair. He often wore a dark suit, a bright shirt, and a wildly patterned tie. Angel was witty and charming, and he looked at the world with wide eyes. He thought of himself as someone special, someone whose story needed to be told.

Shortly after his release, Angel met Adam and Bruce at a halfway house, and the three became friends. They had few things in common beyond the fact that they were intelligent men of color who had served several decades behind bars for murder.

In his early seventies, Adam had spent thirty-one years in prison for murder, robbery, conspiracy, and an attempted escape. He was released in April 2007, one month after Angel. I first saw Adam at one of the many reentry events he attended. Although I don't remember the particulars of the event, I do remember his presence. His forehead was deeply furrowed. His graceful posture, gray beard, and thinly framed glasses lent him an aura of wisdom and respect. To me he looked more like a retired sociology professor or a famous jazz musician than an ex-con. Despite his solemn disposition, he often broke out in spontaneous laughter. While genuine, his laughter was also deceiving. Right at the start Adam told me that he had difficulties taking off his "prison armor." He couldn't "find the zipper." However much he tried, Adam couldn't find his way "home."

In May 2007 Bruce joined Angel and Adam at the Castle, a West Harlem halfway house founded by the Fortune Society. When he was in his late twenties, Bruce shot a stranger following an argument; he spent twenty-four years in prison. Bruce is the most introverted of the three men. Compared to Angel and Adam, he is intimidatingly tall. Trying to make himself look shorter, he walks with a slight hunch. His head is always shaved smooth. At his height, who would want to add an extra inch? He often wears a baseball hat that looks comically small on his large head. Try as he might to appear shorter, he remains six foot six. Bruce is quiet and reserved. He speaks primarily when addressed and even then only sparingly. Bruce seems to have few illusions about life yet strides ahead with surprising balance.

Angel, Bruce, and Adam began their new life at the Fortune Society's Castle. A prominent reentry organization in New York, Fortune, as it is commonly known, has been around since 1968 and has helped thousands of former prisoners navigate the welfare system and find housing and work. In three New York locations Fortune offers a variety of services, including computer tutoring, substance-abuse treatment, cooking classes, and father- and motherhood programs.

Angel, Bruce, Adam, and I are as different as can be. I grew up in an upper-middle-class family in a suburb of a Bavarian city not much bigger than the suburb itself. I moved to Hamburg right after high school and immigrated to the United States in 2001. When I was growing up, the darkest shade of skin in my town was that of the two dozen gypsies that camped out on a field at the city limits for a few weeks every year. The common opinion among the permanent residents was that the gypsies were liars and criminals. Clearly, the gypsies didn't *want* to integrate. Unhappy with the little town's rigidity and impregnability, my mother instilled in me a sense of doubt in stereotypes. At an early age I learned to defeat my fear of the "other" through curiosity. So in a sense, my work as a journalist is a response to my mother's desire to break out of her small world and broaden her view.

As an adult I realized that part of this childhood "exercise" called for the augmentation of empathy for people who can't find empathy from society at large. However naive or impossible it may seem, I wondered what would happen if empathy was our first response to people who find themselves at the margins. (Later I learned that there actually is a movement named "journalism of empathy." Ted Conover, the author of *Newjack*, has taught a course by that name at NYU, as did Alex Kotlowitz, the author of *There Are No Children Here*, at Northwestern University.)[5] In my career as a journalist I have spent time with all kinds of people—homeless alcoholics, people with mental illnesses, blind teenagers, clowns, and fortune-tellers, to name just a few. I didn't *like* or agree with every individual I met, but without empathy I would have never been able to understand them. I think we can learn to respect each other, even while admitting our ambivalence or disapproval.

WHY MURDERERS?

In terms of empathy, murderers are obviously very low (if not lowest) on our list of priorities. Murder is universally considered the most serious crime of all, and the violent loss of a human life inflicts endless grief on the victim's relatives and friends. It is hard to look a murderer in the face. It is infinitely more comfortable to reduce murderers to numbers than to try to understand their lives. Yet considering the rising number of murderers being released from prison, it becomes harder and harder to turn away.

New York's murder rates have decreased dramatically over the last decades. In 2007 the rate had dropped to fewer than five hundred killings a year, its lowest point in more than forty years. But forty years ago murder rates in the city began to rise. (In 1971, for example, 1,466 were killed in the city, and in 1990 the murder rate peaked at 2,245.)[6] My main characters all committed their killings at a time when these statistics were escalating. After serving twenty, thirty, or even forty years in prison, the murderers are returning home to a culture less inured to their crimes.

Given my goal of displaying the different dimensions of rehabilitation, I became particularly interested in people who had spent large parts of their lives behind bars. An extreme crime with an extreme sentence most clearly highlights the issues with which ex-cons commonly struggle, and the longer a person has been imprisoned, the more overwhelming freedom becomes. An extreme crime and an extreme sentence require more complex individual, institutional, and societal strategies of rehabilitation.

One issue that came to interest me in particular is the moral ramifications of murder. No other crime is so transformative, inside and out. Angel once said to me, "Murder is the ultimate crime. Victim and murderer both can't recover." His comment made me wonder whether a murderer can ever be fully rehabilitated. We will see that a murderer's rehabilitation may or may not involve a lifelong struggle with guilt and with society's inability to forgive. My subjects' stories demonstrate that murderers return to our society with a huge amount of psychological baggage and that attempts at rehabilitation and integration put an enormous strain on private and public agencies, on families, and on the individuals themselves.

Although there are many academic studies, memoirs, and journalistic accounts exploring the long-lasting consequences of violent acts on victims, there is little information on the effects that crime and long-term incarceration have on the murderer and on the society to which he or she returns. And to take a step back: murder rarely happens without forewarning. Through three individual narratives my book shows that there are a slew of predictors leading up to the crime. These predictors, in turn, provide important clues about how such a murder could have been prevented. While individuals, family, school, community, and society may have failed at prevention, the examples in this book might help us understand what is necessary for a criminal's rehabilitation. As such, rehabilitation is linked to the criminal's life before prison.

From a public policy perspective alone, it seems obvious that we should care about the 730,000 men and women released from prison each year. If millions of Americans were affected with a dangerous virus that cost us billions of tax dollars, destroyed families and livelihoods, and left a large part of the population homeless and mentally ill, no one would question the government's attempt to find a long-lasting solution. I think we should care about Adam, Bruce, and Angel not only because their stories illustrate the outcomes of applied public policy and criminal justice but because they address our values as human beings and as a collective society. Who deserves forgiveness, and who is willing to forgive? Do we consider punishment temporary or eternal? Should our personal history ameliorate the consequences of our errors? How much can we blame our parents and our environment for our missteps as adults? These vital questions pertain to all of us. I wrestle directly with these questions through the detailed psychological portraits I have drawn of Angel, Bruce, and Adam and show that one answer doesn't suffice.

Rather, each individual deserves his or her own consideration and set of complex answers.

OF REHAB—AND CORRECTIONAL QUACKERY

This is neither a book of public policy nor one of criminal justice. It is a work of literary nonfiction that delves into the everyday lives and emotional struggles of three formerly incarcerated individuals. It explores their journeys to freedom and their various modes of rehabilitation. Not wanting to interrupt the narrative flow, I decided to deliver a brief excursion into America's conflicting philosophies of crime and punishment here.[7] Through their rehabilitative paths, Angel, Bruce, and Adam illustrate and enrich the theories that attempt to define and manage them.

In *Correctional Theory: Context and Consequences* criminologists Francis T. Cullen and Cheryl Lero Jonson define *rehabilitation* as "a planned correctional intervention that targets for change internal and/or social criminogenic [crime-producing] factors with the goal of reducing recidivism and, where possible, of improving other aspects of an offender's life."[8] (Note that the primary focus lies on the reduction of recidivism; I will return to the second goal, the "other aspects," which I consider of equal importance, a bit later on.) Cullen and Jonson argue that "the belief that a core function of prisons should be rehabilitation is woven deeply into the nation's cultural fabric."[9] In other words, if America wants to stay true to itself, it has to revive the rehabilitative ideal, which was stamped out by the draconian get-tough-on-crime policies of the past decades.

In colonial times crime was not dealt with through prolonged prison sentences or correctional institutions as Bruce, Adam, and Angel experienced them. In his seminal book *The Discovery of the Asylum*, historian David J. Rothman writes that suspects accused of witchcraft, blasphemy, or idolatry, for example—the definition of crime then was based on the Bible—were held in small jails only until they were tried.[10] The accused was then publicly humiliated, whipped, fined, perhaps expulsed from the colonial settlement, or even hanged. The three most powerful weapons of crime prevention were thought to be family, church, and community.

The period of enlightenment and nation building coincided with an enormous increase in the diversity and population density of America's cities. (Rothman notes that New York's population grew fivefold between 1790 and 1830.) The colonial methods of punishment were considered barbaric, and a new movement emerged that was concerned with the origins and treatment of criminal behavior. The severe colonial criminal codes were deemed a cause and thus amended, and incarceration was seen as a humane alternative to the old codes. America built its first prisons at the end of the eighteenth century. An offender's sentence was matched with the severity of the crime. When this approach failed to reduce crime, criminal behavior began to be attributed to dysfunctional families and the environmental factors that plagued American cities, such as prostitution, alcohol, theaters, and criminal opportunities. Authorities decided to create special environments, free of corruption, to reinforce the functioning social order. In 1820, two separate penal movements emerged: The Auburn prison established the so-called New York or Congregate System, which aimed to reform offenders through hard labor, religious training, obedience, and silence. At the Philadelphia prison, where the Separate System originated, total isolation and silence were implemented to instill repentance. The purpose of both systems, which were deeply rooted in Christianity, was to rehabilitate the wayward.

After the Civil War America's prison system was in a state of crisis. Unbearably crowded and disease ridden, many prisons had to give up on their concept of solitude, silence, and contemplation. This endemic problem, criminology expert Alexis M. Durham writes, "continues to bedevil modern correctional operations." He points out that the psychological impact of living in crowded conditions "may not appear until after the inmate has returned to society and is no longer under careful observation."[11]

In 1870, leading correctional thinkers convened at the National Congress on Penitentiary and Reformatory Discipline in Cincinnati and suggested a number of principles to reform the system: Prisoners were to be carefully classified; more rewards than punishment were to be administered; prison officials should receive special training; inmates were to be treated on an individual basis and should have access to education and work training. "By providing them with work and encouraging them to redeem their character and regain their lost position in society," offenders were supposed to be reintegrated into society.[12] The creation of indeterminate sentences (which were to make sure that a prisoner was released as soon as he was rehabilitated), the parole board, parole and probation officers, and the juvenile court were all direct results of what came to be known as the "Rehabilitative Ideal."

Criminologists Cullen and Jonson note that the rehabilitative ideal reached its peak in the 1950s and 1960s, when a broad range of treatment programs, including group counseling, college education, behavior modification, work release, and work training programs were introduced and community-based treatment programs were championed.[13] Yet the unfettered belief in rehabilitation waned in the following decades. Cullen and Jonson attribute this decline to the social and political turmoil of the 1960s and 1970s, a period marked by the civil rights movement, the Vietnam War, Watergate, urban riots, and an enormous increase in crime. While liberals grew suspicious of the unrestricted discretion of governmental institutions (such as courts, prisons, and parole boards), conservatives believed that criminals were "coddled" and that the public was being put at risk. With his notorious 1974 publication, "What Works? Questions and Answers about Prison Reform," criminologist Robert Martinson fanned the flames. Citing eighty-two studies on rehabilitation programs and recidivism, Martinson concluded, "With few and isolated exceptions, the rehabilitative efforts that have been reported so far have no appreciable effect on recidivism."[14] In 1975 Ted Palmer published a comprehensive rebuttal to Martinson's findings, reexamining the studies and concluding that 48 percent of the programs studied were, in fact, reducing recidivism.[15] But Martinson's "nothing works" report was "the straw that broke the camel's back," according to criminologists Edward Latessa and Alexander M. Holsinger.[16] Its tone would define the law-and-order movement for decades to come.

Although not all treatment programs were eradicated, rehabilitation as the dominant correctional philosophy was replaced with a belief in deterrence, "incapacitation," and "just deserts." The notion of deterrence is rooted in the belief that punishment in itself reduces criminal behavior. It assumes that people are rational and seek to avoid pain. Incapacitation follows the idea that crime can be prevented by simply locking up criminals. "Just deserts" proponents don't concern themselves with preventing or controlling future crimes. Advocating mandatory sentences that don't make a criminal's release dependent on the discretion of judges and prison officials, they seek to create exact sentences that punish the criminal act: regardless of circumstances, finances, race, or rehabilitative development, each criminal receives exactly the same sentence for his or her particular crime.

It is important to point out that rehabilitation, deterrence, "just deserts," and incapacitation are not mutually exclusive. Angel, Bruce, and Adam experienced not one coherent guiding philosophy but rather a hodgepodge of competing philosophies that have been applied and absorbed at random.

While job training and educational programs for inmates are still available and while prison ministries continue to go strong, the rehabilitative ideal was largely pushed aside by these new philosophies and, significantly, vengeance. A tough-on-crime stance, resulting in mandatory sentencing, three-strikes laws, and the mass incarceration of people of color in particular, determined the approach to criminal justice for decades to come. Bruce, Adam, and Angel were kept in prison far beyond their mandatory minimum sentences. The decision of the parole commissioners was based on some vague notion that the three men's dispositions were "incompatible with the public safety and welfare." Looking at Angel's parole transcripts, I wondered what could have gotten him out of prison after fifteen years, when he first became eligible for parole. He had gathered support letters, an education, and job training certificates to prove that he was no longer a menace to society but was denied parole the first seven times he went in front of the board. Apparently, deterrence, incapacitation, and programming had not yet achieved what they were supposed to do. This case again begs the question of what constitutes successful rehabilitation in the minds of the administration—and in our own.

One of the most obvious problems with the philosophies of deterrence and incapacitation are that what deters one person does not necessarily deter another. In fact, Bruce was not deterred by the prospect of prison. Sadly, he was familiar with it from the street and from his own family. Bruce's example also reminds us that rationality and self-control are not generally strong traits in criminals.

The problem with "just deserts" is that it is difficult to predict who will commit crimes and when; predictive sentencing prevents offenders from being released on good behavior and, overall, results in longer sentences. While proponents of incapacitation may argue that locking up offenders and throwing away the key does, indeed, lower crime rates, opponents retort that these rates are only lower compared to a "nothing works" approach. If a similar amount of money were to be invested in evidence-based correctional interventions, the crime rates might actually decrease.[17]

When Adam was incarcerated in 1976, there were fewer than 263,000 people in prison in the United States.[18] Today there are 2.3 million Americans in prisons and jails and another 5 million on parole and probation.[19] America's correctional system is once again in a state of crisis. "The prisons are 'overcrowded,' we are told (and, in fact, courts have ruled). 'Overcrowding' is a euphemism for an authoritarian nightmare," writes Christopher Glazek in his comprehensive and eye-opening article on the topic. Detailing the manifold obstacles facing ex-offenders, he adds, "Once you go to prison, you never really come back."[20]

Spurred by these daunting numbers, as well as by financial, humanitarian, and public-safety concerns, the last two decades have spawned a growing movement of criminologists who advocate for *evidence-based* rehabilitation. Under the assumption that "crime is chosen but not according to some vague notions of rational choice," professionals have worked to identify "criminogenic risk factors" (such as antisocial values, a dysfunctional family background, criminal peers, risk seeking, and impulsiveness) that have been shown to correlate with crime and recidivism and, most important, that can be changed.[21]

In their influential 2002 article, "Beyond Correctional Quackery— Professionalism and the Possibility of Effective Treatment," criminologists Latessa, Cullen, and Paul Gendreau point out that many of the correctional treatment methods of the last decades are not based on solid scientific knowledge.[22] The long list of what does *not work* to reduce recidivism includes boot camps, programs that focus on humiliation and punishment, wilderness programs, psychoanalysis, acupuncture, and pet and art programs, many of which are goodwill attempts by private organizations. Latessa, Cullen, and Gendreau point to the principles of effective correctional programs established by the Canadian social psychologist Don A. Andrews, which are now widely quoted in contemporary American criminal justice literature. Andrews acknowledges that "risk factors for criminal conduct may be biological, personal, interpersonal, and/or structural, cultural, political and economic; and may reflect immediate circumstances."[23] (Bruce's, Angel's, and Adam's stories illustrate the complex interaction of some of these risk factors.) Emphasizing the importance of individual differences in criminal behavior, Andrews argues that offenders have to be rigorously assessed to determine their specific criminogenic risk factors and needs. These risks and needs have to be addressed through a cognitive-behavioral approach administered by qualified, warm, genuine, and well-supervised professionals in an environment of integrity. Treatment style, modes, and strategies have to be matched with the learning style of the individual. Cullen and Jonson note that programs that conform to the principles of effective treatment reduce recidivism by 20 to 25 percent. Interestingly, they also stress that the propensity to commit crimes decreases with age.[24]

Taking these findings one step further, advocates of America's evidence-based rehabilitation movement believe that treatment should not be limited to our nation's prison population, stressing the need for reentry agencies that provide aftercare and early childhood intervention for children at risk.[25]

One obvious problem with these noble principles and suggestions is that academic findings take time to permeate the spheres of those they target. Although criminologists like Latessa have examined hundreds of service programs for ex-cons and made suggestions on how to improve them, there is still a large fraction of "rehabilitation" programs that work without the existing knowledge of what causes crime and what has to be done to prevent it. Work continues to be seen as both the desired method and result of rehabilitation, despite the fact that it is only marginally linked to recidivism.[26] But even if a reentry organization has the best intentions, its positive results may be skewed. In order to prove reduced recidivism rates and gain private and public funding, many organizations "cherry-pick" the most promising ex-offenders, leaving behind those who need their services the most but who may be the least promising in terms of recidivism.

MEASURING SUCCESS

At first glance, considering the hardships facing a majority of ex-offenders, Angel's, Bruce's, and Adam's journeys read like success stories of rehabilitation: each man served his extensive sentence and was released into the Castle, a halfway house with an excellent reputation. The Fortune Society helped them search for work and housing, get medical insurance, and apply for food stamps; as of this writing, all three have managed to stay out of prison. On the surface the system works smoothly and in favor of those who need it the most. But these "ideal" circumstances make Angel, Bruce, and Adam exceptions to the rule. For most ex-cons the transition into the free world looks much bleaker. Fortune's halfway house offers only sixty beds—not nearly enough to accommodate the tens of thousands of New Yorkers coming home from prison each year. Few of the other halfway houses are as clean and safe, and most offer neither practical nor emotional support. Many ex-cons struggle with addictions and have to spend their days on the street and their nights at unsanitary and unsafe homeless shelters.

But behind Angel's, Bruce's, and Adam's alleged successful rehabilitation unravels a far more complex and untidy story. The men have been "incapacitated" and "deterred" for decades; they have been institutionalized for almost as long as they can remember. The Division of Criminal Justice Services determined their sentences; the Department of Correctional Services decided how and where their sentences were served and what programs they were to attend; religious institutions promised their redemption before God; the Division of Parole dictated their release and determined their curfew and their reappearances before their parole officers and the board. Now the Fortune Society continues this strict regimen, controlling their lives with its various programs, obligations, and daily drug testing. The three men have yet to realize freedom fully.

In the light of all this we have to ask ourselves what effects incapacitation and deterrence, as well as life within an endless chain of institutions and rehabilitation programs, have on the individual. Within this institutional maze, how does the individual balance his or her own needs, fears, and desires? Will he or she ever be allowed to cross over into "our" world? If I interpret Cullen and Jonson's definition of rehabilitation accurately, these needs, fears, and desires dwell in the "other aspects of an offender's life," aspects that, "where possible," should "also" be improved. Yet I have found little to no information on these "other aspects" and virtually none on the moral dimension of successful rehabilitation. Finding a job, housing, and staying out of prison are certainly important. But what about rehabilitation at heart, an individual's (lack of) remorse, his or her insights and moral growth? I would argue that true rehabilitation has to do with the willingness and capacity to take responsibility for one's crime. It is internal. Rehabilitation at heart lies buried beneath statistics, academic principles, and public policy because it is hard to measure and generalize. My book tries to explore this phenomenon with the tools of literary journalism: intimacy and extensive dialogue between journalist and subjects, expository scenes, and an acknowledged subjective view.

Adam, Angel, and Bruce are certainly grateful for Fortune's help, but they are also dismayed about their newly gained "freedom." The men were spit out of one system and into another; their old selves were shattered. Forced to reassemble themselves, they began marking time yet again. After decades behind bars, decision making becomes a real problem, and freedom can be outright frightening. What if I hurt someone again? How does one cross the street, use an ATM, or ride the subway? And how do you shop? Intimate relationships are hard to find after being "away" for such a long time. Despite the assumption that they have served their time for committing their crime, suddenly, the men's criminal past moves once again into the foreground. How does Adam, for example, negotiate his debilitating shame, guilt, and insecurity—those stumbling blocks on his endless road to rehabilitation? How can Bruce carry his burdensome past yet move on? These are just a few, seemingly mundane, yet existential questions that have occupied Bruce, Adam, Angel, and me.

Whereas Bruce and Adam try to deal with their problems internally, Angel deals with his externally. He uses the media (and the media uses him) to help him prove his successful rehabilitation. This book highlights not only the stumbling blocks but also the resources its protagonists find within themselves and in their new world.

Considering their differences in character and coping strategies, it becomes clear why each man's story—his needs, desires, risks, failures, and moral responsibilities—calls for a highly individualized approach. (In that sense my modus operandi honors Andrews's emphasis of the individual.) I observed each man trying to figure out his own measure of successful rehabilitation. Angel, Bruce, and Adam had to figure out which forces to fight and which ones to employ on their path.

As the book's narrative continues, it becomes clear that the only jobs available for people who have spent decades behind bars for murder are the ones offered by reentry agencies themselves, serving the same population the offenders have known—and possibly tried to leave behind—since they were children. Reentry appears to be a microcosm hermetically sealed from the outside world it parallels. This seal is penetrable only when it comes to religious groups. (Not coincidentally, Adam converted to Islam while in prison, and Angel joined the Quakers.) Believing that human beings are created in the image of God, most Christians consider no one beyond redemption. But Adam, Angel, and Bruce move freely only within their religious and reentry communities; beyond those domains genuine *integration* remains an illusion. By inserting myself into the world of my subjects, by listening and engaging in an intimate—and fearless—dialogue, I am attempting to crack the hermetic seal.

Initially, I thought I would follow Adam, Bruce, and Angel during their first year of freedom and then write my book. But I quickly realized that after twenty or thirty years in prison, these men would require much more than a series of traditional interviews. I didn't want to listen only to predigested experiences and describe "the approach" of institutions that claim to rehabilitate. My protagonists' attempts at rehabilitation happened on the subway, at the barbershop, onstage, at the park, at a Halloween party, at work, and over dinner. I wanted to be there when things were happening and ended up shadowing my protagonists for more than two years—from spring 2007 into the summer of 2009. I continued to check in with them periodically in the years that followed. My goal is to provide a visceral sense of their odyssey from prison to freedom. I couldn't have predicted what their new experiences in the free world entailed—their obstacles, the things that puzzled them about "our" world, what delighted them, what scared them, and, perhaps most surprising, what they missed about prison.

Among Murderers examines through my own personal viewpoint the pariah status of three men who have been convicted of society's most heinous crimes and who have returned to the free world. Although I rely on interviews, parole and court documents, hospital reports, and letters to tell the men's stories, I also admit to my personal struggles in coming to terms with their complex characters and crimes. I have immersed myself in their world, hoping to create an entrance to solving a conflict that has long been neglected. By giving a voice to three individuals, marginalized from society by their crimes and prison sentences, and by exploring their discomfiting, jarring realities, I hope to illuminate a much-neglected epidemic.

Naturally, it is not only *their* narrative anymore; it has also become mine. More important, though, their stories point to our society at large. For the longest time we have tried to hide from view this significant part of our population. Now that these former criminals are returning to our society, we need to redefine our stance. Do we allow for the reintegration of murderers, assailants, robbers, and rapists, men and women who have been convicted of dreadful crimes? What do we need to take into consideration as we craft policies that seek to reform and redeem former prisoners—and ourselves? I believe that the most trivial details can expose the most complex psychological circumstances and mysteries of human life. By featuring my observations, conversations, and boundary points, I hope to open up an honest dialogue about crime, rehabilitation, and reentry.

CHAPTER ONE

Freedom Day

And just like that, that was that. No sense of being at all, Angel wrote in the spidery script of a nine-year-old. He titled the new page in his diary *Freedom Day, March 29th 2007.* He was dazed by the abrupt shock of having dropped from one sphere into another in a matter of seconds. The course that had taken three decades to unfold had suddenly advanced with blinding speed: Attica's prison gates closed behind him. *Freedom.*

The prison van took him to a gas station, where he boarded the public bus to New York. *Freedom?* He looked around. Some of the guys on the bus reminded him of the *loser mind-sets* he had just left behind in Attica. *Loser mind-sets* who told the same street stories over and over. Tales of how they robbed old women and dealt drugs, how much money they once had, and what cars they used to own.

"Tell me you own a *business*," Angel would tell them. "*That* would impress me."

The people on the bus all struck him as surprisingly young, and it was then that Angel realized that somehow, somewhere along the line, he had gotten old. More than half of his life had passed. He had spent twenty-nine years behind bars for committing one murder and attempting another. He was forty-seven now.

As more people got on the bus Angel nervously scooted over on his seat, removing his bags to make space. He could see the Manhattan skyline on the horizon. *Looks goooood!* he wrote as the bus entered the Lincoln Tunnel.

When the bus pulled into Penn Station, Angel was tempted to ask the driver for permission to get off. Even the tiniest decision—such as moving without someone else's approval or order—made him feel uneasy. *This is taking some getting used to,* he meticulously jotted down in his diary.

And just like that, that was that. When Angel got off the bus at Penn Station, he had *No sense of being at all.* He had no idea who he was or what he had become.

Angel had secured a bed at the Castle, a halfway house in Morningside Heights, West Harlem, that houses sixty former prisoners. The Castle is one of three New York locations operated by the Fortune Society. Apart from residential services, the Fortune Society offers its formerly incarcerated clients job-readiness and cooking classes, computer tutoring, substance-abuse treatment, and father- and motherhood programs.

Located at the corner of Riverside Drive and 140th Street, the Castle stands out in the neighborhood. It was built from large schist rocks excavated when the first subway line in New York City was constructed, and its facade sparkles with the rocks' characteristic jagged but glittering surface. With its miniature lookout towers, its arched windows, and the bright crenellations that top some of its walls, the Castle resembles a Gothic bastion. It overlooks Riverbank State Park and the Hudson River, which adds to its charm. One could easily imagine the Castle being surrounded by a muddy moat.

A piece of wood bearing the number 630 dangled near the gigantic wooden entrance door on Riverside Drive. Whenever new residents tried to straighten the crooked sign—which was frequently—it always slid right back. The heavy wrought-iron hinges screeched as Angel opened the door.

Angel was carrying his duffel bag in one hand and a music keyboard in the other. He was worried about his keyboard being stolen. After all, he didn't have his own cell anymore; he would be sharing his room with five other ex-cons.

Angel went to his new room to take a hot shower. When he stepped out of the bathroom, he noticed a full-length mirror. All he'd had in his prison cell was a ten-inch mirror. This was the first time in almost thirty years that he saw himself fully naked, that he saw his body in one piece. He turned around slowly to inspect himself.

Angel Ramos has narrow, warm eyes; a wide, knobby nose; and potter's-clay skin, tinged with copper. Thin strands of gray make his dense, black hair sparkle. His unkempt mustache looks like weeds. In some spots it overlaps his ample lips; in others it is sparse, revealing the skin underneath. Angel is short—just about five feet tall—and he has become stocky. His neck has gotten meatier, and he has grown love handles.

"Oh my God," Angel said to himself. "I got fat." He promptly decided to "eat less, move more."

Angel's resolution proved unnecessary. A few weeks after his release, he had already lost ten pounds. He had shed weight just by walking and worrying about everyday decisions. He felt time slipping and desperately tried to keep up. Each day presented him with a flood of entirely new experiences.

When Angel walked around New York during his first months of freedom, he trudged up and down sidewalks and went in and out of subway stations. He tripped over potholes, stumbled over trash, strolled on grass, and hiked up and down the hills of Harlem. This was an entirely new experience. He was walking on uneven terrain. In prison the ground was flat, and his feet had grown accustomed to his state-issued work boots. But outside he didn't seem able to break in his new Timberland boots, let alone the dress shoes he bought. His feet were killing him.

In his first weeks of freedom Angel went to the Welfare Department, the Salvation Army, and the Division of Parole, where he had to report on a weekly basis. On Sundays he walked to Riverside Church to attend his Quaker meetings. Once he ventured east on 115th Street to visit the site of the house where he spent the first few years of his life. It was gone. But the house in which he had killed his victim was still there. The Castle was only a half-hour walk from the house where an outburst of anger had changed his life forever. Two minutes—thirty years—half an hour! Did time fly, or did it stand still?

Surely, Harlem had changed for the better, but parts of it remained gritty. Many of its residents were now locked up. Both East and West Harlem now held several "Million Dollar Blocks," city blocks in which the concentration of currently imprisoned residents is so dense that states are spending an excess of a million dollars a year in incarceration costs.[1]

Young men with pit bulls were hanging out in front of bodegas. Trash spilled from black plastic bags piled up on the curb. Teenagers sat idly on garbage cans alongside the multilane roads that cut through the neighborhood. On Broadway, just around the corner from the Castle, Elvira M.'s Barbershop stood across from Jendy's Beauty Salon, mere steps from Odri's Beauty Salon. With the same repetitive frequency there were Chinese take-out joints, discount stores, and signs that prohibited littering, loitering, ball playing, and spitting—to no avail. On the corner of 137th Street a pediatrician shared a building with McDonald's, the royal blue lettering of the doctor's sign trumped by a large spinning cheeseburger. Single-room occupancies offered dingy accommodations to down-and-out men, and lonesome signs and banners proclaimed enigmatic messages of the past: *Phase Piggy Back, O'Jay's Telephone Answering Service,* and *No Service Available.* The tenor was interrupted here and there by tree-lined blocks and nicely renovated brownstones with flowering boxes.

Angel and I first met in May 2007 on the bus that took us from the Albany advocacy day back to New York City. I had come to report on the event and on the proposed revisions in health care, housing, work, and voting rights. He was one of dozens of ex-cons campaigning for legislative changes for those with criminal records. There were then five million Americans on parole and probation, and in excess of seven hundred thousand people were being released from prison each year.[2] When I sat down on the seat next to Angel, I noticed that his name tag read "Angle." When I commented on the typo, he laughed and briefly released his stuffed backpack to throw his hands in the air. "Angle . . . Angel, what does it matter? I'm dyslexic, so for me it reads right." We shared a laugh, and I asked him what he carried in his big backpack.

"Money, ID, parole release papers, a sweater, a sewing kit, a toothbrush, an extra shirt—you never know if you might have to spend the night or if the bus breaks down or if . . . I tend to be overly prepared," he said, excusing himself. Having spent twenty-nine years locked up, Angel had no idea what to bring for a daylong excursion, so he brought everything he could think of. My question opened a valve. He talked for the next four hours without taking a breath.

After Angel mentioned the length of his sentence, I asked the inevitable: "What were you in for?"

"I killed a friend in an argument," Angel said, adding somewhat apologetically, "I had just turned eighteen." I envisioned a bar fight between two drunk teenagers. Things must have gotten out of hand, I thought. I caught myself giving Angel the benefit of the doubt because of his charming demeanor, his eloquence, and his outspokenness. I would have plenty of time in the future to ask him more questions. I decided to start with whatever Angel was willing to share.

By his own reckoning Angel had changed. Wasn't that what imprisonment, punishment, and rehabilitation were all about? Had prison made Angel a better human being? Would we forgive him for his crimes and welcome him back into our world?

Until his release from prison Angel had considered himself prepared for freedom. He had found God and redemption. He had accumulated countless letters of recommendation from his Quaker friends for his appearances in front of the parole board. The letters asserted that he was ready to be released. He was "corrected," no longer a risk to society but a contributing member.

But the matter of Angel's assumed correction was somewhat mysterious. In 1993, after serving fifteen years of his life sentence, he first became eligible for parole. He was denied. Every two years after that Angel would present his ever-growing folder to the board, but each time he was slammed with yet another two years. He was denied parole six times. For twenty-nine years the parole commissioners considered his release "incompatible with the public safety and welfare." Then, suddenly, after the seventh parole hearing, the board spit him out into our world.

When Angel first went to jail in 1978, the food wasn't too bad, and the correctional officers were, for the most part, "all right." He liked the "old-time career criminals" who took him under their wing to protect him from "booty bandits." (Angel liked to say "booty bandits"; it made him chuckle.) Back then he may have still been able to attend a variety of rehabilitative programs, but for the longest time Angel didn't think he "needed fixing."

Over time the prison food became unbearable and "the cops" dictatorial. The state decimated its rehabilitation programs. In the 1980s the crack epidemic swept in thousands of "crazy people who," Angel said, "turned prison into an insane asylum."

When he finally felt ready to consider what had led him to violence and murder, the only programs available were run by other inmates and outside volunteers. "For the most part," he said, "rehabilitation was up to myself."

But if he was ever going to be released, Angel had to somehow prove his successful rehabilitation, despite a lack of opportunities and the dubiousness of the remaining programs. The folder he carried in his duffel bag brimmed with GED, college, work training, and Narcotics Anonymous certificates (although he claims to have used marijuana only "recreationally" when he was a teenager). He had attended "transpersonal counseling," which was run by a volunteer social worker who encouraged inmates "to look at their inner child." He also went to a slew of Alternative to Violence meetings and to Life Skills programs run by fellow inmates and outside volunteers.[3]

Leaving the task of rehabilitation to the inmates themselves wasn't a fluke; it had become the norm. These programs were not scientifically proven to lower recidivism, but one had to do *something*. The folder needed to grow.

In 2005 Angel was required to attend Aggression Replacement Training at Attica prison. He graduated from a one-hundred-hour program that focused on social skills, anger control, and moral reasoning and prides itself on reducing recidivism.[4] But after almost three decades in prison he didn't feel safe trusting the state. For twenty-nine years he had endured society's unwavering punishment. "Justice without mercy," he said, adding, "By that time, I had already done the work."

Free at last—away from the regimentation of prison—Angel was discovering where "rehabilitation" would really begin: on the bus, on the street, on the job, and in society's judging eyes. He would have to find out for himself what it really meant.

In the summer months following his release I began to accompany Angel on his walks and to his appointments. His struggles appeared mundane. In the mornings Angel didn't know what to eat. "There is five boxes of cereal and I don't know which one tastes good, so I just walk away. Besides, food tastes different today than it did in the past. *Everything* tastes different," he said. His eyes flitted left and right, as if toggling among choices.

Angel preferred apricots, plums, and steak over apples, mashed potatoes, and tuna. In prison he had a pale apple every day and tuna prepared in every way possible. He had no intention of ever eating tuna again. "Fuck fish altogether," he said, laughing.

But in his first weeks out, plums and apricots were hard to find. Not only did Angel have to face children screeching and women talking on cell phones in high-pitched voices, he also had to cross the street to go to the store. And for Angel there were a hundred decisions involved in crossing a street. The mere idea gave him a headache. There were people on either side of him, and he didn't know whose example to follow. *Which way do I go? Do I follow this person or that person?* he remembered thinking. "I was using too much brainpower to make the decision."

If it were simply a matter of ridding his diet of the foods and dishes he hated, life would have been easy. But discarding one thing always meant having to choose another. The first time Angel went to the Fairway Market in West Harlem to buy spaghetti sauce, he was outright terrified. There were hundreds of different spaghetti sauces. He couldn't believe his eyes. He fled back to the Castle without buying anything and put all thought of making spaghetti out of his head.

"I have to learn how to shop," he told me. "How do you buy a suit? How do you go about making a doctor's appointment?" For similar reasons he chose to abstain from having sex. "I just wouldn't know what to do," he said matter-of-factly. "It's all too overwhelming."

Angel found himself staring at a piece of fabric for hours at a time, intrigued by its texture and pattern. When he walked through the park, he did goofy things like sniff roses and exhale with a loud "Aaaah!" He sometimes looked in the mirror just to greet himself. "Hi!" he would say with a laugh, waving at his reflection. Things that might cause other people to curse and stomp could make his day. He fondly remembered stepping on dog poop on one of his first days out. Every once in a while, seemingly unaware, he spit out little verses. "I'm a Latin from Manhattan, but I have the sweets for Brooklyn." In these moments I almost expected him to start skipping.

In his first weeks of freedom Angel became obsessed with doing laundry in the washing machine and with washing dishes. *Which knob do you turn and when do you turn it? Do you first soap all the dishes and then rinse them or do you do one piece at a time? How much did you pay for the rag, how much for the piece of soap?*

Angel was tired during the day, yet at night he didn't sleep well. His body missed the one-inch mattress and the steel slat he had grown accustomed to. The door of his room at the Castle kept opening and closing all night long.

In prison, waking up in a split second was a survival reflex. "The door opens and you automatically wake up," he said. "When somebody comes in your cell and you lay in bed wrapped up in sheets, you can't defend yourself. You are very vulnerable." But at the Castle, to be awakened by every little screech and knock got downright annoying.

Despite his struggles, or maybe because of them, Angel's favorite word became *beautiful*. In the first weeks out he said "beautiful" so frequently that it sounded like someone trying to convince himself that life could really be so. He often said, "Every person is beautiful until proven otherwise." And for good measure he sometimes added, "Then they are still beautiful; I just can't be around them." Angel found Yeats's "Sailing to Byzantium," which he read on a subway ad, so *beautiful* it brought tears to his eyes. He enunciated each word with the heed and force of a sculptor carving stone. It quickly became apparent to me that words mattered to Angel. For twenty-nine years words were all he had. Keeping his word had become as important to him as being able to read and write. Words could fill voids. They could be used to foster relationships. They could keep him busy on long, boring days and help him reach beyond prison walls. Angel discovered that he, too, could write poems, make jokes, and conquer the hearts of strangers. Words could win trust and impress people. With the help of words physical anger could be converted into aggressive enthusiasm. Best of all, words could serve as scaffolding, holding in place and obscuring a personality on the verge of collapse.

I came into this world not knowing anything, Angel's poem "The Dance of Wonder" begins. *Then I found wonder in taste, sound, and the exploration of my body. / But that did not last.*

Together Angel and I explored the city of his youth. We rode the subway, went to Central Park, and walked along the banks of the Hudson River. One of our early trips led us to MoMA. Angel found Picasso's *Violin and Grapes* "so beautiful, it gives me chills." Gauguin's island women reminded him of family, Richard Serra's steel sculptures of "stuff" he had to clean in prison.

At first, Angel always relied on me as his guide. When I took three steps to the right, he would hurry to follow suit. When I turned around, he turned around, too. This was unknown territory to him, and he approached it with an odd mixture of impulse and vigilance. When we passed a stone sculpture by Brancusi, he said, "I want to throw it in the water and ride it." He then went on to examine parts of the escalator welding and its seams with his eyes and his hands. He had learned how to weld in prison and explained to me how he looked at things from an "engineering point of view." He told me that out on the streets he was haunted by imperfections on license plates. Better than most people he knew how a perfect license plate should look. (After all, every New York State license plate has been made at the Auburn Correctional Facility, the prison where Angel served part of his sentence.)[5]

After quickly formulating some James Bond scenarios to account for a helicopter that hung from MoMA's ceiling, Angel looked out the window to study the neoclassic architecture of an adjacent building. "If I had billions and billions of dollars," he mused, "I would build a mile of columns in the desert as a symbol of strength."

But, suddenly, Angel got tired. He yawned. It was already three o'clock in the afternoon, and he, ever fearful of delays, was eager to get back to the Castle.

This is the Angel I first got to know. He was an intriguing character. He was popular among his Quaker friends and among the Fortune Society's employees. But some of the halfway house residents regarded him with suspicion. Some of the men ridiculed him behind his back. I, too, could feel a tension within him, a cord pulling in two directions. How could such a nice, funny guy have killed "a friend"? There must be more to it—a hidden side, a dark corner. There was a lot to explore. It was easy to talk to Angel because Angel did most of the talking. He seemed to take a certain pride in revealing even the smallest details of his life to me. For now, I decided to just let him talk.

CHAPTER TWO

At the Garden

Adam was released to the Castle at the end of April of 2007. He had served thirty-one of his twenty-five-years-to-life sentence for two counts of second-degree murder, robbery, conspiracy, and an attempted escape. I met Adam at the Albany advocacy day in May where I had also met Angel. What I first noticed about him was his meticulous attire. Fashion had always been very important to Adam. A seventy-two-year-old Muslim convert, Adam wore classic secondhand wool sweaters and wire-rim glasses that complemented the color of his silver beard. His wardrobe showed off his athletic build and broad shoulders. His graceful posture, the golden ring on his right hand, and his gray beard and glasses made him look wise and dignified. When he was handed the microphone, he spoke with gravity, confidence, and strength. Because of his aura it took me a few weeks to approach him. When I finally did, I was surprised to find a man who laughed easily and readily shared his sorrows and pain.

Adam experienced his surroundings with unusual intensity. He was aware of every step he took and wondered constantly whether the people around him were as aware of him as he was of them. Adam and I were worlds apart, yet I could relate to him. Aside from the glaringly obvious differences, Adam and I shared certain qualities. We were connected by a state of constant alertness. We both liked to "analyze." Our vigilance protected us and kept us in check, but it also made us slightly neurotic. We moved on thin ice.

Adam's observational skills had benefited him in prison. They gave him something to do, kept him safe, and allowed him to teach prisoners in need of his various modes of introspection. In prison he established "coping programs for lifers," people who, like him, served indeterminate life sentences or who were sentenced to life without parole. His classes addressed the needs of prisoners that the prison system neglected: How does an individual who was sentenced for murder come to terms with his legacy? And how does he go about the possibility that he might have to spend the rest of his life locked up in a vacuum while outside a world is unfolding, becoming more and more foreign each passing year? Can you recover and be reformed when you might have to spend the rest of your life in prison? No one else seemed to discuss these questions.

Adam could feel an ever-increasing void. He was on his own. Prison threatened to draw him into the big, black hole of timelessness and despair. He decided to deal with it himself. Adam believed that there was a way an individual could actually rehabilitate himself. No, not could—it was imperative. That was his responsibility after having committed such horrendous crimes.

One of the first things Adam told me was that he had come to terms with the fact that he would die in prison, and now he missed his "family," his fellow lifers. "I can do this. I can do this till I die," Adam said about prison. "This is no big thing to me." That was his mantra. He kept a scrapbook in which he pasted articles and pictures of places lost, of places he wasn't able to visit. The outside world was no more than a figment of his imagination—hope and hopelessness reduced to strips of paper and glue.

When Adam finally did return to the outside world, he was stunned. He wanted to see as much as he could, lamenting that he didn't have much time left. He had to hurry because of his looming death.

During the two years that followed Adam's release, we embarked on excursions in Brooklyn, Manhattan, the Bronx, and Queens. One of our early journeys led us to the Brooklyn Botanic Garden, which Adam remembered from his childhood. When he was eleven or twelve, he would walk or take the trolley from his home in Bedford-Stuyvesant to the park. He had been a loner as a child and always loved nature, trees, flowers, and birds. Sometimes in the summer he would go to the Garden to sleep under a tree. He didn't know where his love of nature came from; all he knew was that none of the other kids came along.

When I arrived at the Botanic Garden at 10:30 on a Sunday morning, Adam was sitting on a bench across the street on Eastern Parkway. As always, he wore matching clothes and laughed happily when we said, "Hi."

At the Steinhardt Conservatory, a greenhouse complex that simulates different climates and vegetation from around the world, Adam touched everything he saw. The fruits on the cactus in the Desert Pavilion looked like little strawberries. Adam muttered, reading the plaques aloud. It was almost as if I weren't there.

"Endurance and avoidance," he read, referring to the characteristics of cacti. "The survival of the fittest . . . Hmm." Adam always hummed when making space for more thoughts to come.

He admired the Mohintli cactus's slender, velvety leaves and its bright orange blossoms. Touching the hairbrush cactus, he yelped, "Ouch!" Then he laughed, giving me a quick glance.

In the Tropical Pavilion he wondered about the Golden Eye Grass, an inconspicuous-looking plant with a poetic-sounding name. And how different mahogany looked from the outside than from the inside! One couldn't have predicted the reddish sheen it assumed when crafted and polished.

Adam's hands slid down the skinny, smooth stem of a breadnut tree. Hanging down in long tassels, the fishtail palm's berries looked like dreadlocks. Adam poked into the stem of the *Musa brazilia*, a banana plant. The plant had a sore, its plasticky skin peeling off and sap running down its trunk.

The papaya tree bore large, ripe fruit.

Adam smelled the *Clerodendron*, which couldn't have been more alien in appearance. In the middle of a bright-pink, star-shaped flower it proudly displayed a royal blue pearl. The dancing girl ginger stretched her little arms as if to reach out to the carnival flower, whose purple blossoms looked like a jester's hat.

Adam read the description next to the cocoa tree and huffed in disbelief. Fifteen seeds to make just one cup of coffee? The flower next to the coffee tree looked like an open mouth. Just steps from the tree and the open mouth was the cola tree, whose seeds flavor the soft drink. "In African culture," Adam read, "a cola tree is planted for every newborn baby, who then remains its lifelong owner."

No cola tree, or anything else for that matter, was "planted" for Adam. What he seemed to *own* most intensely were his crimes. They were always present, an open wound, throbbing with each step he took. Adam did not need to be prodded to talk about them. They always accompanied us, even on this sunny day in the park. Adam was stuck between worlds.

Adam met his three partners-in-crime in the early 1970s, when he was serving yet another stint for robbery at Green Haven Correctional Facility, seventy miles outside of New York. Just eighteen months after his release, the team started to plan an intricate robbery of a movie house in Manhattan. Although Adam liked "sticking up," he preferred the planning phase to the actual execution.

Kevin, one of the robbers, worked at the movie theater and knew its procedures. The idea was to rob the theater on a Monday morning when two armed guards regularly arrived to pick up the approximately $20,000 in weekend receipts from the safe. The crew did numerous practice runs to the theater. They tied up groups of volunteers to see how long it would take. They staged every part of the robbery to the last detail. But something went wrong.

The turn-of-the-century theater was adorned in art nouveau style, with florid oak paneling and murals depicting classical heroes. Its main auditorium was a massive ellipse with a domed ceiling and elaborate plasterwork. But in 1976, as the neighborhood declined into prostitution and crime, the magnificent movie house fell on hard times.

At first things went according to plan. Kevin let Bobby and Adam into the theater through the back exit while Richie waited in the getaway car. As the theater employees arrived for the morning shift they were tied up with cut pieces of clothesline and taken to the basement, where Bobby was assigned to watch over them. The media described the robbers, who wore ski masks and carried sawed-off shotguns, as polite and considerate. The men told their hostages not to worry and assured them that they weren't going to be hurt or robbed. A hostage later reported that one gunman told him everything would be okay and that he would live to read about it in the paper.

Adam was in the basement to check in with Bobby and the hostages when he heard shots echo down from the theater.

BangBangBangBang!

"Shit!"

Whenever Adam recalls the shooting, *shit* is the word that best sums it all up. "Shit!" he said now, more than three decades later. He grabbed his head in despair as if the event were transpiring as we spoke. Adam had never used his gun. He never carried a gun when out on the streets. When he carried a gun during robberies, it was rarely loaded.

In planning the stickup Adam had not taken into account that one of his gunmen might lose his nerve. Kevin panicked when the guards held their guns in his direction.

"Don't raise the shotgun!" he yelled when the two guards entered the auditorium, where he was waiting to take them hostage. "Don't raise that fucking shotgun!"

But the guards might not have even known where exactly the yelling was coming from or where the intruders were hiding. Kevin snapped.

When Adam came back upstairs, he saw the guards on the ground. The floor was covered with puddles of blood, and the mirrored walls were plastered with pieces of tissue. The guards screamed and reached out their hands, begging Adam for help. Their faces were barely lit by the auditorium's running floor lights. Adam was torn. He wanted to help, but at the same time he knew that he had to get out of there as quickly as possible. Pedestrians had already started to crowd the sidewalk, and one of the hostages had managed to call 911.

The guards both died shortly after reaching the hospital. Adam and his partners were apprehended a few weeks later. After the robbery Adam collected the newspaper clippings about the victims: Thomas Bell, fifty-five, and José Rodriguez, sixty-five—two round, white faces peering out at him from yellowing paper. Both men, captured by a slightly elevated camera, wore grave smiles. They looked as if they were anticipating what was going to happen. Even unharmed, the men looked like beaten dogs. Adam kept the articles and photographs stowed away in a folder in his cell. His victims' pictures and their names had carved themselves into his mind. Thomas Bell and José Rodriguez were with him for good.

The firewheel tree looked as if in flames. Lyrical names—butcher's broom, honeybells, star jasmine, cape cowslip—made me think of taxonomists, peculiar men housed in the secluded bowels of august buildings, presiding over the ordering and naming of life. Names are crucial in comprehending the world. They ensure that plants and people who might otherwise be forgotten remain with us. But names are also a curse, as they inspirit things that we would rather not remember. Once you start naming your victims, the real struggle begins.

A squirrel skidded treacherously along on one of the pipes above us. Wherever we went, we could hear birds chirping. At some point, however, it became difficult to distinguish the call of an exotic species from the screech of a malfunctioning fan. When I shared my doubts with Adam, he was reminded of prison. You could take Adam to the most exotic places in New York and in no time he would be talking about prison. For the longest time he had yearned to be free, but now that he was free, he sometimes missed prison.

In the 1960s and 1970s, before Adam committed the crime that resulted in his being labeled a murderer, the main goal of incarceration was rehabilitation, not punishment. Back then, prisoners were allowed to keep birds and cats. At Sing Sing, where Adam had served a previous sentence for attempted robbery, he fed shrimp to a cat. The next day the cat brought three other cats with him. At Elmira, Adam and the other inmates kept parakeets and gave them Kool-Aid, which, Adam told me, colored the birds' feathers. He advertised his crazy Kool-Aid birds in specialty magazines, and people from the outside came inside to buy them.

Blastin' Berry Cherry, Kickin'-Kiwi-Lime, Man-o-Mangoberry, Pink Swimmingo, Scary Black Cherry, Sharkleberry Fin? Adam told me that the buyers were furious when, after several weeks, the birds' colors began to fade. They complained to the prison administration, and the commissary stopped selling Kool-Aid.

The birds kept the men company. Adam put up pieces of cheesecloth in front of his bars and let the parakeets fly around in his cell. The man in the next cell played his guitar, and Adam remembered how his parakeets used to line up to sing along.

Adam's fantastic prison story ended on a sad note. One morning, he jammed his foot into his shoe and right onto a sleeping parakeet, killing it. "Oh, man," Adam sighed at the Botanic Garden as he recalled the accident. "I felt baaad."

I was struck by how repulsed Adam was by having taken this little life, however small. How bad must he feel for having caused the deaths of Rodriguez and Bell! Whenever the topic came up—and it often did—he said, "I had no intention! It never entered my mind that anything like that would go on. All those years . . . I never shot anybody. If there would have been anything to change that situation I would have."

I was reminded of this story when I later dug out newspaper articles about Adam's crime. One article quoted a hostage as saying that one of the gunmen allowed them to smoke and asked whether the strings around their wrists were too tight. I now wondered whether the person who expressed this concern was Adam. Maybe Adam wouldn't have pulled a gun had he been in Kevin's place. Maybe he wouldn't have lost his cool. Either way, he had planned the robbery and failed to consider its possible consequences; he was complicit in the guards' deaths. And instead of facing up to what he had done, he ran from the law until he was captured. There were worlds between Adam's thinking now and his attitude thirty years ago. Now he constantly expressed his shame, guilt, and remorse and his wish to be able to turn around and change his past. Somewhere along the line he must have learned to face his transgression. What he had yet to face was freedom, the strange bright world he entered after thirty-one years in the dark.

CHAPTER THREE

Street Code

On May 25, 2007, Bruce was released to the Castle. He met Angel and Adam at the first Morning Focus meeting, where residents discuss their plans for the day. It was difficult not to notice the new resident. Bruce was a towering six-foot-six, dark-skinned man with a clean-shaven head. At fifty-two, he had hands the size of dinner plates and heavily scarred wrists from an old childhood burn injury. He wore big, square glasses with bulky frames and pop-bottle lenses that were given to him in prison. His outdated-looking glasses gave him away to anyone familiar with New York's reentry scene: watch out, here comes an ex-felon.

The glasses were courtesy of Corcraft, an institution within New York's correctional facilities that produces furniture and apparel—and glasses—for government agencies, schools, and universities. New York's biggest "rehabilitative" machine, Corcraft claims to "[keep] inmates employed to help prevent disruption" and "[teach] work disciplines and job skills," which, hopefully, come in handy once they are released.[1] Corcraft pays prisoners less than one dollar an hour.

When Bruce was released, Angel had already discovered that he could replace his prison glasses with stylish frames from Duane Reade or Rite Aid. Bruce, however, was stuck with his prison glasses for the time being because he was nearsighted and needed to save up before he could afford a new pair.

Bruce, Angel, and Adam began to hang out because they could relate to each other. They had no need to ask one another what they were in for. Murder, clearly. There is hardly any other crime that gets you twenty-four years and up. Combined, they had spent eighty-four years behind bars, more than an average lifetime.

Bruce, Adam, and Angel didn't feel the need to talk to each other about their crimes. Of course, the men knew the basics about one another: Bruce shot a stranger in an argument, twenty-four years; Angel killed a friend in an argument, twenty-nine years; and Adam was involved in a robbery, in the course of which two security guards got killed, thirty-one years. But they didn't discuss the specifics, the reasons why they committed the crime in the first place, its consequences, or the feelings that came with these traumatic events.

"That's one thing [prisoners] don't discuss: the crime," Bruce told me right at the start. "If you got twenty to life, then they know you had to have a homicide. Once they find out how much time you got, people know." He explained that prisoners are snitches. In prison you had to constantly watch your back. The rule held that if you were provoked, you had to put your foot down. "You gotta come in and set your territory," Bruce said. "It's gotta be known that Bruce will fight." This attitude didn't just change overnight, and hints of it remain to this day. Inside himself, Bruce was still a prisoner. How could he be expected to change from one day to the next?

The trials and tribulations of the new world seemed a bit less threatening when they were approached together. Adam and Angel quickly applied their newly gained knowledge, while Bruce trotted along with suspicion. On his second day out they took Bruce to Fairway to show him how to shop.

Number one: To avoid confusion and terror, you have to make a shopping list. Update your list during the week. Number two: Look for store brands first. Store brands are cheaper and narrow your choices. Number three: To save money, look for value packs of soap and toilet paper. Number four: Don't think too much. Just grab something and head to the register.

Then Adam and Angel put their next lesson into practice: the subway. They got Bruce a MetroCard and showed him how to slide it at the turnstile. At first Bruce didn't get it. He only knew tokens and kept sliding the card the wrong way, first too slow, then too fast. He felt stupid and hoped that no one was watching. He was relieved when he finally made it to the subway. But this was where the trouble really began. What were all those people staring at, and why did they brush him on their way out? Bruce felt "disrespected" and provoked. In prison there was no reason to stare unless you intended to start a fight. The same was true for physical contact. If your safety mattered to you, you simply didn't bump into others. In prison you automatically made space for people approaching you, but in the subway there never seemed to be enough space. The men often felt provoked by their fellow riders. Yes, this *would* take some getting used to.

Once they had gathered strength again, they headed to the bank to try out Angel's new ATM card.

"We were like the three stooges," Angel told me, who, unlike Bruce, was rather amused by his daily mishaps. "Bruce said, 'I'll be the muscle.' Adam was the bagman—the one who carries the money. And I'm the computer guy. I've never touched an ATM, though. But Bruce had seen his sister use her ATM card. Well . . . and Adam doesn't know a damn thing."

Angel couldn't stop chuckling while telling the story. He described how the three of them stood outside the bank scratching their asses trying to figure out which way to insert the card to open the door. When they finally made it into the lobby, they struggled to put the card into the machine. They tried it in all possible directions to no avail. Their attention was so focused on the slot that it took them a while to realize that the machine was broken. "Look! It says on the screen that it's out of order." Exhausted, the three went back to the Castle without having withdrawn any money.

It is ironic that the men's support system could land them back in prison. In New York, parolees are not allowed to associate with other people with criminal records. The argument behind this rule is that this association may be detrimental to their rehabilitation. A parole officer told me: "Parolees palling around with each other leads to gangs, robberies, conspiracies, and ultimately back to prison. That's the idea."

Angel repeatedly reminded Bruce and Adam that if either one of them were ever hit by a car, he would go to the nearest telephone booth, place an anonymous 911 call, and then flee the scene. This was not only to avoid association with another ex-felon but also to avoid police contact (another parole stipulation).

Like their relationships in prison, in which an unannounced transfer could tear them apart, the men's new friendships had an impermanent quality to them. Friendship provided support where support was needed and saturated their idleness—the time they spent without women and work and without a real home. But it was also a result of desperation and the assumption—their own and society's—that three murderers *must* relate to each other, no matter their differences.

When I would come to the Castle to meet Angel, Bruce usually hovered in the background like a ghost. Not a scary ghost, just restless and wary, as if sentenced to relive his past eternally. Eventually, at the end of the summer of 2007, Bruce and I started talking. Our first real conversations were slow and awkward. We would sit down in the Castle's backyard, and Bruce would put my digital recorder in his shirt pocket. He folded his large hands and waited for me to ask questions. It wasn't that he didn't want to talk. It seemed as if he "couldn't find the zipper of his prison armor"—an expression Adam had coined to describe the isolation former prisoners tend to experience in "our" world.

At a coffee shop, over doughnuts and tea, Bruce quickly admitted what he had done. Then he was silent again. Twenty-four years ago he and a girlfriend went to the liquor store to buy something to drink. His friend went ahead while he looked for parking. When he entered the store, he saw that a stranger had cornered his friend and was making sexual advances. The girl was screaming hysterically. Bruce separated the two, and his friend left the store. Bruce and the stranger began to fight, and Bruce shot him. He aimed for his shoulder but hit his chest. "Tyrone Davis," Bruce said. "I always call my victim by his name." That was it.

I was relieved when Bruce offered to give me his trial transcript. Between two pieces of yellowing cardboard with rust-colored speckles were more than three hundred typewritten pages. Handing the transcript to me, he told me that people said he could get rid of it now that he was out. But he opted to keep it. He opted to hold on to his past.

Bruce's trial transcript is far more comprehensive than I had imagined. It didn't only open the door to his particular story; it revealed in detail an experience that for the most part remains in the dark.

The transcript entailed a loaded drama: two eyewitnesses, two opposing arguments, and a leading actor without any lines. Yet no newspaper even took note of the case. On the surface Bruce's case was so commonplace that hardly anyone cared. It blended into the anonymity of daily statistics: men kill men; blacks kill blacks. Men kill with guns. Men kill under the influence of alcohol, heroin, and cocaine. Drunk and high black men kill one another. Bruce was no exception.[2]

Bruce was charged with possession of a loaded pistol with the intent to use it unlawfully and with murder in the second degree for causing the death of Tyrone Davis. The judge offered Bruce a plea bargain if he pled guilty to manslaughter. This was Bruce's first felony. Bruce said the most he could have gotten was $8^{1}/_{3}$ to 25 years. He might have been out after 16 years. But his public defense attorney, Michael Torres, suggested Bruce go to trial. He was convinced he could get him off with less time. After all, no murder weapon was ever found, no physical evidence was recovered, and Bruce didn't admit to the crime. And the only two witnesses, unreliable boozehounds, changed their stories with the wind.

Torres thought it might be better if Bruce didn't testify. So Bruce just sat there and listened. He was effectively absent when the second-most important decision of his life was made.

April 22, 1983. The day the shot was fired, thirty-seven-year-old Vietnam veteran Slover Bouknight, an acquaintance of Bruce's who would later witness the shooting, bought his first bottle of Thunderbird wine as soon as the Monte Carlo Liquor Store opened. It must have been around eight o'clock in the morning. He went to his mother's house, hung out there for a while, and, around eleven o'clock that same morning, returned to the store to buy another bottle. Over the course of the day he continued drinking, alternating among wine, rum, and maybe some vodka. He didn't quite remember. He hung out with friends at the corner of Creston Street by the liquor store when he saw Bruce approach that night. "Gave me five," Bouknight said. He followed Bruce inside the store to borrow some money.

Bouknight's memory of his previous criminal record seemed as hazy as his recollection of the night of the crime. When Johnson, the prosecutor, asked him what he was convicted of, Bouknight answered, "Misconduct or something like that, mischief." Johnson continued his questioning:

JOHNSON: If I mentioned the name, would that refresh your recollection?

BOUKNIGHT: Yeah.

JOHNSON: Reckless endangerment?

BOUKNIGHT: Yeah.

JOHNSON: What was that about?

BOUKNIGHT: Me and my wife had an argument.

JOHNSON: As a result of that argument, what happened?

BOUKNIGHT: I went and got some gas.

JOHNSON: Some what?

BOUKNIGHT: Some gas.

JOHNSON: What did you do with the gas?

BOUKNIGHT: Poured it on the floor.

Perhaps aware that the reckless endangerment conviction would take him in the wrong direction, Johnson finished his direct examination rather abruptly. For Johnson, Bouknight was there to reaffirm that he saw Bruce pull a gun, a claim he had made to the police and the grand jury earlier. He wasn't there to demonstrate that he was an unpredictable, violent, lying sponge—someone who saw a pistol and smoke coming out of Bruce's jacket one moment but later recanted, saying he heard a shot but that it was too dark and he was too far away to see anything, and that the street was filled with people.

Johnson handed Bouknight over to Torres for cross-examination. Torres extracted, in an equally labored fashion, testimony that Bouknight intended to burn his wife and children out of their apartment; that before he went to Vietnam he tried to sell drugs to an undercover agent; that he hadn't had a single job since he got back from the war; and that he still occasionally used heroin and cocaine.

On the evening of Bruce's crime Joseph Vega, a heroin user who had been fired from Center Fence for stealing chain-link fencing, was hanging out with Tyrone Davis. The two men visited Vega's fiancée, who was Tyrone's sister, at North Central Hospital. After leaving the hospital at around eight o'clock, they went to a liquor store at Bedford Park and bought a bottle of wine, which they drank on their way to the subway station. Vega said Davis was "kind of tipsy. . . . You know, he was kind of loud, you know, but he was in control of himself." (The toxicology lab found Davis's blood alcohol level to be 0.27, which according to the medical examiner's testimony leads to "loss of muscular coordination, staggering gait, thickened speech and some disorientation." The lab also found traces of heroin in Davis's blood.) Vega and Davis got off at 183rd Street and walked to Davis's house at 182nd Street and Creston so Davis could use the bathroom. Davis then agreed to walk Vega to the bus stop. On their way they apparently decided to get a bottle of White Rose at the Monte Carlo Liquor Store. At the store Tyrone Davis "complimented the girl" Bruce was with, according to Vega. "Dirty looks" were exchanged, and Tyrone Davis followed Bruce outside.

> VEGA (CONTINUING): I didn't hear what they were saying. The next thing you know they were like face to face and the tall guy, named Bruce Jones, he went to hit Tyrone and Tyrone went to hit him back and the next thing you know Tyrone ran into the street from the side- walk, around the car, back up onto the sidewalk, running down toward Jerome Avenue and as he was running down toward Jerome Avenue and as he was running, he turned around a little to see if he was still being chased—

> MR. TORRES: Objection. It calls for an operation of the mind, Judge.

> THE COURT: Just object, please, without a speech. He turned around?

> THE WITNESS: Yes.

> THE COURT: He just turned around.

> VEGA (CONTINUING): When he turned around, the man that was chasing him pulled out a gun and shot him.

Later on in the direct examination Vega mentioned that Bouknight, who'd been wearing a trench coat that night, pulled out a carpenter's knife.

"I told him it was unnecessary to pull out a carpenter's knife," Vega said, "because if there was going to be [a] fight, it was between the two." After firing the shot, Vega said, Bruce didn't bat an eye. He turned around and ran toward Grand Concourse.

Vega looked at his friend Tyrone Davis, who just stood there, his hands grabbing his chest, before collapsing. Blood streamed out of his mouth and nose.

Vega forced Bouknight, who seemed eager to get away, to return with him to the liquor store and wait for the police. From Bouknight's perspective

Vega became quite violent. "The Spanish guy"—as Bouknight, Torres, and Johnson repeatedly called Vega—"hit me in the back of the head, ripped my shirt off," Bouknight said. "Then he drug [sic] me back down to the corner 'cause I had turned the corner and he drugged [sic] me back down and that's when the police put handcuffs on me."

The bullet had perforated Davis's chest four and a half inches above the left nipple, entered the left chest cavity through the second rib, and pierced the upper lobe of the left lung and the sac that surrounds the heart. It went on to penetrate the main bronchus and the upper lobe of the right lung and exited into a muscle through the fifth rib in his back. Dr. Mella Leiderman, the testifying medical examiner, could not say for certain from which direction the bullet was shot or from what distance. At first it appeared the shot was fired from below and not from short range, facts that might have worked in Bruce's favor. A man of his height would be more likely to shoot a shorter victim from above, and a shot from far away could have established a decreased likelihood that Vega or Bouknight were capable of accurately identifying the shooter. But Leiderman explained that any small change in posture (a slight turn or bend or even a deep inhalation) could change the course of a bullet.

In the cross-examination Vega suddenly admitted that, although the fluorescent light of the liquor store illuminated the dark street somewhat, he could not really make out the details of the process that made Davis collapse. He saw "a flash" and heard "a bang." At this point Davis and Bruce were between thirty and forty feet away from him, and Bruce had his back turned to Vega, who now claimed that he had been distracted by Bouknight, the man in the trench coat with the carpenter's knife, when the shot was fired.

Because he considered the testimony of both witnesses insufficient if not ridiculous, Bruce's defense attorney, Torres, motioned for a mistrial. When the judge denied his motion, Torres asked him to reduce the charges from murder in the second degree to manslaughter in the second degree.

JUDGE: Second? Where, from a fair view of the evidence, do you see that? Would you explain that to me?

MR. TORRES: Well, Judge, in view of the fact there's been no testimony that actually saw the weapon being shot and in view of the fact that both witnesses merely heard a sound, a pop, and saw a flash at a considerable distance, I think the jury could infer that the shooting was done accidentally and not with any intent to cause death or cause injury, physical injury.

COURT: Accidentally?

MR. TORRES: Recklessly. By the same view that Bruce possessed a weapon and discharged it in the direction of Tyrone Davis, they could believe that he did so not with the intent to kill or cause his death, but rather merely with the intent to either cause serious physical injury, which would make it manslaughter in the first degree, or to scare him and as a result of that he recklessly caused the death.

Bruce was sentenced to twenty years to life. While he now admits his guilt and shows genuine remorse for having ended someone's life, he thinks he did not receive a fair trial. No one ever saw a gun on him. There was no physical evidence. His brother, who had observed the incident from across the street unnoticed and from whom Bruce found out that Tyrone Davis had died, had gotten rid of the murder weapon. Bruce was arrested more than sixteen hours after the act at Munchtown. A drug test may have shown that he was high on cocaine when he committed the crime, but no one bothered to check. The only two witnesses were drunk and possibly under the influence of illegal drugs.

It took Bruce two years to reveal to me another, pivotal piece of information, one that the trial transcript had neglected. Over barbeque ribs at a restaurant not far from the Castle, Bruce finished his story. After having separated his female friend and Tyrone Davis, he left the liquor store. The girl immediately took off on foot. Joseph Vega and Tyrone Davis followed Bruce out of the store. Bruce and Tyrone started to argue again. Every time Bruce and Tyrone started to fight, Joseph would stick his hand in his coat pocket as if he were about to pull a gun. According to Bruce, Tyrone was the first to land a blow. He hit Bruce in the face. Bruce pulled a gun. It was then that Bruce realized that neither Tyrone Davis nor Joseph Vega actually had a gun. They were just bluffing. Terrified, Tyrone ran. *I'll fuck this motherfucker up*, Bruce remembered thinking. He chased Tyrone down and shot him. At that point the fact that Tyrone and Joseph had just bluffed and that Tyrone had run away like a coward was more infuriating to Bruce than the insults Tyrone had hurled at his friend.

"Then I was living by a street code," Bruce explained to me at the restaurant. "If you don't have a gun, you don't play like you have a gun. You pull a gun, you use it." Tyrone didn't play by the "street code," but Bruce did. The code held that because he had pulled a gun, he had to use it. After all, his internal sense of propriety was not the only thing at stake. At that point the whole neighborhood was watching.

Bruce's trial transcript and his follow-up story provide a window onto an environment with codes revolving around self-preservation and respect. Bruce had to communicate to his community that he was willing to fight.

Elijah Anderson, now a sociology professor at Yale, spent several years in the 1990s documenting street law in a poor African American neighborhood in Philadelphia for his book *Code of the Street: Decency, Violence, and the Moral Life of the Inner City*. Anderson describes street laws as a response to alienation and racial discrimination by those who make and enforce America's mainstream laws (namely the police and the judicial system).

Street law governs "interpersonal public behavior, particularly violence," Anderson wrote. It is a form of communication whose nature "is largely determined by the demands of the circumstances but can include facial expressions, gait, and verbal expressions."[3] *Joseph would stick his hand in his coat pocket as if he were about to pull a gun. . . . The whole neighborhood was watching. If you don't have a gun, you don't play like you have a gun. You pull a gun, you use it.*

For people like Bruce, who have lived in poor, violent environments all their lives, these laws provide safety, "for if they *are* bothered, not only may they face physical danger, but they will have been disgraced or 'dissed' (disrespected)."[4]

After listening to Bruce's story I wasn't surprised to read in a 2009 Department of Justice study—which followed up on Anderson's findings—that "a youth's expressed street code attitude is a developmental predictor of violent behavior."[5] What struck me was that the street code didn't loosen its grip in prison. I now understood what Bruce told me when we first started talking. He said, "You are coming from a crime-infested environment. You are familiar with the people [in prison] and their lifestyle. They were doing the same thing as you were doing in your neighborhood. We all know each other from the street."

Dismissing your moral code and thinking in an environment that, whenever you take a step forward, pushes you back seems almost impossible. Yet being able to control your impulses, feel empathy, and take responsibility for your actions is the first step toward rehabilitation, the first step necessary to return to and function in mainstream society. Naturally, I wondered who or what taught Bruce alternative ways of thinking. And since I came to see conditioning, violence, and rehabilitation as tightly intertwined, I also wondered how exactly he came to think the way he did in the first place.

CHAPTER FOUR

Talking Murder

Angel seemed mad. I had already apologized twice for being late and didn't know what else to do. When I arrived at the Castle one day in late June of 2007, Angel was sitting alone in the backyard reading one of his old poems. Full of pathos, his poems' main themes expressed his wish to break out of his former self, his isolation, and his attempts to enter our world, if only spiritually. *What do I owe you Oh My Society that you punish me so?* one of them read. *What rights under heaven do you claim to do with me as you wish? Who in this realm is more worthy of your mercy than I?*[1]

A black iron gate stood between us, and Angel and I had to go around the corner to meet. I had brought cherry-apple-apricot cake and grapes because we wanted to picnic in the park by the Hudson River. As we headed to the water, Angel crossed Riverside Drive erratically at a red traffic light. A few months after his release he seemed to have put aside all decision making involved in crossing the street. He told me to follow him, but the street curved at such a dramatic angle and the cars moved so fast that I decided to wait for the light to change. As Angel crossed, part bold, part careless, he looked determined yet lost. He wore big mustard-colored Timberlake boots, and his khakis were far too wide and about five inches too short. If his pants hadn't been held up by a belt they would have been around his ankles. But the belt seemed to serve another crucial purpose. He needed it to attach his pedometer. His Digiwalker counted the miles he walked each day—

usually about two, but today a bit more, since it took us a while to find a spot to sit.

The pedometer was a present from Tanya, a Quaker who had sent him letters in prison and developed a growing interest in him since his release. She had also given Angel a cell phone, vouched for a credit card, and started to pay him frequent visits at the Castle. I had yet to meet Tanya, but Angel had made sure right off the bat that I knew he had a way with the ladies. Once he declared that a woman across from us was looking at him like he was "a box of chocolate." "I'm starting to get bothered by these side glances," he told me another time. When I asked him how he noticed a woman's interest, he said, matter-of-factly, "If she messes with her hair, she's interested."

The bench Angel chose was between the river and the highway. It was strangely high, and our legs dangled as if we were children. Angel's mood lightened. "This is not bad at all," he finally said, gobbling down a piece of cake. "The cake, the sun, the wind . . . it's actually quite nice." I understood now that Angel wasn't mad at all. Maybe he was afraid of meeting. He was afraid of this not being *nice*. Although we didn't discuss what we would talk about, Angel must have anticipated what I wanted to know.

All he had told me by this point was that he had killed "a friend" when he was eighteen. Through the Inmate Lookup Search Engine of the New York State Department of Corrections, I learned that he hadn't told me the whole story. In addition to the murder he committed, the site listed an attempted murder and an escape. Although it provided me with more information about Angel than Angel had provided, it amounted only to a peek through the keyhole. It obscured the circumstances under which he had committed his crimes, and the victims remained unnamed, as did the precise length of his prison sentence. His minimum prison sentence was given as fifteen years, but his maximum sentence was indeterminate: "LIFE years, 99 months, 99 days."

A life sentence means that a prisoner can be denied parole and that even if he is released he could potentially remain on parole for the rest of his life. The additional "99 months, 99 days" are of course rhetorical: a murderer always remains a murderer, even after his death.

Angel wore a pair of mirrored sunglasses. All I could see was my reflection, glimpses of the river, and, once or twice, a barge passing by. He began to talk about remorse.

"I had just turned eighteen, and I committed this crime. This horrible, horrible crime. A terrible thing, and I always regretted it. People talk about remorse, but most people don't understand what the word *remorse* really means. Remorse means more than just saying 'I'm sorry.' Remorse means changing your life. Remorse is feeling sorry in your heart, feeling true regret, irrespective of what people think. Remorse is something that I have learned. I felt bad the moment after I did it. I had crossed the line and I could never go back. I think I wanted to go to prison. I wanted to pay. Which is strange. I confessed. I went to prison for something else, and they asked me about it and I confessed anyway."

On February 27, 1978, Angel and his friend had met at 8:30 a.m. in an apartment on 118th Street and Pleasant Avenue. He had access because he had been helping a "drunk handyman" paint the place. He and his friend found themselves arguing about a kid who had accidentally shot himself in the head. "He had found his father's gun in the drawer, and he had pulled the gun and shot himself. And we were arguing about that—I said it was the parents' fault; she said that it was the kid's fault."

"*She?*" I asked. This was how I learned that Angel had killed a woman, and I was stunned.

I tried to gather myself. "Was she your girlfriend?"

"*A girl* friend, not a love interest," Angel continued, seemingly annoyed by my question. "It was a girl—which is embarrassing to me." He paused before going on to explain he had grown up with the girl. "So we got into this argument, which was stupid. She said it was the kid's fault, and I said it was the parents' fault. And she goes, 'You don't know nothing, you are stupid.'

And I said, 'Don't call me stupid.' She had an attitude, that's what it was. But no reason to kill somebody, because they got an attitude.

"She slapped me and that's all she wrote. I just lost my motherfucking mind."

Angel strangled sixteen-year-old Olga Agostini with a rope he had been using to play cat's cradle.

"I was playing with a rope that I found, you know, making those little triangles in your hand? I was playing with that, and I strangled her with it. The moment I started, I realized, 'Oh, my God! Look what you made me do!' And that became an angle. How dare you put me in such a position."

I noticed myself staring at Angel's hands. I found it uncomfortable to look at his mirrored glasses and see myself while he talked about strangling the girl. His hands are small, wide, and brown, with neatly cut fingernails. They are meaty and round. I lifted my eyes to his face and concentrated on his mouth. He has large, pink lips, speckled with gray, and plaque on his teeth.

"I was thinking, 'Oh, my God! Look what I'm doing.' Almost like, 'How could *you* do this to me? How could *you* put me in this position?'" Angel continued. "I just got angrier and angrier. All of a sudden, she became all my anger that I have ever felt, about my parents, about everything that had gone into my life at that point, all the disappointment. It just kept bubbling forth. There was such a rage. I think in that moment I hated my life. I hated life and everything in it. And I always said that to myself: I think in that moment I hated life and everything in it. That is about as intense as people get."

After strangling Olga, Angel felt a sense of relief. He went to his apartment and waited.

"After I woke up from the moment of intense anger, she was still on the ground in the hallway, and I wasn't sure if she was dead or not. So I went up to her and I started feeling her pulse." Angel touched his neck to demonstrate. "I realized, 'Oh, my God!' Anyway. I was like, 'Oh, shit, what do I do now?' So I went into panic mode. 'I got to remove the body. I can't deal with this right now.'

"Part of me wanted to go to jail and part of me didn't want to go to jail right [then]. And I was trying to figure out how do I explain this? I never dealt with something like that. And I didn't understand what had happened. What I'm telling you now is an analysis of what had happened. In that moment I couldn't have explained to you any of this because I didn't know what was going on. It was just all the rage and everything that has ever been done to me as a child, all that abuse . . . finally . . . I hate my life. That's terrible. To feel that at such a young age."

Angel had no idea what to do with the body, so he imitated what he had seen on TV. He carried Olga onto the building's roof. But having doubts about the hiding place, he returned to Olga's corpse at night. He carried her to an adjacent, abandoned building on 117th Street and removed her clothes and jewelry to hinder identification. He removed a ring she was wearing that spelled LOVE and gave it to one of her friends.

Angel was not immediately caught after committing his first crime. After he killed Olga, he began working as a dishwasher. He became nervous as the enormity of his crime began to sink in.

"I knew I'd get arrested," he said on the bench by the Hudson River. "That's probably why I drank. It's pretty bad [that] I just killed my friend in a hallway. That was bothering me, and I think that's why I drank. I never drank; I always smoked pot. That's why I went out, to get away from—to go somewhere else, somewhere different, outside of my normal self.

"I was a dishwasher." Angel mimicked a Chinese accent. "A dish-washaa, you know, like in this movie? What's it called? Well, doesn't matter." He grinned. I was surprised by how easily Angel was able to switch from the dire subject to a joke. I was more affected by Angel's murder tale than Angel was himself. I began to doubt the sincerity of the story's remorseful introduction.

I wondered if maybe it *is* possible to distance yourself from your crime and your past to the extent that the murderer seems like a completely different person. Maybe it was even necessary if you wanted to "fit in."

At eighteen Angel couldn't read or write, and being a dishwasher was one of the few odd jobs he'd ever had. On his third workday Louis Magan, an older colleague, invited him to a bar after work. But first he showed him his gun, a .22 caliber.

"You snap it open," Angel explained to me. "It has six barrels, but I don't know about guns. He had showed me the gun earlier in the elevator. So I took a butcher knife. If he has a gun we must be going to someplace where you got to be armed. Okay, I got armed. I took the butcher knife from the drawer and I wrapped it in newspaper and stuck it in my pocket, and I was praying that it didn't cut me."

Angel and Magan made their way to a bar near the Port Authority. On March 11, 1978, the city was cold, and trash lined the streets. Garbage removal had been suspended for weeks because the Department of Sanitation's vehicles were being used for snow removal. It had snowed twelve times already that winter.

"It was the first time I ever went to a bar," Angel continued. "I had not eaten, and I got drunk very fast. And then somebody shot himself in the hand and [Louis] left me there. He left with a prostitute. And I'm in a corner in the back, and I thought I got to go past those guys. So we got into an argument over that—about him leaving me in the bar. 'How dare you leave me? What's wrong with you? The guy shot himself in the hand. How you gonna take me out and just leave me!' Duh! I was drinking, he was drinking, we got into a shoving match. I sliced his throat and stabbed him, and I ran. He was reaching for the gun. He stuck his hand in his coat, that's when I grabbed my knife in the pocket. Because it was cold, I had my hands in the pocket. I grabbed my knife and I stabbed him and I ran. I thought I'm going to get shot anyway. You see it in the movies: the guy gets cut, he falls down, he's dead. In real life you stab somebody, and he keeps walking. What the hell do you know? You watch TV. It's terrible." Angel laughed again. "Television prepares you terribly for reality."

After the stabbing Angel ran home. The next day a coworker called to tell him that the police were looking for him.

According to Angel the two weeks that elapsed between Olga's murder and the attempted murder of Magan were a blur. By the time he got into the argument in the bar that led to the stabbing, the police had already found and identified Olga's body. They knew that Angel had given Olga's LOVE ring to one of her friends.

Angel was arrested the following day and charged with murder.

On March 15, 1978, the *Daily News* ran a piece titled "Nab Youth in Slaying."[2] John Lewis's article appeared next to a picture of two clowns entertaining children during a classroom visit.

> Angel Ramos, an 18-year-old East Harlem youth, was charged yesterday in the death of 16-year-old Olga Agostini of 2133 Madison Ave., whose nude body was found wrapped in a plastic bag Thursday in an abandoned building at 517 East 117th St.
>
> The girl, who was strangled, was last seen alive by her sister on their way to school Febr, 27th at 8am. She was reported missing by her mother, when she failed to return home by 10 o'clock that night. Ramos was arrested Monday night.
>
> HUNT MAN IN OTHER CASE
>
> In recent days, rumors have been circulating in East Harlem that six girls, all acquainted, were missing.
>
> Lt. Herman Kluge of the Sixth Homicide Zone said that while a number of girls have been reported missing in the area, police know of only one who was a friend of Olga's. He said she was recently in the area accompanied by Juan Troche, 34, whose last address was 326 E. 116th St.—an abandoned building.
>
> Police want Troche on charges of impairing the morals of a minor.

After Angel had finished his murder story, a story he said he had never told to anyone, we quietly made our way back to the Castle. Over the past few hours the park had turned into an aggressive amusement zone, with families barbecuing, kids screaming, couples making out under trees, and reggae music blaring from nearby car stereos. Something about the atmosphere compelled Angel to begin speaking about his Puerto Rican background.

"We have problems," he began. "Latin people have their own problems. I look down on them. They just have certain behaviors that you don't want the world to see. I'm embarrassed by a certain way of acting and certain attitudes—a certain loudness, certain manners of dress, and certain manners of speaking, just acting in a manner that is not gentlemanly and appropriate."

We walked across the bridge that connects the park to Riverside Drive. It was time to say good-bye. I was drained. But Angel simply gained momentum. As we reached the corner where we would part, he said that he felt like hugging me. His whole face lit up. He appeared heartened by the intimacy of our conversation and hugely relieved after having shared the seminal event in his life.

I subconsciously took two steps back. We did not hug.

Usually I don't have trouble sleeping. The night after Angel told me about taking Olga's life, however, I slept terribly. I dozed off, but suddenly I was awakened by images of Angel's hands throttling Olga's neck. I saw the lifeless body of a young girl being stuffed into trash bags and hauled across a dark street. I saw Angel undressing the girl and struggling to pull off a ring that read LOVE.

In light of these visions Angel's poem—"What do I owe you Oh My Society that you punish me so"—read differently. Ever since I had met Bruce, Adam, and Angel, I wondered what a murderer had to do to be forgiven. What did Angel have to do so we could forgive him for strangling Olga? Not wanting to put the burden on Angel alone, I also wondered about our own role, as society and as individuals, in all this. I knew that rehabilitation could not be accomplished by punishing the murderer indefinitely.

CHAPTER FIVE

Poster Boys

I first learned about the Castle through Rich, a former drug kingpin who had served ten years for three counts of armed robbery. Rich represented himself as one of the Fortune Society's poster boys. He gave me my initial tour of the premises.

Rich rushed down the stairs to welcome me, wearing a red button-down linen shirt, baggy blue jeans, and Timberlake boots. He smelled of aftershave. At first his angular features seemed almost brutal, but the impression quickly faded when he cracked up at his own jokes.

"You look good, hon," he said, beginning the Castle tour. The first thing I noticed by the entrance was a bucket filled with condoms and a billboard listing names and duties. "Look. Whose name is this?" Rich asked, as if subjecting me to a reading test. His name was at the top of one of the lists. He supervised the crew that cleaned the cafeteria. "I just make sure they clean all right, you know." ("They" being a group of his fellow residents.) He grinned, gazing at me out of the corner of his eye. He waited for me to react; then he chuckled. "Nah, I don't clean," he snorted. "If I had a whip I'd put them in the show and whip them." On my first visit to the Castle Rich went through every list on the halfway house's various billboards. He had me read names, activities, and rules.

Rich pointed at the photos decorating the walls and had me identify the people I had already met. He rattled off any additional information that came to mind. The man was a machine. It was hard to follow his hectic agenda. He whisked me to a room with a large flat-screen TV and several couches and chairs. Along the way he introduced me to everyone we encountered. Sarah ("She used to suck ten dicks a day," he whispered), Aazim ("He's blind, ya know"), and Janine, one of the counselors.

The Castle has its own counseling services. Most of its residents share the same parole officer. A staff of eighteen supervises the men and women at all times. The residents and their visitors have to sign in and out, undergo daily drug testing, and attend thirty-five hours a week of "productive service," which may consist of work (for those who can find it), vocational classes, job hunting, and volunteer work. A computer lab is housed in the basement, and the cafeteria offers three meals, as well as coffee, soda, and snacks. A support group meets for thirty minutes twice a day in the cafeteria. At the Morning Focus the residents share their plans for the day; at the Evening Focus they reflect on the day's rewards and disappointments. On Thursday nights the residents meet for approximately ninety minutes in a large conference room where Castle residents discuss the larger problems and conflicts that come with transition and cohabitation.

"No 'rape-os' live in the Castle," Rich remarked out of the blue, as we were leaving the building to go to Riverbank State Park right across the street. "What do you think? The apartments in the neighborhood run for $4,000 a month."

Rich had finished his Castle tour in lightning speed, imparting as much detail as security allowed. On our way out I took a second look at the hand-written sign in the entrance hall: "In this Castle we all rule." After Rich's tour the sign's assertion didn't quite ring true. Like any other place, the Castle is composed of leaders and followers, and it excludes some individuals that no one wants to embrace.

Having lived in the Castle for eight months, Rich had long passed the initial "emergency phase" in which men shared rooms with six beds. (In fact, Rich claimed that his influence was so far-reaching and that he was so well respected that he never had to share a room with five other men as did Angel, Adam, and Bruce.) Gradually, as the men stayed out of trouble, they moved up to rooms with two or three beds and, later, if they were lucky—or as "influential" as Rich—a little studio of their own. The residents were allowed to come and go as they pleased but had to adhere to either the seven o'clock or nine o'clock curfew, depending on their parole stipulations. They received help finding permanent housing and navigating the welfare system but had to undergo daily drug testing and attend certain functions.

At first I found Rich funny, smart, and devious. I thought this combination would make him an interesting subject for this book. But after interviewing him over the course of two years, I changed my mind. Too many of our conversations were "off the record." When Rich talked about his crimes, he left out the most horrific parts. (It wasn't until I read his parole hearing transcripts that I found out that it was a matter of luck that his robbery victims survived the ordeal he had put them through.) Rich often seemed revengeful; one of his main motivations in life seemed to be maintaining control. I include him here because he taught me about the Fortune Society and the Castle, introduced me to many of its residents and staff, and, most important, because his character touches on the question guiding this book: what constitutes success in rehabilitation?

On the surface Rich *was* successful. He had a number of girlfriends and eventually found himself an apartment in a relatively good neighborhood in Manhattan. He worked as a private trainer for women he chatted up in the park and landed construction jobs that paid three or four times the minimum wage. Yet he always seemed to ride the shaky fence between lawfulness and transgression. He lacked empathy and remorse for the many crimes he committed and the lives he destroyed.

Shortly after his release from prison, Rich started to develop a friendly relationship with David Rothenberg, the man who founded the Fortune

Society. Rich enjoyed making fun of Rothenberg. "How do you guys find all these women?" He mocked Rothenberg behind his back, using a helium voice. "Motherfucker, you really asking that question? Who the fuck you mean? I could pick up a model!"

David Rothenberg fit well into the Castle's august ambience. He was a prominent yet slightly aseptic New York character with a royal flair. A former Broadway producer and publicist, he once had the looks of a young Robert De Niro. In the 1960s he worked with celebrities such as Richard Burton and Elizabeth Taylor. In 1967 Rothenberg produced *Fortune and Men's Eyes*, a play that dealt with homosexuality and sexual slavery in prison. Its appearance dovetailed with a problem that had just begun a precipitous rise: America's prison population would quintuple over the next four decades.

Attracted by the empathetic spirit of the play, swarms of ex-cons turned to Rothenberg for help. Rothenberg saw the need for an organized support system and founded the Fortune Society. Since then, thousands have walked through Fortune's doors. Although some returned to prison, others have managed to create more or less successful lives for themselves.

Rich didn't care about Rothenberg's notoriety. He had decided to utilize him and Fortune to help him create a successful life for himself. He was glad to have found an organization that helped with all the necessary paperwork associated with welfare and Shelter Plus, a program that provides rent assistance to homeless people. He also obtained Rothenberg's cell phone number, which he called once or twice a week to ask for free tickets to Broadway shows. Never mind that Rothenberg was gay and that Rich had nothing but aversion for homosexuals. He had gone to fifty shows in the last eight months and continued to ask for more tickets. Often he took a date, sometimes two. In return Rich attended the Castle's public functions. Ever charming, he appeared at health fairs, advocacy meetings, lectures, and fund-raisers, ridiculing Rothenberg behind his back.

Rich prided himself on knowing what wealthy people wanted to hear and was able to switch easily between poster boy and bad boy, between upright citizen and crook. Although he represented himself as the epitome of successful rehabilitation, to me he was quick to admit his motivation: his role earned him favors and privileges at the Castle. But after several months in this function, the question of what he could do for Fortune was overridden by a demand: what could Fortune do for him? One could sense that being a poster boy was wearing thin on him and that he was hoping for a replacement.

As I arrived at the Castle for its fifth birthday celebration and fund-raiser in June 2007, I was once again awed by its opulence and beauty. The halfway house's immense wooden entrance door reminded me of the medieval castles I had visited in Germany. I signed in and made my way to the backyard, where the event was to take place.

Angel was chosen to give a speech at the event. He dubbed himself "the Prince of the Castle." The anniversary celebration doubled as a fund-raiser for the halfway house's expansion. The plan was that in three years there would be a second, environmentally green "Castle," 11 stories high, with 114 additional apartments. The apartments were to be occupied by a mix of residents: people who had become self-sufficient, who had "graduated" from Castle number one, and by low-income residents from the community. But for now there was no money to build, and, except for a small temporary gazebo, the backyard was bare, with no trees or shade. Just grass, asphalt, and hot wind.

Although the lot was anything but cozy, it was a far cry from what it used to be when Fortune first bought the property. Completed in 1913, the building was once known as St. Walburga's Academy of the Society of the Holy Child Jesus. For half a century it served as a boarding and day school for girls, then briefly as a yeshiva, before being abandoned for more than four decades. When Fortune acquired the building in 1998, drug dealers and users had taken over the back lot. The organization cleaned up the corner and lot, thereby contributing to a cleaner and safer West Harlem, a story its leaders proudly share whenever they are given the opportunity.

I looked around and wondered where Adam was. I guess he didn't enjoy this kind of event. His interest was advocacy, not marketing and mingling with wealthy donors. I had last seen him at a reentry event, where he spoke about connecting outside organizations with prisoners. He still wanted to help his "family," those lifers he had left behind in prison. I guess Adam, with all his doubts and fears—his anger about public policy—would not make for a good poster boy.

Bruce helped to set up for the event. He put the flower decorations on the folding tables and helped Aazim, the Castle's portly cook, carry out the food. Although Bruce felt insecure and out of place among the wealthy, white fund-raisers who had begun to assemble in the yard, he was glad to be free and to have a role he could attend to. The flower bouquets looked oddly delicate in Bruce's huge black hands.

Angel looked handsome and charming in a gray suit and tie. He was jokey and chipper, but he seemed too nervous for a prince. It was his first fund-raising event and his first public appearance, and he wasn't quite sure how to perform. Should he give the speech he had practiced ahead of time, or should he speak from the heart, risking gaps and stutters while sounding more sincere? He decided to put off the decision to the last minute.

Rich seemed a bit nervous also, fiddling compulsively with his cell phone. For him promotion and fund-raising weren't the issue; he was juggling several girlfriends that summer and was afraid to miss a call. Kristen Kidder, then editor in chief of *Fortune News*, the agency's publication about prison life and reentry, prodded Rich to exchange niceties with the Castle's funders.

"Just treat them like you were welcoming them at your house," Kidder suggested.

"This *is* my house," Rich responded, sounding bored and defensive.

Angel's hands trembled a bit as he welcomed the funders. The atmosphere was drenched with awkwardness. Dressed in suits, dresses, and hats, the visitors seemed out of place on this empty lot in Harlem. A thousand little windows from neighboring buildings stared down on us like dark, vigilant eyes. A dozen wealthy white men and women and a handful of dark-skinned ex-cons in various states of rehabilitation waited quietly for the speeches to begin. True to his motto, "I put smiles and weight on people," Aazim zigzagged back and forth with bowls of alcohol-free punch and trays of miniature cheeseburgers. Also present was David Rothenberg. Tonight the short man with a delicate frame and reddish dyed hair was putting the final touches on his protégés. He tried to tell Barry Campbell, the assistant to Fortune's executive director, JoAnne Page, how to button his coat. Barry, his long dreads drawn back in a thick ponytail, didn't usually wear a suit and seemed uncomfortable. He unbuttoned his coat, then rebuttoned it. "Not this way, *that* way," David said.

"You what, Dave? A fashion consultant?" said Rich, who had chosen the seat next to mine. When David didn't respond, Rich repeated, "You what, Dave? A fashion consultant?" David still didn't respond. He briefly attempted to get up to assist Barry in buttoning his suit, but then he sat back down. "What do I know," he said.

People settled stiffly onto folding chairs.

"Good evening and welcome," Angel began. Inexplicably, he seemed to adopt a slight Spanish accent. The microphone was too high, and he would have had to stand on his toes to reach it. But he remained flat on his feet, and it was hard to understand him. His voice faded in and out.

Although he would later laugh about "the shakedown" of the wealthy, Angel went on to praise the Castle sincerely. "It's been wonderful and great," he said of his first weeks out. "But always scary." He went on to encourage the women and men in the audience to give people like him a second chance. He sprang one of his stock lines. "I just want to have the same problems you have." This time he added a little variation. "Tax me to death!" he shouted, throwing his arms in the air. The tension broke and the audience laughed with relief and applauded.

Rich had heard it all before and was looking for something with which to entertain himself. "Hi, my name is Rich," he whispered in my ear as if practicing an act. Pointing to the concrete-filled buckets that held down the gazebo, he snickered, "I used to tie these around people's necks and throw 'em in the river." He then stepped to the side to speak into his cell phone.

Angel thanked the audience for coming and received a hug from JoAnne Page on her way to the lectern. Page, her gray, frizzy hair emanating like steam, described the Castle as "the enzyme of transformation." She acknowledged that the first million had just come in from the city council and thanked the council's representative before adding that despite the generous infusion, it was just the beginning.

"Guess what?" she said, smiling and folding her hands. "We need your help!"

There followed more applause, more hugs, more awkward conversation. Beads of sweat were visible on the audience's foreheads. It was almost seven o'clock, but the heat hadn't let up.

Barry invited the guests on a tour of the Castle. While Rich had managed to silently vanish, Angel vacillated, unable to decide whether to accompany Barry and the others. By the time Angel made up his mind, the group had already left the backyard. He caught up with us just in time to hold the elevator door, reassuring a woman who said she suffered from claustrophobia.

"I feel the same way," he whispered gently. "We are almost there."

Our first stop was the Emergency Phase One section, one of the Castle's several three-person rooms for homeless men.

There was a stove, three cots, three backpacks, and three small fridges. "To avoid conflicts," Barry added.

"This looks like a dorm room," one visitor cheerfully proclaimed.

Angel had just been moved one floor down to Emergency Phase Two. He now shared a room with a man named Micky. "Micky," Angel told me, "behaves like he is still in prison." He rarely left his room. He watched TV and pumped iron and did little else. Micky and Angel hardly spoke.

After passing Emergency Phase Two, Castle residents moved into one of the forty private rooms that resembled Rich's.

Rich's room had a view of the park and the river. He had put a wax table-cloth with brown flowers on his little table. The table was set for two. This struck me as odd, as private visitors were forbidden in the rooms. Three photos of a woman in a revealing black dress were strategically arranged on the table. Under the bed were weights, several pairs of sneakers, and Timberlake boots. On the wall hung two rustic pictures, one of a romantic mountain cabin, the other of a stone well in a lush meadow.

In Rich's little showroom everything seemed to have its place. Even the three bottles of air freshener were neatly lined up on one of the bathroom shelves. Rich took great pride in having his room shown to potential funders. He told me that was because the other men lived "like animals."

Rich had left the fund-raising event as soon as he considered his obligations fulfilled. Most likely he had made plans during his earlier cell phone conversation. Despite the pictures on the wall his room seemed lifeless.

"What I like about this guy," guide Barry Campbell said about Rich, "is that he missed the computer age, and that's why he has a computer on his nightstand and the TV stored away under the sink."

Except that the computer was unplugged and by all appearances unused.

Gradually the crowd dispersed. The evening's business had given way to an awkward informal social setting in which everyone smiled woodenly and struggled for conversation. Some took the elevator, while Angel and I walked down the stairs with some of the others. As I admired the walls of rough, untouched schist on the side of the staircase, Angel remarked, "If this was mine, I'd sandblast these walls."

There was one last thing Barry Campbell wanted to show the potential funders: the drug-testing machine, a giant black apparatus that looked like a combination antique camera, optometric device, and magician's box.

To an extent the machine was a less harmful, amalgamated embodiment of the American philosophies of rehabilitation and punishment. It controlled (incapacitation), deterred (if you wanted to stay out of prison you had to stay sober), and, considering its placement, offered the illusion of assisting with rehabilitation. It was there to prove that Fortune cared—and maintained a tight grip on its residents. The potential funders weren't asked to support just any Harlem halfway house; the Castle was the crème de la crème of American halfway houses.

Angel quickly recognized the opportunity for an impromptu performance. He disappeared into the niche and swiped his ID card. He pressed his eyes against the "binoculars" on the large black machine. Then the machine started speaking. It ordered him to look straight into the light and to follow a pointer with his eyes. After a minute or two the machine spit out a receipt with his name, the date and time, the recorded velocity of his eyes, and the size of his pupils. The receipt categories read as follows:

Diameter

Amplitude

Latency

Velocity

FIT index

Have a nice day!

As the evening came to a close and the sun finally retreated, Bruce started carrying in the flowers. He was told to keep some for himself. He smiled insecurely and took one of the bouquets into his room. Angel was still chitchatting, telling a middle-aged blonde about how he became a Quaker while incarcerated. Quakerism demanded honesty, he told her, as if his commitment to religion were further proof of his rehabilitation.

"We Quakers believe that God didn't suddenly stop talking two thousand years ago. When you just quietly sit down and listen, he'll speak to you. He speaks to all of us." The woman patiently listened, throwing in a "Really?" here and a "Hmm, I didn't know that!" there. When Angel paused, she said, "Thank you for sharing," and left.

Tonight Angel had passed the test. He would become Fortune's poster boy.

"Could you find a sweeter, nicer guy?" Rothenberg marveled when I spoke to him after the event. "He is the sweetest, nicest, gentlest guy." He added, "Well, I don't know what the crime was." He admitted finding Angel so nice that he asked him to accompany him to a movie and that he considered him a friend now. "He is wonderful company," Rothenberg said. "He's smart, and he has got good values."

Rich, on the other hand, warned me that Angel was "crazy." Having spent a decade in prison and having dealt with criminals all his life, he prided himself on knowing every type of criminal. "You get into dangerous shit," he warned me, following it with his characteristic cackling and snorting.

CHAPTER SIX

Dinner with Bruce

One of the first things I heard about Bruce was that he had a way with cheese-cake. Rumor had it that it was celebrated in all of the prisons in upstate New York. Aazim called Bruce "The Institutional Junior," referring to the Brooklyn restaurant famous for its cheesecake. In prison Bruce would bake cheesecakes most weekends, particularly during football season. He used a regular pan and the little stove in his cell. He put a lifter on the stove to keep the cheese-cake from burning and let it sit there for about an hour and a half. Sometimes he added a can of mashed-up sweet potatoes "to turn the color."

"I used to do it for therapy," he explained.

Bruce's therapy consisted of six ounces of cream cheese, eight ounces of sour cream, one tablespoon of vanilla extract, one can of condensed milk, and two cups of sugar. For the crust Bruce crushed plenty of graham crackers and mixed them with butter. Bruce perfected his recipe through a "trial and error process." After he moved from prison into the Castle, he was nervous about the outcome of his cheesecakes. After all, he wasn't accustomed to using a regular oven.

To make his first cheesecake in the free world, one August morning in 2007 Bruce got up at five o'clock and sneaked down into the deserted Castle kitchen. He was relieved when the cheesecake turned out well and other residents asked for more. Once he saved me a piece. While I ate it, he stared intensely at me, as if trying to determine what grade I would give his cheesecake by the way I chewed and by my facial expressions. Without exaggeration, on a scale from one to ten, I would give it a ten.

Preparing a meal in the free world was a lot different from cooking in prison. To prepare a typical prison dinner, Bruce would put rice, calamari, octopus, and beans in a trash bag and drop the bag in a heavy-duty bucket filled with water. Then he would put a "stinger"—a spiral, water-heating device—into the bucket and go out into the yard for an hour. When he came back the "stew" would be done. This was much better than mess hall food. To be sure, there were certain foods in the mess hall that were okay—baked chicken, for example. But this was served only once every two weeks. Baked, ground, or fried, any type of chicken was better than Beef Yakisoba or Rice Diablo. No one with a little bit of money and a palate would go to the mess hall for dishes in which the ingredients were unrecognizable and, whatever they were, tasted awful.

Bruce's decisions pertaining to food became a bit of a problem on the outside. It took him a while to realize that he didn't have to eat calamari, octopus, and tuna anymore. At first he stocked up on tuna, peanut butter, and jelly—the staples of his prison cell "pantry." When he came out he bought twenty cans of tuna but then barely touched them. Once he bought some chicken without bones. It sat in the fridge for a week because he didn't have a sharp knife to cut it. He kept asking himself, "Why did I buy it?" He didn't know how to prepare whole chicken breasts, and he seemed unable to figure out where he could have them sliced.

It wasn't that Bruce was disappointed like Angel, who had envisioned "free food" so much tastier than it ended up being and who, as if searching for the ultimate meal, couldn't get enough of trying new dishes. For Bruce it was more a matter of choices and of shedding his jail attitude. Although the rules Angel and Adam had determined for him helped somewhat, he still had to decide what he wanted to eat. If not octopus and calamari in a bucket, if not tuna or peanut butter and jelly—then what?

Angel tried to make suggestions, but these suggestions didn't always work. One time that summer the three of us had gone on a tour of Williamsburg, Brooklyn. Adam had read in prison that the hip neighborhood was the new East Village, and, remembering the East Village's heyday, he was curious. We walked south on Bedford Avenue toward South Williamsburg, one of Brooklyn's Hasidic neighborhoods. While Adam trotted along, mouth agape, and Angel cheerfully chattered and marveled at everything he saw, Bruce seemed uncomfortable. He didn't say a word. Not only did the heavy iron bars in front of the Hasids' windows remind him of prison, but the people's stares also really bothered him. To have coffee and cake at one of the Hasidic bakeries on Lee Avenue was out of the question, so I decided to take the men to a bagel café back in North Williamsburg. But Bruce was overwhelmed by the many different types of spreads and bagels. He rubbed his forehead as if suffering from a headache. Eventually, he followed Angel's example (who had smoothly followed my example) and ordered a bagel with scallion cream cheese. But he was appalled when he discovered that scallions were onions and not seafood. Unable (or unwilling) to see Bruce's struggle, his shame and desperation, Angel snapped when Bruce threw his bagel into the trash.

This episode notwithstanding, Bruce clearly appreciates food. His cheesecake and his stories about cooking and baking in prison made me trust him. The preparation of food requires appetite, focus, and intuition, qualities Bruce and I share (even if I can't keep up with his baking skills). When I ran into Bruce at the Castle and sat down with him in the cafeteria, he remained reserved. But outside of the Castle, over tea and cupcakes, Mexican food, or a barbeque dinner, Bruce opened up.

He hadn't really talked about his crime for years. But he knew that if he wanted to establish real connections in the free world, he had to tell people that twenty-four years ago he had shot and killed another human being. His deeply ingrained feelings of guilt and shame made Bruce uncomfortable. Who could or should he talk to? The people he used to hang out with were either dead or locked up, or they belonged to a drug-ridden past with which he didn't want to reconnect. Bruce felt all right among the people at the Castle, "the criminal element," but the Castle was just a living arrangement based on a shared past. He would need to establish new social connections outside of the Castle. But what would that be like? How did it work, and what could he talk about? Bruce had spent the last twenty-four years in prison because he killed another man. He couldn't get out of his shell. Who was he without this experience? He was no longer the drug-addicted, empathy-lacking young man who acted on impulse, but he also didn't want to be just the ex-con. Something had happened in between, and he was free now. He was the result of the last fifty-two years. But how could he explain, and where should he begin? What would be a good moment? It wasn't easy to find the right words, let alone that most people didn't want to listen.

At the Castle people kept telling him, "You've got to let it out," without specifying what "it" was. Whenever he let "it" out, "it" was still there. It never ceased to exist. Letting it out was just another symptom, like a cough. You can cough all you like, but the virus remains inside you, where it continues to proliferate. Sometimes Bruce would bring it up, but then he would stop himself. At other times, his listener, afraid of contamination, would stop him.

It was ironic that no one wanted to discuss his criminal past. After all, it took him more than ten years finally to admit to having done wrong, to appreciate the fact that he had taken someone's life. When he was convicted, his father told him not to let what he'd done destroy him, to keep his head up. So he would do anything to avoid losing face. Admitting and feeling your guilt doesn't keep you intact. It tears you up. For the longest time Bruce thought he could avoid it—until he met Ms. Bracy.

Ms. Bracy, a counselor at Otisville prison, was "an older black lady with a good heart who really cared for black men." She was nice but firm, a devout Christian who didn't try to convert Bruce. She just took a liking to him. He was planning to go to the parole board continuing to deny what he had done. But Ms. Bracy wouldn't have it.

"At some point you have to accept responsibility for what you did," she said. She didn't ask much of him. At least, it didn't feel like it at first. She told him to take some time in his cell and reflect. Bruce liked Ms. Bracy. Her door was always open. He would drop by her office, and she would welcome him. He could talk to her. She was a good listener and wouldn't judge him. Then he would go to his cell and think. But after eighteen months he was transferred to another prison. He was taken away the same day he found out about the transferal, and he never saw Ms. Bracy again.

Bruce often thought of Ms. Bracy. He was grateful, but her legacy wasn't an easy one. Maybe he would have liked to talk more to people, the way he used to talk to her, but who could he talk to? Prisoners and ex-convicts hardly talked to one another about their crimes.

Opening up even a little meant a lot to Bruce. Ultimately, it meant that he would have to be able to tell the whole story. He was able to talk to me because our roles were clearly defined. I wasn't afraid to ask specific questions to do my research, and Bruce was happy to contribute. Although I guided the conversation through my questions, it seemed to me that Bruce knew exactly what he wanted to give. I didn't push him in a certain direction, nor was it a coincidence that our conversations always came back to the same topics: his crime, his guilt, and his process of becoming a different human being; food; and his concerns about connecting with "the other," be it white people or simply people without criminal records.

Bruce and I continued our dinner excursions. One night I took him to a Mexican restaurant on Broadway, just a couple of blocks from the Castle.

"What is this, Sabine?" he asked me, pointing at one of the dishes on the Mexican menu. "Can you order something for me?"

"What do you want me to order for you?"

"I don't think I would like it. I don't like avocado. I just want a soda." To the waitress he said, "Just give me a Red Bull."

I ordered chalupas with steak. Bruce, always suspicious of food he hadn't tried before, said to me, "Give me the one with steak," and I ordered for him.

"So no one ever talks about the crime?" I said, following up on what he had told me earlier.

"Nah."

How can you live your life without talking about its most defining aspect? How can you reconnect and "fix yourself" if an important link in the chain of events is missing? We have to look at how it all started to understand who we have become.

"Most people, they don't want to talk about it," Bruce said. "Once they find out you killed someone, you know, they leave that alone."

Bruce halfheartedly ate his chalupas and ordered a second Red Bull.

"Do you sense people's fear when you talk to them?" I asked. If he snapped once, what guarantee was there that he wouldn't snap again?

"A level of caution goes up," he said, adding that he didn't blame them.

The truth is, sometimes Bruce was afraid of himself. He thought he would never know for certain what he would do if he suddenly found himself in a threatening situation. And he hadn't really had enough time yet on the outside to find out. In prison it was easy. If someone offended you, you set an example. You took him to the bathroom and taught him a lesson. But Bruce knew that these street laws didn't apply to mainstream society, and he proudly shared with me an incident that allowed him to practice his new rules. More important, the incident proved that he was able to contain himself.

While he was waiting in line at the Housing Authority, some guy came in and cut in front of him. The receptionist was angry on Bruce's behalf, but Bruce kept telling him that it was not important. "Well, I'm gonna tell you a story," Bruce said to the receptionist. "Twenty-five years ago, I went into a

Dinner with Bruce

store to make a purchase and I got in an argument. . . . Sometimes you gotta think for other people." The receptionist was impressed. "I wanna shake your hand," he said. "Now that you told me your story I realize that some things aren't that important."

Although Bruce was committed to changing his way of thinking, he still had problems imagining himself a free man who had paid his debt and who—suddenly—was a law-abiding citizen in control of himself. He was still afraid to have his self-control tested. He still couldn't fully trust himself.

"Do you think it's likely that you'll be put in a situation where you feel threatened?" I asked him.

"Living in an area like this, yeah," he said about West Harlem. "You never know. You might bump into somebody, and it might lead to something else. You might go into the store to change a twenty-dollar bill and buy something and somebody might approach you. Do you understand what I'm saying?"

"But I don't feel that way when I walk through this neighborhood," I said.

"I mean, if somebody approached you to rob you—"

"I would give him everything I have. I wouldn't fight back," I finished his sentence.

"With my low life savings, I might have to fight for mine," Bruce said, chuckling.

I understood in that moment that if you were poor and were just released from prison into a neighborhood that wasn't much better than the one you grew up in, the variables that may cause you to land back in prison were endless. Given his past experiences and his present surroundings, Bruce had to exercise much greater self-control than I ever would. It is a privilege to be able to say, "I would give the robber everything I have. I wouldn't fight back." While I could *afford* an attitude like that, Bruce had to painstakingly *learn* it.

I spooned some salsa on my dish. Bruce usually didn't like spicy food, but he got curious after watching me put yet another generous spoonful on my tortilla.

"Sabine, what is this stuff?"

"It's salsa with cilantro and avocado. You want to try it?"

"Nah, I'm good."

"Are you afraid it's too hot?"

"No, I'm good."

Bruce mentioned that he had recently discovered the Dinosaur Restaurant under Riverside Drive, where they served some excellent "honky-tonk food." I promised that next time we would go there. It was clear that Mexican food had not quite worked out.

It was almost nine o'clock, close to Bruce's curfew and his Evening Focus meeting at the Castle. As we left the restaurant, he began to question my authority as a writer. He wondered whether a person such as I—white, young, German, middle class, with nothing but "book knowledge," as he put it—could really understand where he was coming from. "You are on the outside looking in, and I'm on the inside looking out," he said.

I understood his concern. I will never be able to understand his culture in the same way he does. And to pretend that I could would be outrageous. To illustrate our different perspectives, I pointed to a group of young men standing at the corner.

"I'm sure there is a big difference between hanging out with these guys and observing them as part of a satellite image," I said. Immediately I regretted my analogy. A satellite image seemed so superficial and pretentious compared to the insight both Bruce and I had to offer. Nevertheless Bruce got excited.

"Yeah, you see so much more if you look at a satellite image. You see the whole thing!"

An African American man passed us. "Hey, man!" Bruce nodded.

"Did you know him?" I said. Bruce said no. He often greeted black strangers, never white ones. His skin color united him with people he had never seen before. Suddenly I felt separated from him by a great distance.

As if to put my trustworthiness to the test one final time, Bruce asked, "Do you know what these guys are doing?" He pointed at one of the populated corners on Broadway. I have always resisted the assumption that every black man who hangs out at a street corner in Harlem is either selling or buying drugs.

"Selling drugs," Bruce said matter-of-factly, as if reading my mind. "On every single corner."

We had reached the subway station where he was to drop me off before heading back to the Castle. His brow furrowed with concern. He bent down to give me a hug. "You a'ight?" he asked. I said I was. "You sure?" he asked. I nodded. "Be good, a'ight? Be safe."

CHAPTER SEVEN

Job Readiness

Angel felt like throwing a brick. A few weeks after he was released, he began to experience anxiety in closed spaces. Whenever he was inside the Castle, he found himself cleaning obsessively. Something he had suppressed began to creep up in him. But what? He wiped surfaces and picked up little pieces of paper and cigarette butts. He was astonished by his own behavior. Obsessive cleanliness wasn't a problem he had had in prison, and he was determined to find out its motivation.

Angel thought that once released from prison he would be a free man again. When he first got out, he had big dreams. He felt like a young man. He wanted to get an apartment, a job, and a woman. "I'll find me a girl with kids. I don't care." He just needed some time to adjust to the world, some time to breathe and wander. Angel passively granted parole the authority to structure and control his life. He stoically accepted his parole officer's decision not to extend his evening curfew. The officer had said she would prolong the curfew to nine o'clock three months after his release but then inexplicably changed her mind on the ninetieth day. He seemed almost indifferent when he was denied a pass after his Upstate Quaker community awarded him a grant to spend a few summer days at a spiritual retreat in Silver Bay. "I already got over it," he told me the day after the decision was made. "Everything positive is discouraged."

One summer evening, as we sat in the Castle's backyard, Angel fumed, "I have all these people running my life and none of them is competent. If you think about it, I'd be one of the last guys you want to stress out."

This comment struck me as odd. It reminded me of what went through his mind when he killed Olga. "Look what you made me do!" he thought to himself when she went limp. It was as if the responsibility to keep his impulses in check lay outside of him. While I could relate to his anger about a reentry system that was, at times, Byzantine, useless, and even counterproductive, I did not understand how it could be the system's responsibility to prevent him from snapping again.

Right after his release Angel was forced to join a long chain of "job-readiness" classes. Welfare gave Angel $134 in cash every month, and Shelter Plus Care, a housing subsidy program of the Department of Housing and Urban Development, contributed $260 toward his $475 monthly rent at the Castle. The remaining $215 was covered by the Welfare Department (renamed Human Resources Administration, or HRA, to emphasize its new objective). To be eligible for the $215 HRA rent subsidy and the $134 in cash, Angel had to embark on a seemingly endless journey through a maze of institutions. In search of support, he patiently trudged through many of New York's state and nonprofit agencies that render services to ex-offenders.

Angel's day at WeCare (Wellness, Comprehensive Assessment, Rehabilitation, and Employment) began at nine o'clock in the morning. He was assigned to the "fast track," meaning that he was ready, willing, and able to work. Between 9:00 and 10:15 a.m. he was supposed to work on his typing skills and refine his résumé, a task he had finished weeks earlier. Without further assistance he was then expected to look for jobs online.

Funded by HRA, WeCare operates on a yearly budget of roughly $50 million. According to its website, WeCare serves more than thirty thousand men and women in the New York metropolitan area. It claims to be "a highly successful new paradigm in the delivery of welfare to work services."

WeCare, the site explains, "helps public assistance applicants and recipients with complex clinical barriers to employment, including medical, mental health and substance abuse conditions, to obtain employment or federal disability benefits."[1] Although his intake form states that Angel "does not appear to have psych [sic] related work restrictions," he was stuck in WeCare's system for a full three months.

Like its acronym, WeCare appeared friendly at first. Its walls were painted in lush spring colors and adorned with posters of flower bouquets. It seemed almost merry—all burgundy, mint green, and yellow, brightly lit and clean. Its classrooms were outfitted with rows of black state-of-the-art flat-screen computers. But after having spent several weeks filling out forms seven hours a day, reading handouts listing the characteristics of good job behavior, practicing his typing skills, listening to daily lectures about budgeting and applying for jobs online, Angel realized, "This is not about me."

He had met people who had gone through more than four twelve-week cycles (or one year) of WeCare workshops and still hadn't found a job. Angel started to loathe WeCare. "It's a waste of my valuable, valuable time," he said. "Let me put it like this: if they gave me the choice to smash my hand on a door or to go to this class, I'd smash my hand." He complained about the windowless rooms and the six minutes it took him to get out of the building if he wanted to smoke during his fifteen-minute break. Once passionate about computers—in prison he took every opportunity he could to work with them and had even learned how to write computer programs and build databases— he quickly started to detest them. About WeCare he said, "It's the first time in my life that I'm in front of a computer screen and bored to death."

Work has traditionally been seen both as the main method and the desired result of rehabilitation. The idea was first directly expressed and experimented with in the Auburn prison, founded in Upstate New York in 1817. Through quiet, collective work, vocational training, religious education, and discipline, the Auburn authorities claimed to reform the prison's inmates.

The Auburn system became the standard of American prisons in the decades that followed.

It was not until the end of World War II that penologists, experts on prison management and criminal rehabilitation, began to assess and classify criminals to determine the exact nature of the individual's criminality and to prescribe therapeutic, academic, and vocational "treatment" accordingly. But this "rehabilitative ideal" stagnated in the mid-1970s, when New York sociologist Robert Martinson concluded in a seminal survey that "with few and isolated exceptions, the rehabilitative efforts . . . have had no appreciable effect on recidivism."[2] Martinson's claims meshed with the get-tough approach of the following years, and lengthy incarceration replaced rehabilitation as the favored way to protect society.[3]

While work is important, there is little evidence that work in itself reduces recidivism.[4] When I spoke to criminal justice experts about ex-offenders, rehabilitation, and work, they all seemed to agree: work alone is not going to do it; people aren't criminals because they don't have a job; to keep people out of prison, one has to apply a holistic approach, using methods that have been scientifically proven to work. Yet government and community organizations like WeCare, CEO (Center for Employment Opportunity), and STRIVE (Support and Training Result in Valuable Employees) put their primary focus on work. And even those agencies that do offer a more holistic approach to rehabilitation—like the Fortune Society and the Doe Fund—use work as a signifier of practical and moral success. The Doe Fund's workers sweep city streets wearing blue uniforms adorned with an American flag and the slogan "Ready, Willing & Able."

Compounding the fact that work alone does *not work*, job opportunities for ex-cons are scarce. While WeCare claims to *find* work for welfare recipients, its job bulletin board was unpromising. The day I visited, the large board featured two job offerings (both for a medical billing assistant), which Angel confirmed was the average number posted at any one time. The welfare recipients in Angel's class had to rummage for work on their own. Angel did what he could by posting his résumé, registering for job alerts, and applying for jobs on NYpost.com, careers.com, careerbuilder.com, indeed.com, craigslist.org, and numerous other websites. He responded to postings for low-wage positions such as maintenance worker, janitor, mail-screening associate, clerical assistant, front desk clerk, customer service manager, and youth counselor. From the more than two hundred applications he sent out in ten weeks, he received only one callback but didn't get the job.

In prison Angel thought that it wouldn't be too hard to find a job once he got out. He believed he had come a long way. At eighteen he hadn't been able to read or write. He wet his bed and suffered from uncontrollable outbursts of anger. At forty-seven he had studied at the college level. He told me he had read several thousand books. He earned numerous certificates while incarcerated—a Vocational Appliance Repair Certificate, a Certificate of Proficiency for Computer Operator, a Certificate in Library Training, an IPA (Inmate Program Assistant) II Training Certificate, and several welding certifications—but in the outside world these credentials counted for little.

"Irrelevant," Angel said. "They might as well be toilet paper."

Angel had a serious criminal record, which anyone could easily access online, and virtually no outside work experience. He earned a computer operator degree from Sullivan County Community College in 1995, but since he was never employed in this profession, he had little opportunity to practice what he had learned and to keep up with the constant changes in the field. Rehabilitated or not, Angel could not find a job.

From 10:30 to 12:30 the WeCare students listened to lessons on work ethics, budgeting, time management, and analytical thinking. One exercise taught how to use an ATM machine. A sheet walked the students, many of whom did not even have bank accounts, through the various steps of withdrawing and depositing money. Another one of the exercise forms laboriously explained what interest rates are and then asked the respondent to calculate the yearly interest for eight consecutive years on a beginning balance of $9,000, an amount that for welfare recipients must seem like a mockery.

At WeCare Angel's tedious morning routine repeated itself between 1:30 and 5:00 p.m. with more job hunting, résumé building, and typing. These afternoon hours were the worst. Although Angel acknowledged that many of his fellow students were "broken" and might benefit from WeCare's curriculum, to him the lessons seemed superfluous. WeCare, "the giant superstructure of sucking up souls," made him angry. According to his and Bruce's description, WeCare amounts to a babysitting service for mentally challenged adults. There was no drive, no concrete goals, no individual encouragement. "At WeCare they are very professional in not listening to you," Angel said.

Adam had been able to avoid WeCare. He didn't depend on public assistance because he received monthly Social Security survivor payments from his late wife, Marietta, the woman he was married to when he went to prison. After he went away, Marietta broke up with him, but she never divorced him.

Bruce, however, got stuck in the system as well. He carped about his fellow students' hygiene, their lack of motivation, and the dearth of attractive women in his class. "The women there were *busted*," he said. "When you come out of prison after twenty-four years, you don't want to see these kind of women." He then went on to praise WeCare's good-looking female employees, acknowledging that he considered them off-limits. But no matter the drawbacks, once HRA referred you to WeCare, a job was the only way out.

Sometimes the students at WeCare had to practice mock interviews in groups of two and then evaluate each other on one of the copious forms given to them each week. Angel was bored stiff. He had long perfected his interview skills and his résumé while most of his fellow students were still barely able to form a clear sentence. And, in fact, Angel did stand out. The day I picked him up from WeCare I hardly recognized him. He blended in with the crowd of businesspeople rushing around Hudson Street and seemed out of place among his fellow students. WeCare required its students to abstain from wearing baseball caps, do-rags, T-shirts, and sneakers. The suit had, of course, been Angel's idea. I noticed that he had yet again shaved off his mustache. Many of WeCare's students were missing teeth, were covered in faded tattoos, and had visible scars. Most looked as if they had just gotten out of bed.

As Angel and I returned to the Castle, just in time to comply with his seven o'clock curfew, he performed an imaginary job interview for me. We sat down in the backyard, and I asked him whether he would prefer to change into something more casual, but he insisted on keeping the suit. He first explained how to respond to the two most critical questions on job applications if you've spent the last thirty years in prison. One question referred to past employment, and the other one asked, *Have you ever been convicted of a crime?*

"You put down the penal code of the crime—125.5 for murder, for example," Angel explained. "Don't put the crime itself. Write: 'Will explain further at interview.' This is a place of business, and you don't want people to gossip. This shows, 'I'm looking out for you already.' That's a technique. 'Imagine how I'm going to look out for you once I *do* work for you.' It's great psychology. Plus, people get interested. They want to know, 'What the hell is 125.5?' You want the guy to talk to you. Then it's your time to sell yourself. When he asks you about the crime, you go, 'Well, when I was eighteen years old, I got involved with some bad people. Somebody died; I was convicted of murder, and I was given life.' Not fifteen-to-life. *Life!* 'However, I was released for good behavior. While I was in there, I did this and I did that.' You go through your spiel. You talk about your social skills, your soft skills, your hard skills. You calm that person down. In other words, I went to jail, and it's not a big deal. You shouldn't be afraid of me. Once you see that on his face, it's no longer an issue. You move on to getting that job. What skills can I bring to this job? What can I do better than the other fifty applicants? I bring a whole different perspective. I think outside the box. I work harder than most guys. I love working. I've proved that I'm worthy of work. I can handle difficult people. I've been handling difficult people all my life. I have people skills. Then he sees that I'm not typical. I'm already blowing your bubble what prison is all about. It's all marketing. So when they ask you what was your last employer, I write Department of Correctional Services. Yes, I did work for the Department of Correctional Services. It's not the whole truth, but the literal truth." Angel had not given up hope.

The truth involved another thing that had bothered Angel since he got out. As a Quaker he made a pledge to himself not to lie, and behind bars this was rarely a problem. If he didn't want to work for a day or so, he was allowed to stay in his cell. In prison he felt he was his own man—within obvious parameters, of course. He was used to these parameters. Outside, however, he realized that lying, or at least bending the truth, was a crucial part of getting by. He knew that the only way out of WeCare, either temporarily or permanently, was to lie. He was aware that he could go to the doctor, for example, and demand a work waiver. Posttraumatic stress disorder, anxiety, obsessive-compulsive disorder, or claustrophobia, all common ailments among people who had spent large parts of their lives locked up, were diagnoses that could have justified a waiver. But Angel knew that he was able to work and wanted to find a job. Besides, he felt like he wasn't suffering from these ailments at the time. So he had to sit in the windowless classrooms until he couldn't stand it any longer. After the twelve-week cycle was over and another one was about to begin, Angel decided to quit.

As soon as it got wind of his decision, HRA threatened to cut off his $215 rent supplement and his cash allowance. Yet with the help of the Fortune Society, Angel managed to convince HRA that the organization's job placement program was a valid replacement for WeCare. He signed up for Fortune's Career Development class. Bruce and several other Castle residents would be there, and so far Fortune had not disappointed him.

Fortune's Career Development classroom was located on the seventh floor of a tall building on West 23rd Street in Manhattan. From the hallway the classroom's glass front revealed bile-green walls, ragged brown carpeting, and an opposing wall of large windows covered entirely with shades. Two dozen chairs were arranged in rows facing a white board and a television set. A printout on the door read

> THROUGH THESE DOORS
> WE GUARANTEE ONE THING . . . TOUGH LOVE
> EVERYTHING AFTER THAT
> IS EASY!!!

At Fortune, *Tough Love* was administered by instructor Mitch Brown, a black man with a hulkish frame, a shaved head, and two meaty rolls on the back of his neck. On his left arm Brown had a prison tattoo of a scroll listing the names of his many children, followed by "Daddy loves you." During his lunch break he told me that he was on parole until 2011. In his last stint he spent fourteen years in prison on a variety of robbery charges, adding that he had engaged in criminal activities since he was thirteen. He served time for selling drugs, carrying guns, and committing assault. "I multitasked," he said with a laugh, turning to his fellow instructor, with whom he shared an office and who also had served time for robbery. "You hear me?" he called out, cracking up. "I said I multitasked." His colleague chuckled as he scarfed down his Cheetos.

Brown thought his prison experience served as a credential. While incarcerated he earned prison certificates in Youth Aid, Child Advocacy Counseling, and Parenting. "All I got, I got while I was locked away," he said. While "locked away" he also worked with youths at a Scared Straight program. "They were just like me. That was hittin' home," Brown explained. When I asked him about his decision to go straight, he said that we all grow, but for some it takes time.

At the Career Development workshop at Fortune, Brown was confronted with a wide variety of ex-offenders. Angel's class included teenagers who were sent to comply with their ATI (Alternative to Incarceration) program, former drug addicts, men and women who were mentally ill, and men who, like Angel and Bruce, had spent a large part of their lives locked up for murder and were determined to get their lives together. Like the instructors at WeCare, Brown worked largely from sheets that categorized skills needed in the workplace. On the third day Brown read each of the roughly forty different skills on his list, laboriously explaining the characteristics employers valued in employees, such as *Decision Making* and *Leadership*. After three hours he was barely halfway through the first list. Because Brown had a hard time coming up with a synonym, he went off on a tangent. "*Prioritizing Needs . . . ,*" he began. "Imagine, if you go to the store and you feel like having ice cream. But you ain't got no money. And you also want some meat. What you do?" He elaborated for five minutes before he got to *Efficiency*. But Brown didn't just stick to the lists. He also sprinkled in some personal advice. "You gotta tell your chum when his breath smells like shit," or "You gotta speak better verbally." Brown periodically interrupted his lecture to write up those who had fallen asleep or to lecture Mr. Stevens, a seventeen-year-old who seemed to be perpetually late to class. (I was not able to find out Mr. Stevens's first name. Brown tended to address men by their last name and women by their first name.)

Brown wrote "Mr. Stevens" on the board below a line that read "500-word essays" and ordered him to stand in front of the class. Mr. Stevens, whom Brown also called "Youngie," wore a T-shirt that showed a roaring lion festooned with rhinestones. His pants hung so low that he had to walk and stand with his legs slightly spread. His head also hung low, and he had difficulty looking into Brown's eyes. During the first five minutes of Brown's lecture Mr. Stevens didn't move; he just snorted at irregular intervals.

"How is it you don't get here on time?" Brown prodded.

No response.

"Help me understand."

No response.

"Look into my eyes!"

No response.

"Pull up your pants."

Mr. Stevens snorted.

"I'm walking you through the day. How long does it take you to take a shower?"

No response.

"Come back when you are ready."

Mr. Stevens's attitude was not much different from mine when I was a teenager. Maybe Mr. Stevens was a nice kid if taken seriously and not embarrassed in front of a class of adults. Brown sent Mr. Stevens out of class to see one of his coworkers. Mr. Stevens eventually returned and soon received a second write-up on the board for nodding off. Mr. Stevens's essay on responsibility had now grown to one thousand words. Not surprisingly, Mr. Stevens didn't return the next day.

Bruce thought that Brown enjoyed provoking people with "his essay shit."

"This guy is what we call in prison a bozo," he whispered into my ear.

Unlike Bruce and Mr. Stevens, Angel was repeatedly praised for his professional outfit. Occasionally he snapped open his black leather briefcase, which was overflowing with documents, to pull out a piece of paper or add yet another. The briefcase still contained some old questionnaires from WE CARE. Some questionnaires were left blank and others were filled with his childlike chicken scratch, brimming with spelling errors.

Mr. Stevens, Angel, and Bruce were not the only men at Fortune with exceptional needs. At one time I sat next to Xavier, a Hispanic man in his fifties who had spent two decades in prison for drug trafficking and conspiracy. We got along well and talked several times during the break and once for an hour over the phone. Xavier was polite, well read, and educated. He had been trained in prison to develop software for the military. Now released, the military didn't want him, and much of what he had learned was too specialized to be applied to other fields.

Then there was Mr. Xu, a fifty-seven-year-old Chinese man who spent one year in prison for operating an illegal gambling joint. Mr. Xu seemed to have problems following the class. When he didn't respond to one of his questions, Brown asked him, "What language you speak?"

"Chinese."

"You know they speak different languages in China," Brown explained to the class. "Like Mandarin and Korean." He called in Jen, Fortune's Chinese American intern, to translate.

"Ask him," Brown said, "if he understands me."

Jen translated. "He says he understands about 70 percent, but he can't write in English." Jen was sent back out and Mr. Xu was ignored from then on. When he fell asleep in class in the afternoon, Brown yelled, "Gotcha!" and wrote his name on the board. He now owed a five-hundred-word essay, due the next day, about the importance of staying awake in class.

After class I spoke with Mr. Xu. He actually spoke English quite well and didn't have a problem understanding when addressed slowly. He told me how his conviction changed his life. "It turned my family around 180 degree," he said, gesturing as if flipping a plate upside down. He then pulled out a piece of paper. Since he couldn't write in English one of his classmates had written down a couple of sentences for him: *I'm sorry that I fell asleep in class. It will not happen again.* Mr. Xu chuckled and said that he would just write these two sentences over and over until he reached the required word count.

Mr. Xu told me that he didn't even require a well-paying job. On his (imaginary) job application form, which he filled out with the help of another student, he wrote, "Restaurant. Wherever there is a job. Okay. Cooking, cleaning, whatever." I later asked him whether it would be easier to apply for a position in a Chinese restaurant, and he started stuttering, "My face, my face . . . " He touched his face. I looked at him and wondered what was wrong with his face. "How can I explain?" he said. "My face . . . " After some back-and-forth I understood that because of his conviction, Mr. Xu had lost face in the Chinese community.

The classroom-hallway situation reminded me of a fish tank. Because the wall bordering the hallway was made of glass, those inside could see what was going on outside and vice versa. I watched job developers rushing by to access the file cabinets in the hallway and instructors lecturing misbehaving students. I tried to decipher intricate handshake rituals between Fortune employees and clients: grip, clasp, hook, slap, pull, and bump. Or hook, pull, slap, clasp, and bump. Often the adjacent offices were bursting with laughter and chatter. The classroom door constantly opened and closed. Job developers called out students for evaluations; Ron Harris, Brown's boss, stepped in to see how the class went; and whenever Brown would see a former graduate walk by who had managed to find a job, he waved him in to give a quick motivational speech.

Brown distributed job applications among the students without further instructions. I noticed that they rarely asked what they were supposed to do. They simply bent over and started writing. After half an hour Brown collected the applications. He created three piles. The "hell no" pile, the "maybe" pile, and the "I'm gonna work with you" pile. Mr. Xu's application landed in the "hell no" pile. "You ain't starting a poker business in my restaurant," he said, adding that you weren't supposed to put down your crime on the job application. Angel already knew that the penal code and "will explain further if granted interview" was enough, and Brown tossed his application in the "I'm gonna work with you" pile. When asked whether there was a slight chance that an employer would consider the penal code evasive and become suspicious, Brown said, "No, it makes 'em *curious*." It is important to note that except for a short stint at STRIVE, another job placement agency for ex-offenders, and his few months at Fortune, Brown had virtually no outside job experience. He seemed to take a certain pride in this. "I never worked a day in my life," he said to his students. "My rap sheet? You can flip mine like . . . " He made a gesture as if unfurling a long scroll.

The blind were leading the blind, I thought. But then again, who else is going to offer Brown a job? If Fortune advocates the employment of ex-cons, naturally the first step was to hire someone like Brown and give him a second chance.

Another staple of Fortune's Career Development class was the so-called mock interview. Again Brown introduced the exercise with some practical advice. "What do you respond if an employer asks you, 'Why should I hire you?' Say, 'I'd be an asset to your company,' " he said, and wrote *access* on the board. He paused and looked at the board. "How do you spell *asset?*" he asked the class. "A-S-S-E-T," one student volunteered. Brown gave a couple more examples of exemplary interview behavior: do not extend your hand before the interviewer extends his; do not take a seat unless offered one; and put some tissue in your pocket to wipe your sweaty hands. (He later distributed yet another list, this one with supposed reasons why employers decide not to hire applicants. Among the twenty-four examples on the handout were *Limp-fish handshake; Has dirty hands or face; Has a persecuted attitude ("They are out to get me!"); Too much concern for salary; Lacks career plan;* and *Has re-communication skills* (which, according to Brown, described an applicant who repeated the same thing over and over again). Brown believed his students should say "Yes, ma'am" and "No, sir" and wear a shirt—preferably "white, light blue, or chocolate gray"—and tie to the interview. On the fourth day of class he finally considered his students well enough equipped for the mock interview. He counted them and divided them into pairs. Lisa, a middle-aged woman who kept nodding off in class, remarked that she didn't have a partner. Brown pointed at me and said, "You go with Sab-, Sab-, Sab- . . . " Before

I could pull my chair up to Lisa, Brown waved me over to ask if I could control the class while he stepped out. "Keep it down, ya know," he added. I told him that I would feel uncomfortable with this responsibility and sat down with Lisa to practice.

Lisa looked like a bride in her white dress trimmed with frills and lace. The illusion, however, was seriously jeopardized by a little green towel she occasionally produced in order to wipe her face. She also compulsively filed her nails. Without looking up, she said, "Okay," signaling me to start the interview. Lisa's responses to my questions were incredibly slow and labored. Asked about a situation she handled particularly well in her last job, she proceeded to tell me a convoluted story about the nursing home where she was sent for community service after one of her last convictions for shoplifting. The crux of the story was that, when one of the patients asked her to smuggle some booze into the nursing home, Lisa reported it to her supervisor. "I think I handled that well," she said proudly.

The next day Lisa offered codeine pills to one of her fellow students who had complained of a headache. Later that day she was accused of stealing some subway cards. Brown had forgotten the fifteen cards, which were supposed to be distributed among the students after class, having left them on a classroom chair. Lisa noticed the cards and dropped them off with one of Brown's coworkers, who realized that three were missing. When confronted, she said, "If I had stolen the cards, I would have taken all of them."

Bruce thought that the situation was Brown's fault. He should never have left the cards unattended. He leaned back and whispered in my ear, "You knew I was a snake when you brought me home. You are dealing with people who have a criminal nature!"

When Brown thought that the class had practiced the interviews enough, he sent everyone into the lounge and asked them to wait for a more "professional" mock interview. This time the interview would be conducted by Ron Harris, Brown's boss, and recorded on video, so the students could watch and critique one another. The video room was a small office space unsettlingly similar to a police interrogation room. A large rectangular light was mounted on the ceiling directly above a plain wooden desk. The only decoration on the otherwise bare walls was a calendar with a picture of mountain goats. Lisa was called in. She had put away the nail file but still carried her green towel. She continued to avoid eye contact. Her answers to Harris's questions appeared to be as slow as before. "She needs help. She definitely needs help," Harris declared after she stepped out.

When I returned to the lounge, Mr. Xu was still waiting to be called in. He was under the impression this was going to be a real job interview and was crushed when I told him it was just another practice. He had been sure that Fortune already had a job waiting for him.

At Fortune the main emphasis was on how to behave during interviews and how to fill out forms, whereas little or no attention was paid to what the men and women were capable of doing for a living—let alone what they *wanted* to do for a living.

In class Angel was continuously praised, and no one actually knew how jumbled and unpredictable his career wishes were. He would go from studying political science to business to computer science to architecture to becoming a youth counselor or janitor in a matter of days. Unlike Bruce—who told me during one of the breaks that he wanted to go into maintenance, preferably at night, when no one could look over his shoulder and he was all by himself—Angel seemed overwhelmed by the prospect of having to make his own decisions. He was waiting for someone to steer him in the right direction.

Angel faced Fortune's Career Development class with the same sense of acceptance he initially had for HRA and WeCare. Although he thought that while in prison Brown had mainly worked on his muscles and had yet to divorce himself from jail culture, Angel believed that Fortune would help him find a job. But halfway through the two-week program he admitted that he was no longer sure if he even wanted a job. But if he had a choice, he would prefer to work with computers. "At least you can't hurt them," he said.

It was another hot summer evening, just a few minutes past seven o'clock, when Angel and I retreated into the Castle's backyard to snack on cookies and strawberries. We were the only ones outside, the others preferring to cool off in their air-conditioned rooms. Angel ushered me to two lounge chairs facing away from the bars that separated the backyard from 140th Street. If being indoors made you anxious and if you didn't want to be reminded that there were parole regulations hindering you from taking a stroll over to the nearby park, the bar, or the ice cream parlor, this was the only place to be.

Angel started talking about being afraid to take someone to a dark alley. Take whom? To what dark alley? What if, he asked, someone followed us? What if the other person were harmed because *he* had chosen to go through the alley? What if he were unable to provide protection? What if he had failed in his leadership?

Again he started talking about prison and how much more protected he felt while locked up. Angel didn't mention that he was afraid of others. He seemed to be afraid of himself. In prison he was protected from himself.

I was reminded of the many rules WeCare and Fortune had established for their clients and how some of them echoed the regimen he had experienced in prison. None of the classes addressed Angel's, Bruce's, and Adam's fears. Perhaps a job-readiness program isn't designed to deal with these kinds of fears, but the work environment may very well be one of the most stressful places in which we find ourselves. Crumbling under pressure and losing control on the job are not farfetched: according to the Department of Labor, almost two million Americans report having been victims of violence in the workplace each year. (In fact, murder is the leading cause of death for women in the workplace.)[5]

"Job readiness" and work could be starting points to explore the men's needs and fears. There are no guards on the job who keep you in check, but your performance is constantly being measured and compared.

In addition to the fear of causing harm to another human being, an ex-con might simply be overwhelmed by the countless unfamiliar rules that accompany his or her personal and professional life on the outside. What if you accidentally broke a rule because you weren't aware it even existed? In prison if you lost your job, you were still fed and clothed. You would always have a roof over your head.

"[In prison] I ran my life for the most part," Angel said, just as we had finished our cookies and strawberries. "Of course there were cops and walls. But they were like environmental factors. You come to accept them. [Outside] I don't know what the rules are. I don't know how to behave. I have no way to judge anything. I know how to survive in prison, but it's not a prison out here."

CHAPTER EIGHT

Prisoners Still

In the summer of 2007 the Fortune Society worked hard to distract its residents from their daily plight. Sugar, music, and trips to the water park were offered to take the sting out of New York's relentless summer heat.

The fund-raiser and anniversary event was followed by a health fair, where residents and their families ate mounds of cake with neon-colored frosting in the air-conditioned cafeteria, while outside on the empty lot vendors offered information on health care. Teenagers and adults filled their pockets with condoms wrapped in foil adorned with the colorful logos of New York's subway lines, while children with painted faces ran up and down the hallways playing tag.

David Rothenberg arranged a classical concert at the Castle and provided a seemingly never-ending supply of tickets to Broadway shows. In August 2007, during the season when those who have the time and means leave New York's unbearable mugginess for more temperate grounds, Fortune invited its residents to a water-park outing in Pennsylvania. Angel and I were both stuck in the city and were quick to sign up.

Sometimes, when there were no events scheduled, Angel, Bruce, Adam, and I would just hang out at the Castle and talk. Most likely something interesting would unfold. At the very least I would meet some new people.

"What's going on here?" I asked Angel and Adam one summer afternoon as we sat in the shade in the backyard. There were people carrying video cameras. A dozen men in green prison uniforms paced nervously back and forth. Angel explained that to raise funding, Fortune had rented out the big conference room to an educational film crew. The film was intended to teach prisoners how to become responsible fathers. For the day, the actors, all of them ex-convicts, had assumed the role of their former selves to help those who were still locked up.

The atmosphere was tense. Some of the "prisoners" sat down on the benches next to us to smoke, and Angel suddenly recognized one of them as a former fellow inmate. He was able to identify him only because he wore a prison uniform.

Adam paced up and down like a caged lion. Being around so much dark green made him anxious and sick. He had been flustered this afternoon because he had purchased an Amtrak ticket online with his sister's credit card and then noticed that the ticket was in his sister's name. He was pained by the prospect of going to Grand Central to correct the problem, facing the crowds, the shoving, the noise. Crowds made him sweat. *Oh, baby, am I doing this right?* he would ask himself. He scrutinized himself as if his every move were being observed by the crowd. Whatever I said to calm him down had no effect. An insurmountable wall separated us.

Angel didn't like to be around men in prison uniforms either, but he was too busy getting his stuff together for his welfare appointment to really notice. Or maybe he was just better at distracting himself than Adam. His new briefcase—"Ten dollars, I couldn't say no!"—was full of envelopes, loose sheets of paper, pens, a digital tape recorder, a disposable camera, and a bottle of Brut cologne. I was surprised. The dark suit, the white shirt, the tie, and the smooth black leather briefcase communicated order and professionalism. But inside the briefcase chaos ruled. Angel's briefcase echoed its owner's condition: smooth and professional on the outside, but spilling over with chaos within. Among the confused assortment of things were some important documents that he had yet to look at.

Looking for his welfare appointment letter, Angel noticed that he still needed proof of the rent he paid to the Castle. He ran inside to see if one of the administrators could help.

A few minutes later he returned triumphantly with a receipt for his rent payments. Adam had finally taken off to Grand Central, and I wasn't allowed to accompany Angel to his welfare appointment. I decided to wait for them in the Castle cafeteria. There I ran into Aazim, the Castle's cook. Like Angel, Bruce, and Adam, Aazim had spent a big portion of his life in prison, but unlike them he looked much older than he was. It surprised me when he said he was only fifty-one.

Aazim is a big, wheezing man. He looked out over the kitchen counter, his eyes, in an advanced stage of glaucoma, milky brown. He used to be a Castle resident but had long ago moved out and married Mahdiya, an attractive woman who looked no older than thirty. The two were expecting their second child. As was often the case with Mahdiya, she sat at one of several plastic tables in the cafeteria with the couple's one-year-old daughter.

Aazim and Mahdiya had converted to Islam while they were incarcerated. I took the opportunity to ask them why they became Muslims and how they found each other.

Aazim and Mahdiya both found Islam to be an uncomplicated religion, one in which gender roles were clearly determined. Where Mahdiya emphasized the protection and structure provided by Islam—the man is the provider; the woman is there to support her mate and to take care of the house and children—Aazim stressed its potential for freedom. He seemed to like the idea that under Islamic law a man is allowed to have several wives. Although he said that he was happy with Mahdiya, he defended the notion of polygamy. Mahdiya agreed with him. Her voice was clear and calm; she seemed like a woman who has come a long way. The religion allows several wives "for legitimate reasons," she said. "It might help at times. You don't feel like having sex when you are pregnant. I'd rather have my husband sleep with a legitimate person than with a stranger." She added, "A co-wife could help when you are sick."

Having found in me a patient listener, Mahdiya eagerly shared her sad history. But it was always hard to remain focused on one topic at the Castle's cafeteria. Most people there were notoriously needy. I never sat at a table alone for more than five minutes before one of the residents would assume that I was dying to read his poems or listen to his political rants, his prison knowledge, or both. Sometimes people just wanted to share the heartbreaking story of their lives. They needed someone to listen to them. Mahdiya was no exception. She quickly told me that she had experienced abuse at home and did not know any boundaries growing up. This led her to a life of crime and eventually to prison. She added that she always felt exposed and didn't like how women on TV were portrayed as sex symbols. Islam offered her refuge. Aazim interrupted Mahdiya.

To illustrate his bond with her, he offered a "humorous" story about chasing her around the house with a shiv and locking her up in the bathroom. I managed to piece together the couple's bond. Mahdiya and Aazim didn't hold what they did in the past against each other; they forgave each other for their crimes; they both understood seclusion, frustration, and fear; they lent each other moral support. Their bond was reinforced by a religion that provided refuge and reliable rules. Mahdiya and Aazim had found something to hold onto.

I asked Aazim to show me around the kitchen. This pleased him. The attention was back on him. He took the opportunity to demonstrate his greasy Clearview 300 machine, which he used to magnify paperwork. To illustrate the severity of his glaucoma, he told me he could recognize me but couldn't tell whether or not I was smiling.

He presented the talking measuring cup, the talking spoon, and the talking meat thermometer. He insisted on demonstrating the thermometer. He took my hand and pressed the stiff length of the thermometer against my palm. Then he wrapped his large hand tightly around mine to hold it in place and keep the heat from escaping. My palms were cold and sweaty. Aazim's chalky eyes stared at me. The one or two minutes it took for the thermometer to pronounce my body temperature in a cold, robotic voice felt like a lifetime. Aazim laughed. "See?" he said. "It talks." The temperature it gave was so low, however, that it indicated I must have been dead for several hours.

On the day of the outing to Dorney Park and Wildwater Kingdom in Pennsylvania, the residents scurried about the Castle's backyard waiting for the bus to depart. It was nine in the morning, and the heat was damp and oppressive. Yet Angel wore a gray suit, a beige shirt, and a tie. As was his custom that summer he also sported mirrored cop sunglasses. I arrived an hour early because Angel's parole officer had not granted him a one-day pass to leave the five boroughs. Angel had hoped until the last minute that he could go. He seemed disappointed. I was disappointed as well, but I had signed up for the trip weeks before and didn't want to drop out. I thought at least Bruce would go, but he said that he needed the weekends to rest and do laundry. Besides, having his two-person room to himself seemed like a great luxury. Maybe, he said, he would just lie in bed all day.

Adam had gone up to Albany to visit the widow of a reverend he had met at a prison ministry.

Angel and I walked through the Castle's backyard to get to the street. When Bruce and Adam saw us approaching, they snickered, "Here he comes, Binder & Binder. You going to your law firm, man?" The men were referring to a television commercial featuring two lawyers in suits and ties and hammy, overly serious expressions. Angel ignored the ribbing.

We walked down Broadway to buy cheesecake and find a comfortable place for a morning picnic. We found a bench by the Hudson River. "Oooh," Angel said, sniffing the air. "Oooh! Something has died here!" He laughed. While looking for another unoccupied bench, he mused whether a dog or cat had been run over by a car and died in the bushes or whether someone had disposed of their deceased pet in the woods.

It always surprised me how Angel spoke of death. One time when he was discussing the murder he committed, he interrupted his train of thought to point out a ball floating on the Hudson that he had mistaken for someone's head. "I thought for a moment there was somebody floating. I thought it was a floater. I don't wanna see it. It would be my first floater, and I don't wanna see it." He returned to the thread nonchalantly. "So I have always been embarrassed by my past, but some people are not."

I wondered whether a killing ever ceased to haunt the killer and whether a remorseful murderer was ever able to separate the death he caused from other deaths around him—a run-over cat, a family dog, or an apparent "floater"—or whether the trauma of murder was always triggered by the smell, sound, or image of death. Angel seemed to have distanced himself from the crimes he committed. I also wondered whether the time he served in prison—the endless confinement, punishment, and deprivation—separated the crime from the free world to an extent that made it harder to actually *feel* the life he had taken. Bruce and Adam always carried their past with them. Maybe Angel was so life-affirming and chipper *because* he had left his past behind. Either way, being with Angel, Adam, and Bruce made it hard for me *not* to think of murder and guilt when confronted with death. At this point I knew about their pasts. I had started to get a sense of what had led to the killings. I knew there were numerous factors that contributed to their actions. I couldn't forget about their crimes. I could have never made a blasé comment about death in their presence.

It was time for me to go; the charter bus was waiting. Angel smoked a cigarette nervously on the sidewalk, when Tanya arrived. Tanya was one of Angel's Quaker friends—the one who had given him the check card, cell phone, and Digiwalker. She and Angel were going on an excursion. Angel wanted me to meet Tanya, but Tanya did not want to get out of her car. From what I could see through the window, Tanya was a white, heavy-set woman with gray curly hair. We said hello awkwardly through the car window. With the summer Tanya's visits had become more frequent.

I boarded the bus while Angel stood outside smoking a Newport. He could see only our silhouettes and could not hear the men's comments. He had positioned himself behind a one-way mirror, unaware that we were able to see him clearly from the bus.

"Angel looks like Secret Service," one man said. One of the supervisors added, "He can't come to the water park because no one under four feet is allowed in." Angel, it seemed, was not accepted by his own, but somehow he had carved a niche for himself, finding acceptance elsewhere.

CHAPTER NINE

The Penis Dialogues

In the early fall of 2007 Adam fell in love with Minnie Leonardt. Adam savored Minnie's name, pronouncing it as if each letter were a different type of candy. He had been planning to take her out to dinner for weeks now. But each time I asked him about his plans, he said, "I got to get up enough courage." He usually added, "Minnie Leonardt . . . ," and paused, engrossed in his thoughts. "Minnie is nice. She knows how I feel about her. I like Minnie a great deal." Then he yawned as if the mere thought of the challenge exhausted him.

Adam wanted a love affair that would make him forget all the time he had lost or at least put it into perspective. But after thirty-one years in prison he found the thought of being intimate with a woman overwhelming. Where to begin after more than three decades of sexual deprivation? Now free, how could or should Adam reconnect to something that for the longest time had been confined to the realm of his fantasies?

At the Castle I heard men talk about "not getting hard" with their new loves because the women weren't as tight as the grip of their hands, men who couldn't come because the women did not meet their fantasies. "They don't look like the pinup girls in magazines," one man told me.

Apart from the possibility of a sexual encounter, dates brought many challenges, some of which Adam experienced in his first few months out. At one of his advocacy meetings he met a retired professor of social work whom he liked. He took her to the Brooklyn Botanic Garden and to the Brooklyn

Museum. At the museum café Adam told the woman to sit down at the table while he went to get coffee. When he came back the woman was gone. Adam later found out that she suffered from Alzheimer's. Having forgotten why and where Adam had asked her to sit—maybe she even forgot the man who took her to the museum—she simply wandered off.

Then Adam went on a couple of dates with a Korean woman whom he called "Bird." Bird shared his passion for jazz. But she soon revealed that she suffered from manic depression. She, too, disappeared shortly afterward.

Adam thought that maybe it would be easier if he just went to a prostitute. But this was no better. The prostitute took him to her apartment. "Take it out and let me see," she said. When he opened his pants and took out his penis, she was startled. "Ohhhh, what is this? This is a *new* model!" Adam assumed she was trying to be funny. Nevertheless, he paid and left without having sex.

At this point Adam had told none of his new friends that he had cancer "in one of the worst places possible." It had started about five years ago in prison, when he began having trouble urinating. He went to the doctor and was given aspirin. The pain progressively worsened. Many months later, a sympathetic male nurse sent him to the hospital. There Adam participated in an experimental cancer treatment trial and had part of his penis removed.

"It doesn't look the same," he said. "They waited too long. They fucked me around for a whole year. The doctors said, 'You should have come sooner. We wouldn't have to do all this cutting.' That's the shit that happens in prison."

One of his friends in prison had tried to comfort him after the operation. He showed him clippings of John Wayne Bobbitt's reattached penis after his wife's attack with a kitchen knife. "Some women might find it appealing," the friend said, adding that Bobbitt got more sex than ever. "Some women will find it a new innovation," he reassured Adam.

But Adam wasn't sure whether Minnie was one of these women, so he waited instead. But waited for what? For a woman who viewed his disfigured penis as "a new innovation"? Adam had already "waited" for thirty-one years. He was seventy-three now, and time was running out. But so much had changed while he was away. Today's women appear more emancipated than their counterparts did thirty years ago. Besides, what *did* Adam know about women? The women he used to know were different. *He* was different. His knowledge regarding women was outdated. Emotionally and intellectually Adam had matured, but practically his experience was close to zero.

"You jump on top of a woman and that was it. Wham bam thank you ma'am." What he had learned when he was a teenager defined how he saw physical relations with women. The few things Adam knew about sex he had learned from older women he slept with when he was twelve or thirteen. At home and at school no one spoke about sex—not his grandmother, not his aunts, and certainly not his teachers.

"Hey, come here, come here, come here, come heeeeere!" he said the women would call from their houses. I wondered why an adult woman would want to have sex with a twelve- or thirteen-year-old. Had Adam mixed up his age? Maybe he had been sixteen? I asked Adam to confirm his age several times on different occasions, as his memory sometimes played tricks on him. But he was insistent: "twelve or thirteen."

Yet Adam was never a ladies' man. When he went to prison at age forty-two he was married and had two sons. His wife, Marietta, was "a country girl" who, at first, found his criminal lifestyle exciting. Adam remembered being very attracted to Marietta, but it didn't occur to him what a woman would and could feel during intercourse until many years later, when, in prison, he read the Kinsey Reports. By then, he and Marietta had long separated. Adam was never able to apply his knowledge about women's sexual desires.

It was not that Adam didn't have the opportunity to get involved with real women in prison. There were magazines with ads from women looking for pen pals, but because he didn't know how long he would be incarcerated, the correspondence always dwindled. There were visitors who tried to hook up their female relatives with inmates, and there were women in volunteer groups who ended up marrying prisoners. Once you got married, you could request conjugal visits every few months. But Adam was always suspicious of women who got involved with prisoners. "Most women who come into prison with the idea of developing a relationship with a prisoner have problems developing a relationship with men on the outside," he said. "And that cuts down on the kind of people you come in contact with."

Nevertheless, Adam educated himself about sex in prison, and he never gave up nurturing his fantasies. He fantasized about women who came to visit, about magazine girls, about romances from the past. The things he would do with these women boosted his spirits.

One might find it curious that Adam and I talked about sex with such openness. But Adam made it easy to talk about sex. His comments about women and sex never felt sleazy; his only motive was to be understood. He once told me he wanted me to tell his *whole story.*

In prison Adam would talk to his penis, and his penis would respond. When Adam and his penis talked about women, they did not always agree. It would happen that Adam would fantasize about a woman, and his penis would take all the fun out of it. One day, over lunch at his favorite Italian restaurant down in the valley, Adam reconstructed his penis dialogues for me.

"Oh, that was a bad one there," his penis would say, referring to a woman from Adam's past.

"What do you mean it was a bad one there?" Adam would respond. "It was all right."

But his penis always had the last word. "All right my ass. *That* was a good one," it would counter, reminding him of yet another woman who hid in a corner of his mind.

Adam's yearning was for companionship as much as it was for sex. But after so many years in prison, after so many years without touching another human being and without being touched, Adam was at a loss. Pain, loneliness, and disease had left their marks. Considering the injuries and indignities he had suffered, I sometimes found it surprising that he still *dared* to love. But Adam felt that now was the right time for a grand love affair.

Adam met Minnie at a community organization where he was invited to give a speech about the link between outside organizations and people within the prison system. A writer and photographer, Minnie sometimes did freelance work for the organization. At first, Adam wasn't particularly impressed. But to his surprise her face kept reappearing in his mind. In the beginning he didn't even know why. "A strange attraction," he admitted. "She doesn't underscore her features, she dresses in drab colors, wears no makeup." At first sight, Minnie was not the typical dream woman. In her late forties or early fifties, she looked almost mousey—certainly not the type Adam normally would be attracted to when browsing through magazines or walking through the city. But Adam found himself back at Minnie's office week after week. They chitchatted, and she proved to be a good listener. They were able to laugh with each other. Adam's visits with her felt casual, safe, and free. Whenever it was time to leave, he regretted that once again he hadn't managed to ask her out, having failed to work up the courage. But his short visits allowed for the easy illusion of eternal love, while the idea of asking her out on a date carried the potential for the unpleasant reality of rejection—or, equally terrifying, acceptance, in which case Adam would once again have to face the dilemma of his penis.

Maybe the way a date was set up would determine its outcome? Maybe if he took along his two friends?

One night I received a phone call from Angel. He wanted to know whether I knew Minnie Leonardt because Minnie Leonardt, he claimed, knew me. I could hear Bruce and Adam chortling in the background. Angel also burst out laughing, and the three men started shushing each other like girl-crazy teenagers. When I said I didn't know Minnie, the men whispered among themselves. Then Angel told me they were thinking I could call Minnie and ask her to join us at his birthday dinner. I explained that calling someone I didn't know would make me uncomfortable but commended them on the idea of inviting her along and encouraged Adam to call her himself. I was curious to meet Minnie and to see if Adam—or Angel or Bruce—would find the courage to invite her along.

CHAPTER TEN

At the Barber

A dried corncob hung by the entrance of Odri's Beauty Salon. The jet-black hair that covered the floor merged into a dense black fur as it reflected on the mirrored ceiling. Turquoise tiled walls and cabinets brought to mind the colors of the Caribbean. Awkwardly taped to one of the mirrors was a crucifix. A dried apple sat on the shelf. Someone had cut a hole in the wall to accommodate the TV, which was tuned to a game show that competed with tropical love songs from the radio.

Angel went to the barber once a month when his hair started curling. In prison he had used his own clippers to cut his hair. You could not really trust another inmate with scissors, and Angel didn't agree with the prison barber's policies. Although paid by the state, he would demand extra money from some of his fellow inmates. "One, two, three, chop it all off. Next guy," Angel said. But some of the inmates had preferences. They wanted to look good. They came with pages torn out of magazines, wanting their hairline shaped or their thick, curly hair to appear light and feathery.

"I really don't understand for what," Angel said as he sat down on the barber chair. "You don't want to look cute in prison." So one, two, three, chop it all off it went.

"I don't let just anybody near me with a straight razor," Angel said, explaining that Denis from the Castle had recommended Tony the barber. Angel trusted Denis, and that's why he could trust Tony.

I noticed that Angel had shaved off his mustache yet again. In his first year of freedom Angel couldn't make up his mind—one week he would have a full mustache; the next it would be gone. The following week, however, the mustache would start to grow back.

Angel asked Tony to guess what he did for a living. "*Es abogado?*" Tony asked, going on the suit, tie, and button-down shirt. Angel had been observing how businesspeople dressed and communicated and enjoyed copying them. To be mistaken for a lawyer pleased him. He certainly didn't want to look like an ex-con. Angel wanted attention. He wanted to be liked. In that spirit he explained to Tony that I was writing a book about him. Then he urged Tony to give me his name so he could be in the book as well.

Angel closed his eyes again. Tony's scissors mowed through his hair, revealing more gray with each snip. Angel's voice, usually strident and precise, faded into a quiet, slow drawl. He spoke about the holy water he recently bought at a *botánica* and how he still had a tendency to be superstitious. Our conversation, like his curls, drifted in the air.

It was hard for Angel to think about hair without thinking of his mother, Dolores. Dolores had always been superstitious about her son's hair. She would follow him to the barber and sweep it all up and take it with her, so no one could use it to cast a spell. When he came home from the streets at night, a tub full of hot water stood ready, infused with oils and floating with leaves and flowers.

"People pay a lot of money for this stuff," Angel kept saying, sitting on the barber chair with his eyes closed. He sounded hypnotized as he defended his mother's behavior. Dolores's steaming concoction was meant to cleanse Angel of evil spirits. In her mind there was a lot of work to be done.

Angel had put off talking about his mother. What I learned about her had come from the parole package he gave me in the summer of 2007. The package contained psychiatric and school reports detailing his violent childhood. It wasn't until our visit to the barber many months later that Angel finally began to talk about his upbringing.

As a child Angel stuttered and frequently suffered from headaches and angry outbursts. He misbehaved in school, was unwilling to work, and made no friends. He was frightened and depressed. When he was eight or nine years old his school referred him to Mount Sinai for psychological treatment. Mount Sinai recommended follow-up treatment, but his mother did not take him back. Instead, she took him to another doctor, from whom Angel was to ask for sleeping pills to support her addiction. A hospital report referred to Dolores as "an obese very disturbed Spanish speaking woman with thought disorder and hallucinations." It noted that Angel's "stepfather and mother are rigid and primitive."

Angel never questioned his mother's obscure practices. He would get into the tub, and it would feel good. It felt so good that he didn't even consider that taking a bath was often followed by an inexplicable beating. There was never a pattern to his mother's outbursts. You might as well enjoy the few things in life that you love. And Angel loved his mother's baths.

After some baths Dolores would beat him with an electrical cord. The blows would hurt even more because his skin was damp and soft from the oils. Had he played hooky? Taken food he wasn't supposed to take? Stayed out for too long? There was no way to tell. And why worry about consequences of bad behavior if the punishment was so brutal and arbitrary? This would be the overriding lesson Angel took from her punishment.

Dolores gathered Angel's negative spirits. Then she threw them in a cup filled with water to drown them and put them under Angel's bed, where they would be closer to hell.

There was always smoke in the house. Depending on Dolores's mood, the burned materials were meant either to bless the house or to deter evil spirits. "She burned all kinds of shit," Angel remembered. He briefly opened his eye while Tony the barber sprayed his hair with water to tame it. "I'm surprised I don't have cancer," Angel laughed.

Of his presumed biological father Angel has only two memories. One time he accompanied his mother to pick up ten dollars from Felix Ramos. Ramos said the money was supposed to be for Frank, Angel's younger brother. The mother got furious. She tore the bill apart and shoved it under the door. The next time Angel saw his "father," Ramos was in the hospital. Shortly after— Angel must have been seven or eight—Ramos died of gangrene. At that point his mother had already moved the family in with the "new man," Atiliano Oyola. The mother's new boyfriend looked vaguely familiar to Angel. Like Angel, Oyola had fairly light skin and green eyes, and he was short. His brothers Junior and Frank were tall and burly, their skin much darker than Angel's and Oyola's. They resembled Felix Ramos, but Angel believed he looked like Oyola.

Angel often wondered whether he was the secret love child of Dolores and Oyola. It would be nice to know. Angel had always felt out of place. Even today, he says, it would be a great relief to have his assumption confirmed.

Angel thought that Oyola favored him. When I asked what made him think so, he told me about two memories. One time Oyola took him out to buy a *pastelillo* (a kind of pastry). Of all the siblings, the new father had chosen Angel to walk with him across the bridge from Ward's Island. This made Angel feel very special. It was also the first time that Angel saw hail. Another time Oyola bought Angel a little plastic helicopter.

Yet Oyola did nothing to prevent Dolores from beating Angel. He would always take the path of least resistance. When Dolores threw herself into the East River to commit suicide, Oyola simply laughed. "She was a fat woman and she floated," Angel said, chuckling. "[Oyola] laughed. And I always find it funny that she tried to kill herself and couldn't because she was too fat."

The family was poor, and Dolores sometimes kept chickens and rabbits in the Harlem apartment for food. One time Angel took one of the soft bunnies to bed with him and accidentally suffocated her in his sleep.

To me this echoed the story of Adam accidentally killing one of his Kool-Aid parakeets. I found it telling that Adam expressed his remorse, saying how terrible he felt having killed the little bird, while Angel told the rabbit story almost nonchalantly on our way to the subway, a minute before we said good-bye and parted ways.

Angel's whole childhood was laced with violence, pain, and shame. Each story he had to tell had violence as its main theme. The early parts of his life appeared like a chain of one cruel event after another. Not surprisingly, Angel grew increasingly violent.

Having lost control over her ten-year-old son, Dolores sent him to live with her eldest daughter, Carmen, in Dorado, Puerto Rico. Carmen was the result of a rape that occurred when Dolores was just thirteen years old. She was first raised by her grandmother in Puerto Rico and later by an aunt in New York. At the age of seventeen, she got married in New York. Carmen's three daughters are about the same age as Angel and his two brothers.

I called Carmen because she was the one who had unsuccessfully tried to turn Angel's life around in his youth. She said that the rape, along with Puerto Rican *brujería* (witchcraft), drove Dolores insane. When a neighbor died, someone poured the water used to wash the body in front of her mother's house in order to bring her harm. The grandmother did not get sick, but her teenage daughter, Dolores, did. Dolores lost her mind. Carmen acknowledged that her mother was sick but also "a beautiful soul." She said, "When she was well, you could find the sweetest person."

Carmen didn't think her mother's beatings were "that severe," or that Angel's upbringing was much of an excuse for the direction he took in life. "I don't know how to say it, but I grew up almost under the same conditions and face it, I . . . don't have a temper. I don't fight. I don't do anything. And I don't know how to explain it. It's like living in a jungle, and the strong will survive. I wasn't strong enough so I had to get out."

Angel, Carmen said on the phone, "did a lot of nasty little things. Since he was born, he was mischievous. And he's such a good talker that he could talk anybody into anything."

Angel seemed to do well in school in Dorado, acquiring some basic reading and writing skills in Spanish. He got along with his cousins. Yet he stole from stores in the town where Carmen's husband had just opened a printing business. At first, the merchants kept quiet out of respect for him. But once one of them opened his mouth, the others followed. Carmen's husband got angry.

"My husband came home," Carmen remembered, "and he just said, 'I can't take it. You know, we have a peaceful life, and he's upsetting it.'" The couple sent Angel back to New York.

This is a small fragment of Angel's past. Our conversation apparently pained her, and she didn't remember much, or perhaps she didn't want to.

It's possible that a few more years in Puerto Rico under Carmen's loving and consistent care would have turned his life around. Angel believed as much.

At the age of twelve, shortly after returning to New York, Angel was placed on a five-day suspension from school after he threatened to kill one of his teachers with a hammer and almost threw a chair at another one. School guidance counselors admitted it had happened before. Previously Angel had threatened to kill a paralegal in his bilingual class. In fact, he openly spoke to his teachers about blood, bombs, and killing and about "not being alive by the age of fifteen."

Although suspended, Angel returned to the school the day after the hammer incident, running through the hallways screaming and, this time, threatening to kill himself. The school called the police. Angel was in such a rage that it took four officers to subdue him. The officers called an ambulance, which took him to the emergency room at Metropolitan Hospital. One psychiatrist described Angel as a "small, well-developed, nice looking twelve year old P[uerto] R[ican] boy who appears younger than his stated age," and who was "of at least average intelligence." Irwin Moor, the supervising psychologist who administered the test, noted that Angel's knowledge of body parts was off. "Speech is rapid," one report reads, "spontaneity present." Reports also list his constant fidgeting, his insomnia, his suicidal thoughts, his illiteracy, his bitten-down nails, his mother's beatings, and his bed-wetting. Yet it was decided that hospitalization was not necessary. Psychotherapy was recommended. But Angel claimed to have "secrets he could never divulge." The hospital thought he would respond well to treatment, but Dolores did not take him back.

Looking at Angel's childhood as a whole, I believe that incidents of external and self-inflicted violence recurred uncontrollably. Until he committed actual murder and was put into jail, where ironically his bed-wetting instantly stopped, no one seemed able or willing to help.

Angel's teenage years followed the pattern laid down by his childhood. His sister Maria, the only person whose love he never doubted, became a drug addict and a prostitute. One time she took her little brother with her to the "cathouse." But where were the cats? Angel wondered. He just saw a bunch of skimpily dressed girls, a guy, and a bulldog. Maria introduced him to her pimp. Angel didn't know what a pimp was, but from the way Maria talked about him, he seemed like a great guy.

A few years later Maria died a brutal, mysterious death. Angel thinks she was murdered, but no one knows for certain. Chased or distraught, she ran into oncoming traffic on Westside Highway in the middle of the night. Or she was dropped from a bridge. Either way, she was hit by a car and died on the spot.

At age seventeen, Angel shot his older brother Junior in the testicles.

Junior, the bully who threw his seven-year-old brother Angel in the pool, where he almost drowned. Junior, tall and handsome, who had a way with women. Junior, who broke hearts left and right and who always managed to get "her digits."

The boys' mother was about to come back from her vacation in Puerto Rico, and while Junior partied with his friends, Angel tried to clean up the house. He had saved some money from salvaging copper, robbing parking meters, and selling pot to pay the bills and to fill the fridge. Junior and his friends had made a mess and eaten everything Angel had bought. Angel had had it with his older brother. He wanted revenge.

"My brother is a big guy, and he's always been a bully," Angel told me. "We always had conflicts. I always thought that I should be in charge. It was just a dominance game." Angel laughed as he related the story of his crime. "We got into an argument and I shot him twice. I shot him once in the stomach. And you see in the movies: he's supposed to fall over and fly, but reality is not like that. You shoot somebody with a .22 and it's like nothing. He went, 'Ah!' and came toward me. And I was like, 'I'm gonna beat you silly.' Because every time I fought with him, whatever instrument I brought, he's always taken it away from me and beat me with it. Every time we got into a fight and I would bring a stick, he would take the stick away and beat me with it. The equalizers I brought into the fight were never enough. This was the first time I had brought a gun. 'You are not going to do this to me.' The second time I shot him [I had intended to shoot him] in the leg; and what happened was, I didn't aim low enough and I shot him in the testicle. Then he fell on the ground. I didn't want to hurt him. I was like, 'Don't mess with me now.' If I had claws I would have scratched him. It was really [like] that. The look he gave me when he fell on the floor. Oh my God! It was the first time he feared me. I never want to see that look on anybody again. That's what stopped me. That look! Like, 'Oh my God! You are going to kill me!' Reality had set in: This is serious. This is not a game. Then I ran away. He was right there in front of my aunt's house. So he went to my aunt and she called the ambulance. 115th and 2nd, first floor with my grandmother." He added, "She was as old as dirt."

Angel was charged with shooting his brother. His stepfather bailed him out, and a court date in family court was appointed, but Junior did not show up and the case was postponed.

Carmen remembered calling her mother after the shooting incident. Dolores was crying. Carmen went back to New York and tried to talk to Angel.

"I was saying you have to control your temper," she remembered telling Angel, "and he says, 'Whoever does it to me, even my own mother, is going to pay for it.' He's already got this thing in his mind that whoever does anything to him is going to pay. Nobody could do anything to him and get away with it. Without him taking revenge."

Carmen had never been able to talk to Angel about his crime. When I brought it up on the phone, she grew increasingly standoffish.

"He has never talked to me about it," she said. "And I never asked him when I visited him in jail, 'Did you do it?' I never brought the subject up. It's so gruesome that I didn't want to know about it."

The two times Carmen visited Angel in prison were sad, awkward, and superficial. Angel did most of the talking. He told her he studied a lot and was going to college, but Carmen was suspicious. "He's a sweet-talker," she said to me. "He could sweet-talk anything." To Angel she just said, "That's nice, that's nice."

His mother, Dolores, didn't like to talk about Angel's crimes either. She was still determined to rid her son of demons. When she visited him at Rikers Island, where he was awaiting sentencing for the crimes he had committed, she told him that she had gone to see an *espiritista* (spiritualist). The espiritista told her that Angel had little demons attached to him and charged her twenty dollars.

"You should have given me the twenty dollars," Angel told his mother. "I would have told you the same thing." She gave Angel one of the looks he had learned to read well over the years: "You are not that old that I couldn't bust you in the head."

Although subdued, Angel's anger was still apparent today. His poems contained lines like "Anger, a Place Where I Don't Live Anymore" and "So I will not judge you, that is up to God. / I can only smile and nod." But in real life Angel could quickly get overagitated and angry. With the same passion that he showed for finding beauty in the world, he could show anger—anger at his brother Frank (whom he called the "donkey"), anger at the government, anger at other Castle residents, and even anger at me. I was always surprised by how upset Angel would get about relatively minor issues.

Once he went to the store and bought a fourteen-dollar pen, which turned out to be broken. "I wanted to go and beat that guy to death," he said, referring to the salesman who sold him the pen. "I wanted to beat that guy and hit him over the head with that pen."

What Angel considered moral transgressions also made him furious. He once preached to me about the obligations of marriage. He admitted that he looked down on people who had gotten divorced, who "disrespect the institution of marriage." He said that he learned honor and integrity in prison. "Yes, I still look down on people that are getting divorced." Angel's voice grew more and more fervent as he spoke. "It should be very hard to get divorced," he said.

I couldn't help but feel offended. "I am divorced," I said calmly, hoping this would make him stop. "Things happen, things that I couldn't have known."

"Well, then don't get married!" he spat.

Once, at the Castle, Angel almost lost it. One of the residents called him a bum. "I wasn't going to punch him," Angel told me. "I was starting to think in the darker way, of taking him off the block. I actually thought about it. I thought about it afterward, and I was like, 'What the fuck is wrong with you?' I was going to take him off the block and leave him there, come back, pack up my clothes and go on the run. I had all intentions of doing it. I just had enough. Because I thought this guy's seriously gonna hurt me and I wasn't gonna let it happen." Angel decided to confront the guy instead, and the issue was resolved.

At the Barber

It came as no surprise to me when Angel told me one day that the person he was most afraid of in this world was himself. One night he told me how he had felt split in two as he committed his crime. While he tightened the rope around Olga's neck, another part of him watched from above. The watching part analyzed what was going on below but couldn't intervene. This was how he came to realize he was the most dangerous person in the room.

"Put it this way," he explained. "When you've killed someone, you've done the ultimate; you've crossed that line. The only person that I was truly afraid of was me. Because I knew that I couldn't trust me. And once you're afraid of yourself, what more do you have to be afraid of? I'm more afraid of me than I am afraid of you."

With a small, quiet clipper Tony started shaving Angel's neck and the last little details behind his ears. A large scar on his head became visible. Angel's meticulous grooming procedure took twice as long as when I get my hair cut. I looked at the clock. It was already seven o'clock. The barbershop, now packed with people, had turned into a social club. The day had come to an end. Across the street Ray's Liquor Store turned on the chain of colorful lights attached to its awning. The little lamps flashed cheerfully. Just outside the barbershop its red neon sign bounced the letters U-N-I-S-E-X onto the dark gray sidewalk. While the men crowded the front of the store, the women disappeared into the back. "Loco, loco!" one screamed. The others chorused her with screeches.

CHAPTER ELEVEN

Causalities

One day I sat in the Castle cafeteria waiting for Bruce. I was chitchatting with Greg, an older residential aide with a few sharp teeth that jutted out between large gaps. Greg had lived at the Castle a long time ago. When I told him I lived in Sunnyside, Queens, he proudly proclaimed that he knew the neighborhood like the back of his hand. To prove it, he listed every fast-food restaurant on Queens Boulevard between 39th and 47th Streets.

"There is McDonald's at 39th Street," he said. "Then comes Burger King at 40th and White Castle at 43rd. I know. I know. I know *all* of Queens."

Next to us sat a Hispanic boy with curly black hair. His name was Louie. Louie was seventeen and had a baby face and an innocent smile that gave him an unweaned and naive yet charming appearance. He interrupted Greg's monologue. Who was I . . . *miss?* What was I doing here . . . *miss?*

Louie punctuated each sentence with *miss* as a sign of respect and to present a positive attitude toward superiors. *Miss* and *sir* were the magic words that signified the new goals he was so desperately trying to reach. It was obvious these goals were new to him and not yet anchored in experience. I had the impression that they were uncertain still.

I introduced myself to Louie and told him that I was writing a book about some people who lived at the Castle.

"How about you?" I asked. "What are you doing here?"

Louie said he had just moved into the Castle to escape the gangs in his East New York neighborhood that were pressuring him to join. I knew that this couldn't be the full story and that he had to at least be on probation or part of Fortune's Alternative to Incarceration program to qualify for a bed at the Castle.

Suddenly the wind picked up, jerking the branches of trees outside against the Castle's walls and rattling the window frames. Greg closed the windows.

"You know," Louie said, "that the trees can make the wind blow, miss?"

For reasons lost to me Greg started insulting Louie. Louie was just a dumb kid who thought he knew it all. "Trees making wind!" he huffed. "That's the dumbest thing I've ever heard."

"No, no," Louie insisted. "The trees can actually cause the wind to blow, miss." Louie ignored Greg.

I was struck by his insistence but wasn't clear myself on what made the wind blow, so I said, "I think it's the other way around."

Louie listened carefully and smiled while Greg continued to insult him. I admired his ability to remain unfazed by Greg's outrage. I assumed he must have been used to this sort of treatment. In his place I might have thrown something at Greg or at least stomped out of the room.

I asked Greg what Louie had done that upset him so much. He mumbled something about the young generation and how they never listened and always talked back and had no respect for their elders.

"Did you listen to older people when you were young?" I asked Greg.

"No," he said with a laugh.

"I'm so glad I am where I am today," Louie said out of the blue. He sighed.

Louie was the oldest of eight children. He was raised by a single mother in one of New York's most drug-infested neighborhoods. He was full of hope that the Fortune Society would help him out of his predicament. He seemed to do everything his caseworker told him to, joyfully. Finally there was someone in his life to steer him in a positive direction. This young man was ready to take on the world.

Louie used to hang out with the wrong crowd. His family was poor, and he sold marijuana to support himself. "This one I don't deny, miss," he said, suggesting that there was something else that he refused to admit. The cops threatened to raid his family's apartment, and Louie, trying to protect his mother and his younger siblings, gave the cops his stash. After the marijuana story, Louie told me about his second conviction. Supposedly, his friend stole an Xbox from a subway rider in Louie's presence. Louie said that he was still trying to hold his friend back when two cops on the platform pounced on them. Louie's friend blamed the whole thing on him, and Louie was charged with robbery and sentenced to several years on probation. "I'm just glad I'm still alive and that I got out of there," he said about his former life.

Then Louie told me about his grand plan. By the summer he would have his GED. Then he could be a role model for his younger siblings. He would get his driver's license and become a security guard. When I asked him why he wanted to become a security guard, he said, "I just imagine it must feel great. You just stand there and say, 'No, sir, I can't let you in here.' Polite, you know, but . . . 'No, sir, move back, please.'" His face turned serious, like a child playacting at being an adult. One of his hands slid down to his hip and grabbed an imaginary object.

"What kind of guard do you want to be?" I asked.

"One that drives these vans, you know," he said, growing increasingly excited.

"Armored vans? You want to be an armed guard?"

"Yes!" he said, slightly annoyed at my obtuseness.

When I expressed doubt that people on probation could carry a handgun in New York, Louie was shattered. He couldn't yet grasp the consequences of his crimes.

Shortly after I met Louie, Bruce told me about his own childhood, and although there was a gap of almost forty years between them and although they came from different ethnic backgrounds, their stories resonated with each other. Both men were raised with multiple siblings by a single mother. Both grew up in crime-infested and drug-ridden neighborhoods, and both dropped out of school. Most important, neither of them understood the consequences their actions could have on themselves or others.

For a reason I couldn't name, Bruce and I had both been avoiding the topic of his childhood. Unlike Bruce, Angel often mentioned his terrible childhood and only at the beginning refused to go into detail. Even if he didn't openly talk about it, it quickly became clear that his childhood played a role in his remorse-and-forgiveness narrative (*Brutal Childhood Turns Innocent Boy into Killer/Prisoner Turns Productive Member of Society*).

Angel was keen for me to read whatever concerned his life. He gladly answered any follow-up questions and was eager to add detail and color. Angel was a storyteller and liked to present himself as the tale's hero. Bruce and Adam, however, seemed less detached from their stories. Their story lines were muddled. The men were still in the middle of their developing narratives, fighting their way through. But they also seemed to realize that a narrative like Angel's was too simple to capture the whole truth. This made them appear to me more genuine than Angel—and, as a result, more tragic. It might also account for why it took me almost two years until I finally asked Bruce directly, "What was your childhood like?"

Bruce chuckled, as he often did when he was insecure or felt awkward, and I suddenly saw Louie in his face. Whereas Louie had struggled to look and sound mature, Bruce was fighting to keep his face from turning childlike. He had to lock his facial expression into a frown to be able to tell his story. Like Louie, Bruce was one of eight children raised by a single mother. Although his father held a steady job with the postal service, he drifted in and out of

Bruce's life, reappearing briefly in crisis situations, trying to steer the boys back on the right path, or before school started to take them shopping. Bruce was one of five boys, all of whom became addicted to drugs and were incarcerated at some point in their lives. Bruce's mother pleaded with her free sons to join her on her frequent prison visits "to see the wall," as she put it. Bruce never went. He had no interest in seeing "the wall."

At twelve he joined a group of neighborhood kids who robbed freight trains. They sold their booty—mostly furniture and crates of fruits and vegetables—to an older man on the block.

"What was the best thing you ever stole off a freight train?" I asked him. Bruce's frown turned into a grin again.

"Boxes of cereals," he said, chuckling mischievously. Again I saw Louie in his face.

At first his mother, who worked full-time as a seamstress in a factory and whose income was supplemented by public assistance, reprimanded him for bringing stolen goods into their home in the Bronx. "Don't bring this shit here," he remembered her saying. "This is my house!" After a while she realized that she was powerless against her five sons and gave up.

When asked whether his mother was loving, Bruce responded, "I mean, you gotta define that when you say, 'Was she loving?' I mean, nurturing love? I would say yeah, but when you look at it, how can you be loving with eight kids? She had to go to work every day. She had rules. We had to clean the dishes, take the garbage out. If you didn't do it, she would whip your ass. My oldest brother, she put a lot on him. She would make him an example. When she went out, she would give him the orders: Take out the garbage, do the dishes. She come home, she expected you to be done."

In the summers Bruce's parents would ship him south to his grandmother's farm in North Carolina. He made a little bit of money picking cotton and tobacco, milking the cows, feeding the hogs, and plowing the fields. At the end of the summer Bruce had to buy his school uniform with the money he earned. The slow-paced and simple environment, the animals, and the struc-ture and solitude presented a stark contrast to Bruce's life in the city, with its continuous buzz and omnipresent violence and temptations. The closest store to the farm was an hour's walk. In the countryside there were no drug kingpins showing off their fancy clothes and cars. "If we had stayed down there, I probably wouldn't have gotten into some of the trouble I got in," Bruce reasoned.

Back in the Bronx, Bruce committed crimes within a stone's throw of his apartment; after robbing freight trains he "graduated to selling drugs." He got caught up in gangs, including the Black Pearls and the notorious Black Spades, who claimed to have invented hip-hop and later evolved into the more peaceful Universal Zulu Nation. Bruce started to carry a gun when he was fourteen or fifteen, "so that guys who don't live in your neighborhood know not to come in your neighborhood." At around the same time he started using heroin and selling drugs. Compared to schoolwork, selling drugs was easy. You could make thousands of dollars in a couple of hours. And then you could buy yourself an even cooler gun. "Buy gun, sell gun, get more money, buy another one," Bruce explained. His role models were accomplished drug dealers. They had nice clothes and cars. They had money. To see his mother making an honest living, to see her struggle day after day, was no inspiration. In fact, it was quite the opposite. Her struggles couldn't compete with the glamorous lives of the older dealers who came to show off their possessions.

Bruce's mother died of a heart attack in 1979, when she was in her late forties. She was spared having to see four of her eight children die within the next few years. One son was shot on the street in the Bronx, one died of AIDS, one succumbed to a stroke, and one of her daughters died of mater-nal bleeding.

Bruce kept being arrested for selling and possessing drugs. He was repeat-edly taken to central booking, where he was either fined or dismissed and released. In his early twenties he went on trial for shooting and hurting another man in an argument over a customer Bruce had allegedly taken from him. The man pulled a knife and Bruce pulled a gun. The rival drug dealer didn't appear at the trial, the case was dismissed, and Bruce got off. His lawyer at the time warned him about the possible consequences of his destructive behavior. He gave him a business card from the Fortune Society. Bruce took the card but never went. After all, it wasn't an order, only a piece of paper.

At twenty-five Bruce was put on probation for selling drugs. His probation officer told him that he was a walking time bomb. She sent him to therapy and to programs, but he only went once or twice. "Everybody is not out to hurt you," Bruce remembered his parole officer saying. "You don't find somebody where you can let things out, one day you get into an altercation. It's gonna explode and you are gonna hurt somebody." Bruce proved his probation officer right. "In '83 I got into an altercation and it exploded."

It took Bruce years to connect and order the chain of events and to grasp the causes. It came to him one day, while lying on a cot, locked up in his prison cell, where he was serving time for murder. *Oh shit,* he thought. *She told me.*

Louie's and Bruce's stories helped me understand the role of chance and how one person can become a murderer while another one, with help, can eventually become a law-abiding armed guard. Their narratives echo several findings that academics have pointed out for years: children and youths exposed to poverty, drugs, guns, discrimination, and adult criminals are more likely to turn to a life of crime than those who come from a safe middle-class background. In 2000 the Study Group on Serious and Violent Juvenile Offenders—an initiative of the Department of Justice's Office of Juvenile Justice and Delinquency Prevention—published a survey of sixty-six studies that identified the most common predictors of violence. The report arranged the violent-crime predictors in five domains: individual psychological factors, family factors, school factors, peer-related factors, and situational factors.[1] Many of the "criminogenic risk factors" that are related to these domains can be found in Louie's and Bruce's stories. If a teenager is involved in stealing or selling drugs, the risk that he will one day commit a violent crime rises. Low academic achievement seems to be a predictor, along with gang membership and having delinquent siblings and peers.[2] Many studies suggest that children who have been physically abused are prone to become criminals and that parents who don't supervise their teenagers or who discipline them inconsistently—sometimes ignoring their children's misbehavior while at other times punishing them for it—set up their children to commit a violent offense. Teenagers who are hyperactive and aggressive and who like to take risks are more likely to commit a violent act later on. These criminogenic risk factors can be aggravated through situational factors, such as having consumed alcohol or drugs or being judged or "disrespected," by the victim or bystanders. Obviously, the more risk factors an individual is exposed to, the more likely he or she is to commit a violent crime.[3]

There is another interesting aspect, apart from the men's criminogenic risk factors and needs. Louie had reached a critical point of the "age-crime curve": burglary and robbery rates peak at Louie's age, at around seventeen years old. But they rapidly decrease after that, possibly allowing some youthful offenders "to grow out of it." But one can grow out of it only if one doesn't "graduate" to more violent crimes. (Murder rates remain at a high plateau between the ages of eighteen and twenty-four and after that drop off slowly.)[4] Not to diminish the life-changing impression Ms. Bracy has left on Bruce, but Bruce could possibly have also, at least in part, grown out of his criminal attitude as he became older.

Recognizing the different factors that have led people like Bruce, Angel, and Adam to commit violent crimes and understanding how these factors interact can help us determine how "a perfect storm" could be averted. In other words, rehabilitation begins in the cradle.[5]

CHAPTER TWELVE

The New Coat

Adam, Bruce and I were on our way to the Men's Wearhouse. It was a fall day in 2007. The season's first snow, salt, and sun had bleached the asphalt a glossy light gray that reflected on the buildings' street-front glass. For half a day New York looked brand new.

"We meant to ask you a question," Adam said as we were crossing Sixth Avenue. "Under which circumstances would you commit a crime?"

"Self-defense?" I said, well aware it was a feeble response.

"Nah," the guys said. "That ain't no crime."

I had to agree.

"So you never committed a crime?"

I hesitated. "I smoke pot sometimes," I said, adding that I never carry any pot with me when out on the streets.

"*Sometimes,*" Adam mocked. This must have registered as a nonoffense to him after having spent more than three decades locked up for two counts of homicide, armed robbery, conspiracy, and attempted escape.

"Okay, what would you do if you found a bag full of money on the street?" he asked.

I told him that I would take the money to the police. When I tried to explain that I wouldn't be able to enjoy money that didn't belong to me, Adam cracked up. His skinny seventy-three-year-old body shook with laughter. He couldn't stop. Bruce chuckled as well. But for the most part he was sidetracked by female pedestrians. "Can I take you out for a coffee? Can I buy you a coffee?" He spouted his new mantra, a broad, sweet grin stretched across his face. Adam continued to question my answer. It appeared he had given this a lot of thought.

"So what if it were three in the morning and no one, *no one*, was on the street, no cameras around, no passing cars. Would you still try to return the money?" The truth is I would. When I picture myself on an abandoned street in New York in the middle of the night, two things come to mind. First, I see a thousand eyes watching—no, spying on—me in the darkness. Second, who abandons a bag full of money on the street? I would immediately suspect a trap. It occurred to me that I've become incapable of committing a crime. When I shoplifted clothes in college, it was more of a dare. I had moved to Hamburg to be far away from my family, and stealing was part of an existentialist gesture. I wanted to prove to myself that *nothing really mattered.*

"Money doesn't really make me happy," I answered. "I wouldn't take any risks for money. It would be different if I found a bag of career on the street," I joked. Adam nodded. His expression turned serious. In this moment I must have been light years away from him.

At the Men's Wearhouse Adam greeted each salesman individually. He knocked on counters and reached out as if to pat their shoulders. "How you doin' today? How you doin', man?" His demeanor was exceedingly warm and friendly, as if he were meeting old friends. But the salesmen regarded us with suspicion—Adam, the handsome elderly Muslim; Bruce, a Lurch with big square prison glasses; and me with my funny accent, trotting along pale and small. As Adam tried on a couple of coats, the salesmen eyed us like hawks. Adam glanced into a mirror, and as he took in the reflections of all the observers, his gaze dropped down to the price tag. He let out a surprised "Pheew!" The coats were all $200 and up. Adam turned away from the mirror and frowned. "You look good, man," Bruce told him. The coats, though, seemed far too light for a New York winter. When I expressed my concern, the salesman huffed, "No, miss, I know for certain that this coat is warm. I have the same one." Warm or not, the coats were too expensive and too wide. "They are too boxy," Adam said. He wanted a coat that complimented his slender and athletic build. He wanted a coat that did justice to his daily devotion to yoga and the exercise bike. This coat had a job to do. It had to reestablish his identity, an identity he had worked on diligently ever since he was a child.

Adam's mother died young and left him nothing. He said she had died of "a bleeding heart" when he was one and a half. Raised by his grandmother, Adam and his sister grew up in deep poverty. When Adam said "deep poverty," it sounded bottomless and sad. When I asked him to elaborate, his voice seemed to fade, and his eyes lost focus. He muttered that he never knew his father. His grandmother was so poor that she couldn't afford to buy chairs for the children. When he was little, she would wake him at dawn to go steal milk from a horse-drawn cart and some donuts or rolls. Because of his ragged clothes, he was the school's "laughingstock." He remembered taking the bus to the welfare office, crossing through different neighborhoods, and seeing white children that weren't as poorly dressed as he. "How come I don't have shoes like that?" he once asked his grandmother. She smacked him and told him to shut up.

"She was embarrassed," Adam shrugged. "From that moment on I thought, 'I'm going to get my own.' It dawned on me that things would never be any better for me."

Adam started hanging out with older boys who were in the same situation as he, and together they started "sticking up." At first they committed burglaries, stealing suits and shoes to make themselves look presentable. Things quickly escalated from there, and the group started to rob stores. Adam's grandmother didn't like it when he brought home the stolen money and clothes. At age fourteen Adam moved in with an older woman. This was around the same time he was first locked up. Maybe it happened a year earlier, or maybe a year later. Adam sometimes mixed up his sentences and the many prisons he has seen.

In prison he was stripped of his identity. "In the streets," Adam explained, "I am an A. Not an X Y Z. I dress like an A, I talk like an A! And you treat me like an A!" His voice was firm and loud, and his hands swirled around. "When you go to prison, that's *over*. The authorities don't want to hear this. Excuse my language: 'Fuck what you were on the street. You are in prison. We say, *Jump!* And you, muthafucka, better *jump*.'"

Although articulate and soft-spoken, Adam said *fuck* and *muthafucka* a lot when he talked about prison. He said that in prison there are two parties that chip away at a person's identity. On the one hand, there are the authorities that treat you like a dog. And on the other, there are the prisoners that demand toughness. "Any type of weakness is going to make you prey. I was never into violence. I don't like it. It turns me off. I can't *staaand* it!" Adam chuckled softly. "A hard rock, a macho? You know I ain't that. That's not my *style*." Adam's words, his intonation, sounded like a symphony. As a grand finale his voice boomed and his chuckles turned to full-blown laughter. Then his speech softened and slowed again. He whispered carefully, as if not to wake the past.

"Little by little you begin to conform. It hurts deep inside that your identity is fucked with. But over time you become what they make of you."

Adam became his own guardian. He would pay attention to which foot he stepped out of bed with in the morning, to every bite he consumed, and to every word he exchanged with the other inmates and guards. Suddenly, things that had become boring were interesting again. The pain of being excluded from life on the outside eased. Adam began to study everything he saw: the color of the bricks making up the adjacent wall, the bars of his cell. For hours he would gaze at the various shapes created by the rays of light that fell through the window. He would stare at its opaque glass and its narrow bars. The more he looked, the more he began to see. When he ran out of things to see he would lie down under his cot and try to experience the cell from a different angle. Then he would crawl back out and start pacing. He would take six steps from his sink to the bars, then turn around and take six steps back. While the other inmates were out in the yard or asleep, he would walk up and down in his cell for hours thinking and reviewing his day. This is how Adam's mind invented his "inner guardian." His inner guardian was part of him, yet he would hover above him scrutinizing his every move and thought.

In the wee hours of the morning Adam would have visitors. Sometimes he heard their rapping first, but often they would just appear without notice. No one but he was able to see them.

When his crime victims José Rodriguez and Thomas Bell first "appeared" in his cell, they writhed around on the floor screaming in pain, their bodies drenched in blood. The men begged him for help. But over the next fifteen years the nature of their visits changed. No more screaming. The blood was gone. For several weeks they didn't say anything. They just stood there, eerily, in a corner of Adam's cell. Adam would do all the talking. "I'm sorry. I had no intention," he would tell his visitors. "It never entered my mind that anything like that would go on. All those years . . . I never shot anybody. If I could have done *anything* to change that situation, I would have." Eventually the men began to respond. They would say, "Listen: This feeling sorry is never good enough. You need acts of contrition to overcome the bad things you have done. When you feel more about helping other people than [about helping] yourself, we don't come back no more."

At age forty-two, when Adam started serving his twenty-five-years-to-life sentence, there were a lot of acts of contrition to be done, and Thomas and José were there to help him do them. At Green Haven Correctional Facility Adam started working on the prison newspaper. After reading about prison conditions and visiting a prison hospice, he got involved in the prison movement. He decided to help and fight for those who were locked up for life.

Thomas and José would come at night and tell him what books to read. He would discuss with them whatever had happened during the day. "They would give me a lot of boosting and help," Adam remembered. This is how he began to measure rehabilitation: not by the number of institutional programs one has attended but by the level of insight, the acts of contrition, and the inner strength he presented in light of his crime and his sentence.

When Adam first became a Muslim, he did it for the discipline and support. He realized that if he really had to serve at least twenty-five years in prison, he would have to create a more structured path for himself. Thomas and José encouraged him. "You can't fight all that by yourself," they said. "Go study and see what the professionals are doing." Adam decided to seek help from the Muslim prison community. Muslims watch over other Muslims, and Islam is based on strict tenets dealing with what you can and cannot do. Allah is also called "The All-Forgiving," and according to the Hadith, the prophet Muhammad is still considered "the most forgiving person." He defended even those who abused and hit him with stones because, he says, they only did it out of ignorance. Maybe this is why many prisoners convert to Islam, a religion that pairs forgiveness with control and strict regimentation.

Islam helped Adam to stay on track. His inner guardian had less to do with it. Slowly life became a bit easier. Thomas and José visited Adam less often.

Adam made a name for himself when he started a program to help lifers adjust to the idea of leading a life behind bars. Whenever he was transferred, which happened all too often, the men from his previous class would replicate the program, and Adam would start a new class in another prison. Soon Adam's seeds spread through all seventy prisons in the state of New York. In prison he had an identity. Everybody knew his name. According to him, they called him the "father of the prison movement."

Adam was eligible for parole in 2001, after serving twenty-five years of his life sentence. He failed the first three parole hearings—2001, 2003, and

2005—and hadn't even wanted to go to his fourth parole hearing until a guard convinced him to give it another try. He was stunned when the board granted him parole. He returned to his cell and told no one. He was embarrassed. Accepting one's life sentence was the staple of his teachings, and now he was going to be released. Would his students think he had just been bullshitting them? He always told people that if he had to do life, he could do it, and people admired that in him. In prison he had a name. But on the outside he had nothing. Not even a winter coat.

After so many years behind bars, Adam didn't know who or what he was. He was a halfway house resident, an ex-con, a cancer survivor, a widower. He was Angel's and Bruce's friend and a father of two. But here again the terms fragmented. He had never really known his kids. He didn't even know where one of them lived. He and his wife separated years before he went to prison. When she visited him about eight years into his sentence, he didn't even recognize her.

A new coat is as good a way as any to start life on the outside.

We decided to try Burlington Coat Factory, two blocks north from the Men's Wearhouse. On the way Adam told me the halfway house's parent organization recently had invited an editor from a black women's magazine to speak about what today's women look for in a man. This sparked Adam's interest, as he was looking for a woman to spend the rest of his life with. The editor told the men, many of whom had spent several decades behind bars, about condoms for women. Adam cracked up and said he didn't even know that female condoms existed. Women able to take charge and put on their own condoms? Amazing. As he explained to me how it worked, he sounded like a struggling scientist who had just stumbled onto a great discovery.

Suddenly Bruce was gone. It seemed that he had finally managed to get the attention of a young woman pushing a baby carriage. "Can I buy you a coffee?" he had asked her. She stopped and they started talking. Adam and I waited for Bruce in front of Burlington's. Adam hadn't even noticed that

Bruce was trying to chat up women. When I told him, he found it hilarious. He explained that Bruce was trying out advice he had received in another one of their halfway house meetings. The men had been discussing how and where to meet women when David Rothenberg suggested they ask strangers on the street to join them for a cup of coffee. It seemed to have worked, at least for Bruce. Adam went on to tell me about the idiosyncrasies he acquired in prison, the ones he still couldn't shed. He still wore his underwear when taking a shower. I was confused. As a means of protection? Out of shame? He explained: in prison it was a matter of convenience. Keeping his underwear on allowed him to wash it while in the shower.

We looked around. Still no sign of Bruce. We decided to take the elevator upstairs. Adam tried on some Calvin Klein coats from the sales rack. The coats were the color of deer. At $139 the price seemed right, but they were still too boxy. Adam took his time ogling himself in the mirror. He turned, opened the coat, closed it, turned around again, looked at himself from the back, then from both sides. Then he tried on another coat, which seemed suspiciously similar to the one before, and the scenario repeated itself.

Bruce suddenly reappeared, out of breath. "I got her number!" His smile made him look like a twelve-year-old, a charming mixture of embarrassment, exhilaration, and impishness lighting up his face.

Adam paid no attention to Bruce's success story. He continued to look at himself in the mirror, still wearing the same deer-brown coat. Adam had his own woman on his mind—Minnie, the excellent listener who wore bleak clothes and no makeup, Mousey Minnie. Adam was still visiting her at the advocacy agency where she worked as a writer. But he had yet to get up the courage to ask her for a date.

Bruce found a black hat that he liked but concluded that a hat without a suit didn't make any sense. He put the hat back on the rack. Hats were not a priority for him. Like Angel, Bruce had recently discovered a love for wild patterns. In prison the men had to wear dark green every day, and it seemed

Bruce and Angel were making up for decades of monotony. Adam, on the other hand, preferred solid colors.

There remained the issue of the coat, and it was starting to get cold. Bruce, Adam, and I took the subway uptown. A man bumped into Bruce. Bruce turned around, locking eyes, and rolled on. We continued our coat search on 34th Street. I suggested we try H&M. I had recently found a coat for myself there so it was worth a look. Bruce's advances toward women continued as we made our way to the store. "Can I buy you a coffee? Can I buy you a coffee?" But they came to a sudden halt at H&M. There his jaw dropped. To get to the coats on the second floor, we had to go through the lingerie department, which was large and crowded with young women picking out thongs and lace bras—in the company of the two men even I felt like blushing. We were quiet as we wended our way up. We briefly scanned the coat racks, and I felt silly for having picked this store. Army coats and bomber jackets clearly were not what Adam wanted or needed. He admired the low prices but quickly decided to continue his search elsewhere.

I was relieved to have noticed Daffy's discount store across the street. I couldn't wait to get out of the crowds. In the late afternoon 34th Street is crazy, with herds of people dashing fatalistically in front of oncoming cars as if traffic lights didn't exist. Adam remembered how such crowds used to make him sweat like a pig. Whereas a few weeks ago a situation like this would have frozen him with self-consciousness, he now mentioned nonchalantly that if it were Tuesday, he could combine Daffy's with a visit to the nearby Division of Parole, where he was required to report once a week.

At Daffy's Adam marveled at the coat selection. In no time he found one he really liked. It was beige and also reversible. When you got tired of beige you could turn it around and have a blue coat. The coat had everything going for it except the fit. Bruce said it made Adam look really professional and that it was perfect for when he gave another lecture. But Adam wondered whether he would be able to fit a suit jacket underneath. He looked at himself in the mirror again. "Looks good," he said, "really good." When Adam observed himself, he seemed to forget about everything else around him. It seemed as if he were searching for something. It reminded me of the countless teenage hours I spent trying on different outfits, wondering whether they could withstand the discriminating taste of the boy I had a crush on. Maybe Adam was trying to look at himself through Minnie's eyes—Minnie, whom he still hadn't asked out for a date, but who continued to roam his mind.

A saleswoman arrived carrying a lined dark green trench coat. She praised the coat in a friendly yet assertive way. This seemed to work. Adam liked the color and the price—$150.

Adam looked exhausted. He knew that the trouble he went through to find a new coat would not solve his problems. But maybe the coat would allow him to temporarily slip out of his "prison armor." He did look professional in his new coat. But what lay beneath? Who was he, and where was he heading? Would he manage to ask Minnie for a date? Time was running out.

CHAPTER THIRTEEN

A Haunted House

The chain of vibrant events at the Castle continued throughout the summer and into the fall. One afternoon in October, the preparations for its annual Halloween party were in full swing. Like the previous year, the residents were busy turning their halfway house into a haunted house. Outside, a long line of children snaked around the corner. Inside, the men set up the DJ booth and created the path of horror through the conference room. This year's theme was "The Obstacle Course." Kids were invited to climb through a narrow black aisle that curved through the building's ground floor. They would be frightened by radio-controlled mice and rats, flying spiders, and ex-cons hiding in dark window frames. A "mental patient" on the loose and a "doctor" cutting off fake limbs would roam the old chambers, accompanied by recordings of thunder, screaming, and clattering chains. I was told that a more benign aisle was reserved for pregnant women.

Among the day's most celebrated attractions was an old microwave oven with its bottom cut out. It stood on a folding table, covering a circular hole. At first I thought someone had just stuck a bloody mask inside the microwave. Then I saw patches of dark skin and black shiny eyes. His body obscured by a large trash bag, the man behind the mask knelt on the floor. He rattled and moaned at the people walking by.

Because I considered this event part work and part play, I decided to invite my friend Franzi along. A performance artist who enjoys dressing up and whose work encourages people to interact, Franzi likes people, and people like her. I hoped that through her the haunted house would lose some of its gravity.

Franzi was dressed in a purple and orange Ninja costume. She wore a necklace made of heavy wooden balls. Inexplicably, she had tied a thick rope around her forehead. I wore the usual costume I dig out for any type of masked ball: black leggings, long sweater, teased hair, white makeup, and black eye shadow. I considered the costume a frightening version of myself. It later occurred to me that it was a comical image of how my mother used to see me as a teenager: sickly, rebellious, with unkempt hair and perpetually dressed in black.

Franzi had brought a decomposed leg and arm made of plastic. It led me to wonder how people at the Castle separated the idea of murder from real murder. Many of the costumes screamed murder. There were weapons—guns, knives, swords—and a lot of fake blood. Is real murder so detached from its sham version that murderers can dress up as murderers without being reminded of their crime?

"We are not scaring the children to the point where they run away and wet their pants," said Tom Pumo, the Castle's director of Food Services and Event Planning, when I interviewed him a few days before the event. "The kids in this neighborhood are tough," he said. He emphasized the therapeutic quality of the event, saying that ex-prisoners are really serious. He hoped the party would cheer them up.

Franzi was as cheerful as the children around her and didn't seem to feel what I felt. She kept extending her rotten arm at small children while keeping her real arm concealed inside her shirt. When the children reached out to shake her fake hand, she dropped the arm and went, "Oops!" She giggled. Some children laughed, others screamed in horror. I hid behind my camera.

Eventually Franzi misplaced her rotten limbs. Or did someone take them? The last time she saw them, they were under a table in the cafeteria. We began to search frantically. Rich, who had brought his new girlfriend and his two boys to the event, was on a mission. Where was the leg, and where was the arm? Rich turned the place upside down until he finally found Franzi's body parts. Someone had placed them in the TV room with the other props.

I wondered what kind of parents let their children go to a house full of murderers, robbers, drug addicts, and dealers. For the Fortune Society the event was important proof that its halfway house had found acceptance in the neighborhood. The Castle's residents had been fully rehabilitated—that's why parents would allow their children to attend the event. I noticed that most of the children were accompanied by older siblings. Many were with their friends. Some were there by themselves. Among the girls were countless black princesses and nurses, in part representing what they would like to be when they grow up, in part representing what they might end up as. The boys dressed up as wrestlers, superheroes, and vampires. There were also a few blood-drenched murderers among them. A tiny clown strapped down in his stroller looked like he was close to tears. A teenage mother with her two boys was dressed as a pregnant nun. The white rubber ball shone through her black habit.

One girl stood out in particular. She was dressed as a cowgirl. No older than thirteen, she wore a form-fitting plaid shirt tied in a knot three inches above her belly button. She wore a short denim skirt that barely covered her bony bottom. Her curly black hair draped over her tiny breasts and touched the exposed caramel skin of her waist, where a gun holster held a pink and white plastic gun. The gun matched the iPod in her right hand. The cowgirl seemed to be there by herself.

Bruce walked back and forth arranging equipment and putting on the final decorative touches. Unlike Terrence, who hid his face behind a Jason mask from *Friday the 13th* and who knelt in a corner waving a bloody sword, Bruce didn't scare the little children. He wore a blonde wig under an ill-fitting sunhat and a set of rotten yellow rubber teeth strapped to his forehead.

Angel did not dress up. He simply put on his mirrored sunglasses, folded his hands behind his back, and remained motionless in a dark corner. I tried to talk to him but couldn't penetrate his mirrored barrier. His silence and forbidding glasses made me feel uncomfortable. Later, Franzi said that she, too, felt uncomfortable in his presence. "Everybody except Angel tried to be cheerful and play along," she said.

I wondered why Angel acted the way he did. Maybe to him all the blood and weapons seemed a bit too real? This might be a projection of my own feelings. Angel was cheerful and charming only when he had an audience. He felt most comfortable when he was the center of attention. But the haunted house was a team effort. Keeping everybody happy and making one another laugh was its primary purpose. We all did our best.

As for Adam, he briefly loomed in the background dressed in his usual costume: glasses and tastefully matching wardrobe. Then he disappeared without speaking. Nobody knew where he went. "Halloween party?" he said when asked later about his whereabouts. "I didn't know they had a Hallow-een party."

At first I didn't recognize Aazim. His black cowboy hat had transitioned into a black spandex mask. His milky eyes were obscured by elliptical black sunglasses. The kitchen lights reflected in his glasses like cold stars. Aazim's mask merged into a black T-shirt with the image of an angry silver skull that sprawled across his big stomach. Usually a chatterbox, tonight Aazim was silent. The most frightening partygoer of all, he just stood there—blind, mute, and scary. To me he looked like a murderer. I had never asked Aazim about his crime, but judging from the length of his sentence—twenty or twenty-five years, if I remember correctly—it must have been serious.

Franzi suddenly disappeared. A little girl dressed as a princess had been so frightened by the head in the microwave that she started crying. No one knew where her parents or siblings were, so Franzi took the little girl by the hand and led her outside, away from sword-swinging murderers and scary men in masks. She tried to calm the girl, who was sobbing desperately. Later Franzi told me how powerless she felt in her costume. "Dressed as a freak, it was hard to represent a more comforting world," Franzi said. "As I was trying to comfort the little girl, I wished I had been Cinderella—and I wished I had left the rotten arm and leg at home."

Franzi's comment captured the night's dilemma. This one day of the year, for a few hours, the men had the opportunity to escape their pariah status and cross over into the mainstream—and the mainstream could enter their world. Yet the event only resulted in a grotesque parody of their situation. The scary man frightened a girl. She never saw his real face.

CHAPTER FOURTEEN

Waiting for Nothing

As the clerk at New York Supreme Court rummaged through the files to sort out the public documents I had requested, I caught a glimpse of a black-and-white photograph of a young man as it disappeared between off-limits documents. I couldn't restrain myself. "Could I please take a quick look at that picture?" I asked. The clerk grunted and briefly pressed the two-by-four-inch photograph against the window separating us. I tried to take in as much as I could in the few seconds he gave me.

It was Angel's mug shot and the only existing picture of him as an eighteen-year-old. The photo showed the face of a skinny teenager with an Afro who appeared no more than fourteen years old. The light contrast in the picture was stark, making his skin appear much darker than it actually is. His facial expression conveyed a mixture of loss and disregard. It was unclear whether this expression was spontaneous or something he had learned watching movies and practiced on the streets.

The photograph combined with another image I had long carried in my head. A few weeks before Angel killed Olga in the hallway of a neighborhood building, he had carried his baby cousin from one relative to another. The Harlem streets were buried in snow that year. Angel had put his little cousin under his jacket and climbed over towering mounds of white from one side of the road to the other. He felt like a lion, strong and proud. He had been given the big responsibility to take care of this little helpless human in a situation in which almost everything had stopped working. *Just don't fuck with me now!* Angel thought, as he imagined a group of teenagers bullying or even attacking him. He was determined to keep the baby warm and get him to his destination unscathed.

Angel said that for a brief period after he was arrested, the police had searched for an associate. How could such a short, skinny boy have dragged Olga's body from a third-floor apartment on 118th Street all the way up to the roof? And how could he, one day later, have undressed the body, stuffed it in plastic bags, carried it back down, around the corner, and into the hallway of another building? But Angel insisted he alone carried Olga to 117th Street.

Angel's small size and childlike appearance have often belied his capability and strength. One afternoon as he and two other inmates were in their cell at Rikers Island playing cards, Angel told them that he knew how to remove the screws from the cell window. Back then Rikers Island didn't have barbed wire—"They got it after I tried to escape," Angel liked to joke—and one could theoretically swim from the island to Hunts Point in the Bronx. "Theoretically" because the strong currents had swallowed even good swimmers.

Angel swiftly removed the screws and jumped out of his cell window. Three decades later he still remembers how wonderful the grass felt under his feet. "This incredible feeling of freedom," he remembered. "When you are locked up, you go into shock. Like a sparrow. Have you ever caught a sparrow?"

Angel ran to the shore, which was lined with rocks. It was at that point he remembered that he didn't know how to swim. Once again he had failed to consider the consequences of his actions. He was apprehended a few minutes later and transferred to the segregation unit at the Brooklyn House of Detention.

At the Brooklyn House he met Mae, a woman in her early thirties who ran the Adult Literacy Center. Now in her sixties, Mae is still in touch with Angel. She remembers a skinny young man in a corner cell with a temper who told her he had killed a guy who had an affair with his girlfriend. It was not until twenty-five years later that Mae learned the truth about Angel's crime.

Mae noticed quickly that Angel, although unable to read or write, was "incredibly bright." She began to mentor him, and by the time he was sentenced and transferred to a juvenile prison upstate the following year, he had acquired rudimentary reading and writing skills. Mae began to send Angel letters and books to broaden these new skills, and Angel devoured every book she sent him. He started writing poems and prose. Language became a tool that enabled him to redirect (or at least allay) his violent fits. When asked whom he credits with his "successful rehabilitation," Angel always named Mae first and his Attica Quaker community second.

In a nostalgic gesture Mae returned 120 letters Angel had written her between 1990 and his release in 2007. Angel offered the letters to me to read, and I was curious. In them I hoped to find the turning point that led to his recovery, that turned the teenage criminal into a law-abiding adult. While it was important for me to understand how Angel was brought up and how he struggled to put his life back together after twenty-nine years in prison, I also wanted to know who he had been when he committed the crime and who he had become between then and now. He was no longer the teenager with the lost and snotty facial expression. But had he shown remorse? Was his smiling and charming personality—and his popularity among the Quakers and Fortune's staff—proof of his rehabilitation?

Angel's letters to Mae bear little evidence of his confronting the severity of his crimes. Their prevailing theme was not his remorse or his search for forgiveness. Rarely did he write about his experiences with other inmates. He primarily focused on the prospect of his release.

Angel was eligible to appear before the parole board after fifteen years but was denied parole seven times before he was finally released. In what appeared to be an endless cycle, Angel kept preparing for freedom. He filed appeals and complaints and conveyed utter disappointment and anger

Waiting for Nothing

each time things fell through. But after a period of mourning and ranting against the parole board, he would pick himself up once again. He would eventually calm down, making room for yet another thin slice of hope. Once again he would prepare for his freedom and, once again, he would have to deal with the disappointment and anger that came with its denial. According to his letters, Angel's preparations began at least three years before he was first eligible for parole and from 1993 on repeated themselves in twenty-four-month cycles for the next fourteen years.

As if worrying about freedom might ease a prospective disappointment, Angel constantly questioned whether he was even prepared to face release. "Look at it this way," he wrote in 1991, two years before his first parole eligibility hearing. "If they hit me, I go back to doing what I've been doing [because] life doesn't change much. But if [I] am released then I've got problems!!" When Angel ran out of words to express his emotions or when he wanted to add a humorous note to a previous sentence or paragraph, he would include a drawing of a little face. The face sometimes looked happy and sometimes sad. In this letter it looked worried, its eyes rolled up and its mouth gaping. The thought bubble explained: "Rent. Food. Taxes. Oh NO!"

In another letter he wondered about being burdened with neuroses upon his release. After telling Mae an anecdote about a guy who promised himself that he would never wash a pair of socks again in his life and who, upon his release, decided to flush his pair of worn socks down the toilet at the end of each day, Angel wrote: "I look forward to experiencing my set of 'crazy' when I get out. I don't think it will be the sock thing but I often wonder about sleeping in the same bed with someone else. I don't think I have ever done so for more times than I can count on one hand. Twice I think. I always imagine myself having my own room even when married. Sounds strange eh?"

Former New York governor George Pataki—whom Angel referred to as "a shit kicker," "a real asshole," "quite dangerous," "not a thinker," and "not the type of person I would like with his finger on 'The Nuclear Button' or even my belly button for that matter"—abolished parole altogether for repeat violent offenders in 1998. The governor also consistently repressed the release of murderers who, like Angel, were convicted with the promise of parole long before his tenure. "They have classified me as a 'Violent Felony Offender,' a legal designation that didn't exist back then," Angel wrote in one of his letters, hoping that his finding would open a door to the outside.

To prove his successful rehabilitation, he accumulated numerous program certificates. But Pataki didn't seem to care how many certificates he had earned during incarceration. His release policies felt like a game of chance, and Angel surmised that Pataki's administration painted him and others as "some mad dog killer just waiting for the opportunity to eat some child or something."

Sometimes Angel's anger would make room for strategizing once again. He would work on his "killer application" for the jobs he intended to apply for once released, or he would try to prove the parole board wrong.

At some point Angel decided to get the community's approval for his release, "the thought being, of course, that if the community has no objections, then why should the board? It would sort of blunt that dagger they like to wield as an excuse." Optimistically he added, "I got your asses fuckers!" Angel started to request and collect letters from his Quaker community and from the Fortune Society, but again to no avail.

It was not until Mae hired a lawyer at the end of 2004 to help Angel with his parole preparations that she discovered the exact nature of his crimes. "It's not like something I am proud of so talking about it has always been hard," he responded when Mae addressed the issue. "It's just not who I am is all. How one moment of madness can define a person is amazing to me. It's probably why I tend not [to] do it consciously if I can help it. Anyway, it's only a version of the 'truth.' The government is not interested with [sic] anything else."

To Angel, the punishment he received for killing a young girl, attempting to kill his coworker, and trying to escape from jail seemed arbitrary and exaggerated. "If I believed in karma I would swear I had been a Nazi in some past life and now I'm paying for it," he wrote. Not once did he contemplate in his letters to Mae the life he had taken or the lives he had altered forever. Reading the hearing transcripts, I was very surprised to find out that he hadn't apologized to the victims or expressed remorse in his first five parole hearings.

The commissioners usually started out by recounting the crimes Angel committed. This was followed by Angel trying to explain the circumstances as well as he could and in as much detail as he had the opportunity to give. At his first hearing in 1993, for example, he gave his attention deficit, lack of guidance, and poor self-esteem as reasons for killing Olga.

"How does your self-esteem get better when you strangle some sixteen-year-old girl for no reason?" Commissioner Veronica D. Thomas asked.

"Ma'am . . . ," Angel tried. "That was just the effect. I'm not saying that—I don't have an excuse. There is none."

"I didn't ask you for an excuse because we know there is no excuse; otherwise you wouldn't be sitting here, because if it was an excusable homicide, you'd be home. But, I mean, I would like to know what was going on that you were acting out so violently in the community."

"Just the way I was living, ma'am, my ideas, my—just I had no values. I had nothing."

"Why not?"

"I wasn't guided. I mean, it's—you know I've been having problems since I was a child, since I was in second grade, and it seems like I never paid attention. . . . I didn't behave."

Commissioner Thomas brushed off Angel's attempts. "Well, kids never behave. I mean, that's part of being a child," she said, adding, "Well, if every person in this country who had poor self-esteem did what you did, we'd all be locked up."

Commissioner Thomas had a point. Nothing can excuse such a horrible crime. But at the same time her question—"Why did you commit these crimes?"—implied there was something that could. Her question appeared like a trap. Why even ask if there were no excuse? And why respond in such an aloof manner if your opponent had no power? Or is that what she wanted? *There is no excuse—period.* The answer couldn't possibly be that simple. I had been struggling with this question since I first met Angel and believed that it was impossible to answer in a twenty-minute parole hearing among total strangers.

At the second hearing, conducted by Commissioner Irene L. Platt and Commissioner Daniel B. Tauriello, Angel clearly stated that there was no excuse for what he did and continued by saying that he understood that he had been wrong, but that he couldn't undo what he had done, regardless of how much he would like to. At a parole hearing there is no time for philosophical, analytical, sociological, or even personal debate; there is hardly time for anything. Whatever Angel tried was doomed to fail. When Platt ran out of responses she was free to change direction.

"Yeah, but you see," she said. "Before you talked about losing your temper, anger, you know. Obviously you had no care about any other human being but yourself and, you know, went wild when somebody argued with you, but if I read these facts right, there was more to this. You took this body to the roof, placed it in plastic bags, attempted to hide it. You know what I'm—I'm reciting the facts because it shows me a person who more than loses his temper and goes out of control."

"I compounded my folly by trying to hide the fact," Angel admitted.

"Why did you take her clothing off?" Platt wanted to know.

"Identification."

"Did you dismember this body at all?"

This question seemed unnecessary because the files did not indicate anything to that extent.

"No, no," Angel responded.

"Did you ask her for sexual favors at that time and she said no?"

"No, there was nothing sexual."

"What, did you ask her for money?" Platt asked.

I wondered what line Platt would have followed if Angel had said yes. Was that what she wanted to hear? Would that have been a better explanation than low self-esteem, uncontrollable anger, a lack of safety as a child, a dysfunctional family background, and growing up in the ghetto (all explanations Angel had tried at his various hearings)?

At the end of the 1995 hearing Angel tried another strategy.

"I could never really explain the depth of my sorrow, but I believe I'm ready. You know, to continue incarceration would really not be in anybody's interest," Angel said when Commissioner Tauriello asked him if there was anything he would like to discuss. But Angel's response to Tauriello's conciliatory question didn't sit well with Platt.

"Except maybe your victims."

"Well do they really—," Angel tried.

"You really can't help it, right?" Platt said.

I got stuck at this sentence. On the one hand, I didn't like Platt's leading questions; their sole purpose seemed to be to humiliate Angel. On the other hand, I understood her irritation. Angel's response *was* aloof. Unlike Bruce and Adam, Angel didn't show much remorse in his hearings (or at any other moment for that matter).

It obviously didn't help Angel that the next hearing, in 1997, was once again conducted by Commissioner Platt, a Republican and generous donor to Pataki's party. On the board with Platt in January 1997 was Commissioner Sean McSherry, another longtime conservative, who would be indicted one year later as part of a federal probe of alleged parole trade-offs for Pataki campaign contributions. Although charged with promising favorable state parole rulings to the families of convicted violent felons in exchange for tens of thousands of dollars in donations, McSherry was only found guilty of perjury and obstruction of justice. He was sentenced to two years in a federal prison in 1999.[1]

Considering that parole commissioners are supposed to take into account all evidence, previous hearing transcripts and the development of the prisoner, Platt's approach seemed sadistic.

"What you did is you hid part of the body, I believe you dismembered part of it," she alleged once again.

"No," Angel said.

Platt continued with what appeared to be her second favorite topic.

"There was no sex involved? It seems a little strange to me that you took her on the roof, you undressed her, stripped her, that there was no motivation here for any sexual contact. Had she turned you down?"

"It was more of a—the stripping and the putting her in a bag, I think was more of just hiding, as, you know, just trying to cover up. I panicked. It was terrible," Angel responded.

In 1999, shortly before his fourth parole hearing, Angel was transferred to Attica after getting into an altercation with another inmate at Sullivan Correctional Facility. Angel said the other inmate was twice his size and had been mocking him for a couple of years. One day, when the "knucklehead" was serving food in the mess hall, he saw Angel and jumped over the counter to attack. Angel was prepared and was carrying a clothes iron. Angel still cracked up remembering the fear and surprise in his opponent's face when he realized Angel was armed. Angel may have made his point, but his efforts landed him in "the box" (solitary confinement).

When Angel got called to the 1999 parole hearing in Attica, he still had 19 of 120 days of "keeplock" left to serve. Nevertheless, Commissioner Kenneth Graber seemed far more sympathetic to Angel than any of the previous commissioners had been. When Angel said that he was nervous, Graber told him not to rush. Graber encouraged him to continue to see the psychologist he had been seeing after his last parole hearing and to "open up the wounds to see what causes" his violent behavior. He said he saw a lot of progress over his past appearances in front of the board. Yet he denied Angel parole because of his "serious pattern of violent behavior" and the assault.

The hearings in 2001 and 2003 were considerably shorter and repeated much of what had already been said. It was as if everyone had tired of the endless game. Why continue to ask the same halfhearted questions when the answers were limited and the decision had already been made? Even some of the faces were familiar. The facility parole officers remained the same, and so did the parole program aide. Commissioner Lawrence Scott appeared both in 1999 and 2003, and William Crowe in 2001 and 2003. The next hearing included another familiar face: Commissioner Smith, who had attended the hearing in 2001, was now leading the one in 2005.

By that time Angel was well prepared thanks to the lawyer Mae had hired for him. The lawyer pointed out some of the deficiencies in his thinking at his previous parole hearings. But in the letters to Mae before his 2005 hearing Angel focused on something entirely different. "You know what I could use for Christmas?" he wrote.

"A shirt, a tie, and an open-v-sweater, pullover of course. This way I could look presentable at the board."

He picked up the topic again in the next letter:

In terms of size? Using a measuring tape from my sewing kit . . . I have a 16-inch neck and a stout frame. That's 46 inches in the chest area with an arm length of 22 inches (from arm pit to wrist). It would make me a Large I believe. As you can probably tell I have never bought clothes for myself. As for colors? Well I will have dark green pants so what works with that? I would think a dark green sweater with a light colored shirt. Maybe off white or light beige and as for a tie? Well I'll leave that up to you. No black or gray is allowed. Maybe Khaki?

Receiving Mae's package with the clothes prompted Angel to reflect:

Great tie by the way, it goes perfectly with everything else. I have been watching people on TV to try to get a sense of how men are wearing them now. I have notice[d] some interesting stuff. It seems that the people of wealth put a dimple under the center of the bow knot while those of the teaching professions don't. Then there is the size of the bow knot itself. It tends to vary depending on status or perhaps preference. It might sound a bit nuts that I should focus so much attention on such a thing. But I just found it fascinating. I'm willing to bet dollars to doughnuts that there is a book out there devoted to just such observations. Call me crazy but I would probably read it. As you can tell I really did like the tie!

On January 11, 2005, Angel sat in his cell, dressed up and waiting to be called to his parole interview. But no one came to pick him up. The board later claimed that the interview was postponed because of "availability of inmate."

Angel was devastated, of course. So much energy had gone into the preparations. He even had secured himself a room on the outside. He would live with his Aunt Lucy, one of his few surviving family members and the only one who would write a letter here and there.

Angel's seventh parole hearing, which finally took place on February 8, 2005, got off to a promising start. Commissioner William Smith started out by commenting on Angel's outfit. "You appear today in a nice shirt and tie, the second person today to do that, and we certainly—it is a little bit unusual, and we recognize it. And it is an important day for you."

"It is out of respect for you guys," Angel said. "You guys are doing a lot of work."

"We understand that; that is a positive," Smith responded.

Angel appeared to have learned his spiel. He said his previous violations— possession of marijuana in 1985 and assault in 1998—were a result of his hanging out with the wrong crowd. He said he kept Olga's LOVE ring because he wanted to get caught and that he now despised violence, even on TV. "I try to focus on programs that are nonviolent, 'Seventh Heaven' and 'Touched by an Angel,' those kind of things." Smith went so far as to discuss Angel's postrelease plans, and Angel laid out his commitment to Quakerism and his broad set of skills. At the end of the interview Angel did something he had never done before. While in previous parole hearings he had only said that to be sorry was never enough, this time he made a point of apologizing to the victims' families.

I don't think I can leave without apologizing on the record to the victims' family. I know I caused them great harm. The older I get, the more I understand what the harm is. Not only in the immediate moment, but how it continued through the years. I'm still in pain over this, I imagine, I empathize. I want to apologize for the pain I caused her, I caused my family, the embarrassment. It seems inconceivable that I could be so broken. I want you to know I worked my whole life to become whole. I see myself as whole, I truly want you to know that I am whole, that this is a difficult thing, that this does work in a very small case for people who really have that. You guys have to have faith in that; if not I will be here.

Angel's parole request was once again found "incompatible with the public safety and welfare."

A few months after the 2005 hearing, Angel was presented with "an unexpected gift." His Aunt Lucy had died, and he was to go to her funeral. Although in his letter to Mae he said he doubted that *gift* was the appropriate word, he couldn't hide his excitement. Of course, it wasn't the death itself that was cheerful but the prospect of those few hours of freedom granted while attending the funeral. In his letter Angel said hardly anything about the death of his aunt. Neither did he consider the consequences: with the death of Aunt Lucy he had lost his place to stay on the outside—which is crucial when going before the board, because parole's alleged responsibility is not only to look at your progress while incarcerated but to make sure your post-release plans are solid. Proof of housing plays an important part.

On May 12, 2006, Angel arrived at the funeral, shackled and escorted by several officers. He had missed his cousin Marcos, also shackled and escorted by officers, by half an hour. Marcos was serving time upstate for two attempted rapes, an attempted robbery, and a burglary; he had been denied parole repeatedly as well. Angel's parents had long since died, and his brother Frank, who had attempted to visit him only once in the last twenty-seven years, did not even recognize him. "You look a bit like my brother," Frank eventually said, according to Angel.

Sitting alone in his cell after his aunt's funeral, Angel wrote:

> I couldn't believe that the cacophony of strangers I had met were my family and that I loved them dearly but had forgotten with the passage of time. And although the sadness that griped [sic] my heart was so intense as to rob me of breath, I was left with a sense of compassion that turned the world into an even more beautiful place. The lilacs were in bloom in their full glory and it was as if the world opened itself up to me. And although I could not smell not a sent [sic], encased in my metal casket as I was, my heart was permeated by memories of fragrances long forgotten. . . .
>
> I had not realized how much I miss the City till I was leaving it. I remember at one point crossing over the Hudson and seeing the City appear between mountains. I must have been 20 to 50 miles away but I thought as I beheld her "The City!" I had to smile to myself as my breath caught at the majestic beauty of her skyline. At some primordial level it called to me and I could feel its intensity and pulse course through me like a liquid shower of anticipation. I was home or as close to home as I have been in a long, long time. I did not realize then as I drank deeply of her streets that leaving her would hurt too much.

After a preliminary interview with the parole office in November 2006, Angel wrote Mae a letter. In it he said, "I don't attach much importance to what the Parole Board thinks of me or whatever." He continued with what would become his prevalent attitude. He was optimistic and thought that life was all right and that he was all right:

> I'm just in a good place right now. Like I told the parole officer this morning, I like myself and am enjoying life as it comes. Taking my little pleasures where

ever [sic] I can find them. And as to why I did what I did? The simple truth is that I didn't know any better. That was the best decision that I could make at that time. Which speaks to how broken I was when I was making those types of decisions. When she asked me what are two things I would like to change about myself I couldn't think of any. Because I like the man I am and the man I am becoming. . . . If they don't like it, tough! I didn't tell her that but I'm feeling incredible confident in myself and that is that.

Some months after Angel wrote this, he appeared in front of the board for the eighth time. A few days later he was informed that he would be paroled to the Castle in New York City.

What struck me the most while reading Angel's letters was how unrepentant he sounded. Apparently, Angel needed a lawyer to tell him to express remorse and apologize to the victims' families in front of the parole board. Mae only found out the truth about his crime by reading the documents the lawyer prepared for the board. But Mae was charmed by Angel, his keeping in touch, his improvements in terms of education, and his becoming a Quaker. She believed that Angel's case had been mishandled by the Division of Parole and that after being locked up for fifteen-plus years he deserved to be released.

I never really saw Angel grapple with what he had done. Clearly, he wanted to get out. Who could blame him? But in contrast to Adam and Bruce, I always felt something was missing. Adam had decided early on that he needed to make amends and perform "acts of contrition," as he repeatedly told me. Bruce expressed his remorse almost every time I saw him. He also expressed it in front of the parole board. He emphasized his victim's name, making the experience of killing a personal one and thereby acknowledging his total responsibility. His childhood would have never come up had I not asked. Also, his story about Ms. Bracy left a lasting impression on me. There was a turning point, a clear break from his former homicidal self. Angel, on the other hand, had lied to Mae about his crime. He seemed more preoccupied with his appearance than with what he had done. I remembered that when he told me about his crime for the first time he interrupted his gruesome narrative to cheerfully note that he had mistaken some ball in the river for a dead body. He had detached himself from his former self. Angel just wanted the whole thing to be over and done with—and he had plenty of friends who supported him.

CHAPTER FIFTEEN

Growing Old

When I asked Angel what he would do on his "first" birthday on December 10, 2007, he just shrugged and said he hadn't given it much thought. It was his forty-eighth birthday, exactly thirty years after his last birthday on the outside.

His friend Mae and I decided to throw him a little birthday party. Angel had known Mae for a long time, and he considered her a real friend. But I wondered how much Mae and Angel actually shared. Clearly, Mae knew a lot about Angel's life, but what did Angel know about Mae? I felt like I knew Angel, even though I had only met him seven months earlier. I was probably the person he had spent the most time with since his release. He had shared some of his life's most intimate details with me. I knew things about him he had never told anyone else. But Angel rarely asked about me and my life. Our relationship was unbalanced. We weren't friends. I would always remain the journalist and he my subject.

A couple of weeks before his first birthday, Angel had begun working at the Fortune Society as an intake worker and counselor. He conducted first interviews with ex-cons in need of Fortune's job, health, and counseling services. He was friendly with his coworkers, but when I asked him if he would like to invite anyone else to his birthday dinner, he declined.

Angel was not only the first one to find work; he was also the first one to find a girlfriend. His relationship with Tanya had quickly become more serious than anyone had expected. Already Angel was talking about moving in with her. Oddly, though, Tanya wasn't invited either.

The temperatures hovered around the freezing point. The New York winter had officially settled in. Angel had "grown up" over night. He had his first job now and his first girlfriend, and in a way it felt like we were celebrating his eighteenth birthday, not his forty-eighth.

Mae, Bruce, Angel, and Adam were waiting in front of the Yaffa Café. We entered, and the men waited for me to guide the group: a towering African American who ducked to fit through the door frame; a hesitant Muslim with beard and round glasses; a short Puerto Rican wearing an elegant blue cashmere coat at least two sizes too large; an elderly white woman, trim and athletic, with short, brownish-gray hair. I was, as always, nervous. Would the men like the food? What would we talk about? Which table should we sit at? Suddenly Angel's birthday felt like a burden. The men never liked to make decisions; I felt it was all up to me. I chose a Middle Eastern restaurant in the East Village because its decor of fake leopard and zebra skin and colorful Christmas lights lent it a celebratory atmosphere. It also offered a wide variety of vegetarian dishes, which I thought might please Adam, who was a vegetarian and whose own first birthday was approaching.

I chose a table in the far back. We shuffled back and forth for a while until we found the right seating arrangement. Bruce, in particular, couldn't decide where to sit—between me and Adam on the padded bench or at the head of the table? He eventually sat at the head of the table, in the corner. That way he was able to see what was going on in the room. Angel and Mae took seats with their backs to the room. I noticed how Angel always made a conscious effort to confront the things that frightened him. No other ex-con I have ever spent time with liked to sit with his back to the room, unable to see who entered, to see strangers approaching from afar. Angel once told me that he was comfortable sitting with his back to the room as long as he could see my facial expressions. A twitch or a panicky glance in my eyes indicated danger— a danger he was ready to respond to.

Mae ordered a beer, and I ordered wine. It was then that it occurred to Angel that he might not be allowed to be there. One of his parole regulations forbids him from visiting establishments whose primary purpose is to serve alcohol. I argued that a restaurant's primary purpose was to serve food, but Angel knew from experience that it was impossible to reason with law enforcement. In any case, today he didn't seem to mind. He pointed out that he had been to several restaurants since his release and that it never occurred to him to order a drink.

"Sabrina . . . "—Bruce sometimes called me Sabrina by mistake—"What are you having?" I wasn't sure yet, but Bruce kept prodding. "Sabrina, what are you having?" When I decided to order hummus and baba ghanouj, Bruce posed his question to Mae, Angel, and Adam. Angel and Adam were clueless as well. Mae said she would have the pasta with shrimp. Angel said he would also get pasta with shrimp, whereupon Adam and Bruce chimed in that this seemed like a good choice to them as well.

Angel snapped at Bruce, saying he did not want to hear any complaints like the time we had bagels with scallion cream cheese in Williamsburg. Bruce growled back, saying he wouldn't complain, and then the men started chuckling, reminding one another not to take the silverware with them on their way out. In the prison mess hall they had to pick up their silverware after each meal and drop it into a bucket by the exit. Adam said that more than once he had picked up his knife and fork on his way out of a restaurant and remembered that he was a free man only when he couldn't find the bucket.

The waitress brought the wine I ordered, and Angel said that wine always reminded him of death. His mother used to feed his stepfather in a corner of their apartment when he was too drunk to eat. "The stupor in his face," Angel said, shaking his head. "Like a baby." He imitated the facial expressions of an inebriated cartoon character.

Pink Floyd's "Wish You Were Here" came on, and Angel sang along. He furrowed his brow and closed his eyes.

Growing Old

Can you tell a green field/From a cold steel rail?

Angel has a nice voice. I wondered whether this song symbolized his new-found love—mushy but real, abstract yet tangible, in any case, filled with weighty, contrasting emotions. Suddenly it seemed all three men were talking about women they had met and gotten—more or less—involved with. But in Angel's case things were happening so fast, I could hardly keep track of it all.

"We are embarking on a wonderful journey together . . . ," he said. "A wonderful journey!"

Unlike Adam and Bruce, Angel did not mind being directed and immers-ing himself in something that might not have appeared perfect. Tanya, Angel said, loved him "fiercely." He was powerless to resist. In any case, what could be wrong with fierce love, if for thirty years no one had really loved you at all? What could be wrong with a woman who so clearly enjoyed taking control of a man who was used to being controlled, and who, in fact, often felt lost and anxious in his uncontainable new world? Love's sudden attainability after thirty years in prison must have felt like a foreign country. Angel still jerked when Tanya touched him without warning.

Angel's fast-evolving relationship was a reason to celebrate, even if the insecurities, the fear, and the uncertain feelings that came with love were still difficult for him to grasp and at times hard for him to cope with.

Was that why Bruce was hesitant to commit to a relationship? One of his sons, with whom he had just recently reconnected, had introduced him to a woman from Albany. He told her that his father had just been released, and the woman started calling Bruce. He even went to visit her a few times, and she came to visit him in New York, where he took her to Times Square on one of the long buses that fold like accordions. He enjoyed her company but insisted that she was "just a friend." He wasn't yet able to open up. He told her that he had been in prison for killing a man but never went into any detail. Despite the time we spent together, Bruce never elaborated on his relation-ships, and I didn't push him. I accepted and pursued only what he offered.

Whenever I asked him about the woman in Albany, he said, "She's just a friend, not a *girl*friend." It reminded me of how he shrugged off my questions about his common-law wife, the mother of his sons. "At some point you gotta let go," he said, when I asked him whether it was hard to leave her behind when he went to prison. "You know, I've seen guys bugging out over having no females. I'm not gonna let that happen to me." His "wife," a drug addict who had died long ago, came to visit him during the first years. Then she stopped coming. He had a couple of pen pals but those didn't last either. He said he needed to get his life together before committing to an intimate relationship. This made sense to me. Maybe a woman couldn't get through to Bruce until his life and dignity were restored, until he had a job, an apartment, and a future. A woman had to be able to listen to his whole story with all its gruesomeness, regrets, and pain.

At the restaurant the conversation revolved around the usual topic: prison. On the one hand, the three men all agreed that prison was evil and robbed them of much of their lives. On the other hand, Bruce and Angel both said that prison also had good parts. Angel praised prison for the structure it offered him, a structure he had never known growing up.

"I wouldn't give up the experience," Angel said. "Jail taught me how to appreciate life," Bruce added. "It made me a man."

The men often spoke about their lives and inner growth in prison as if they would have never had the opportunity to grow had they remained free. This made me sad.

As he often did, Adam remained quiet. It was in these quiet moments that I felt a deep connection to him. These moments summed up all the sorrow, the lack of opportunities, the lost years, and the wish to be able to start all over under more favorable circumstances. But where do you even begin at this point in life? You might as well remain quiet.

Angel, Bruce, and Adam did not celebrate their birthdays while in prison. Hardly anyone did. What was there to celebrate? That you were born and that you took another person's life? That you were locked up for an indeterminate length of time? Birthdays in prison reminded the men about the passing of time. About getting older without getting out. It reminded them of what they didn't have, things like love, money, and decent food. Where birthdays were about getting presents, about being loved and celebrated, prison represented the ultimate absence of those things.

Having ignored his birthday for so long, Adam's old age took him by surprise. "At the halfway house everybody is trying to launch a new life for themselves," he told me. "It's over for me. I'm going on seventy-five years. If I'm lucky I can squeeze twenty more years out of this. If I'm extremely lucky. If I get ten more years I'm lucky."

When Adam was released, it was spring. He would go to the park across the street from the Castle and sit on a bench overlooking the Hudson River. It was warm and bright, and he could smell the grass. He would see the barges passing by; New Jersey's river communities lie sleepily on the other shore. It should have been paradise. But instead, he sat on the bench and cried, the tears running down his gaunt cheeks. "What are you crying about?" he asked himself. He had no answer. It must have been autumn when he finally realized: In prison time stood still. There were hardly any chronological reference points. No one ever mentioned his age. He never felt old. There were no women who'd label him "too old." In prison there were no birthdays and no children he could have observed growing up. It was life in a timeless vacuum.

At the restaurant I asked whether their experiences varied depending on the prison they were in. They all agreed that Attica was one of the worst prisons. Adam scooped his shrimp onto the fork with his fingers while Angel elaborated on the beatings inmates received from guards. With the ease with which someone might talk about his last vacation to Aruba, Angel spoke about the screams he would hear coming from the cells adjacent to his in the middle of the night. The next day he would see the inmate limping, his body ripe with dark bruises and cuts. Afraid of repercussions, the beaten man would say that he had fallen down the stairs.

Trying to steer the conversation to something more positive—it was Angel's birthday, after all—I asked, "What's a particularly 'good' prison?"

"Napanoch!" they replied in a chorus. "That's why they call it Nappy Napa," Angel added.

Then the conversation turned to Minnie. Adam still hadn't mustered the courage to ask her out for dinner. Mae suggested that maybe a spontaneous invitation to lunch during work hours would be less conspicuous. Having mulled this over before, Adam shook his head and stared down at his empty plate. Not an option either.

Angel wondered again whether they should ask Minnie out together, to make it seem even more casual, less like a date and more like a relaxed get-together. But Adam was skeptical. Minnie might be the kind of woman who would notice. Then the whole thing would come across like a scheme, destroying the effortlessness they had been enjoying.

"I'll be serious as a heart attack," Angel promised, giddy with excitement at the prospect of playing a part in this. But Adam remained unconvinced.

Angel had had enough of the conversation and brought the topic back around to himself. "There is a woman at Fortune who calls me *cara chula*." (It means "pretty face" in Spanish.) "She wants to take me home, but I decided against it, because she's a bit on the heavy side."

We had finished dinner, and it was time for me to go. The five of us walked up First Avenue. "This was a memorable event," Adam concluded as we said our good-byes. His voice sounded heavy with heartache.

CHAPTER SIXTEEN

Silent Forgiveness

I was driving up to Rochester in a rental car to attend the Friday night Quaker meeting at Attica prison and to meet some of Angel's friends. It was shortly before Christmas 2007, and the bare mountains lined with leafless trees looked like the heads of sick, balding men. The snowflakes were too small, too fast, and too many to evoke Christmas but still too few to hide the depressing grayish-brown tinge that dominated the landscape. I could not find a radio station that featured anything other than bad country music, Christmas carols, or Christian sermons. I passed towns that were familiar to me for the names of their prisons: Beacon, Fishkill, Wallkill, Otisville, Sullivan, Elmira, Monterey. . . . There are sixty state prisons in New York alone.

Angel's path to forgiveness began with the Quakers from Rochester. When Angel turned forty, he had lost all hope of ever being released. He grew depressed and considered suicide. "Despair gripped my heart, and I couldn't seem to shake it off. I got tired," he said one day as we sat on a bench by the Hudson facing Riverside Church, where he attended his Sunday Quaker meetings.

Angel went to the prison psychiatrist and told him that the idea of killing himself had become a viable alternative. "How about now?" the psychiatrist asked him nonchalantly. "Now you are feeling okay again, right?" Angel left the doctor's office without medication or a sense of relief. As he put it, "a switch in mind and soul" saved his life. He stopped lifting weights but decided to choose life. "Me and God, we be mates," he said with a chuckle, quoting a line from *Crocodile Dundee*.

When the social and the physical body are forced to retreat and "despair grips the heart," spirituality gains importance. Angel opened his heart to the Quakers, and the Quakers opened their hearts to him.

The Religious Society of Friends—dubbed "Quakers" by detractors—was first conceived in mid-seventeenth-century England by George Fox. Fox mistrusted paid clergymen and the church's hierarchical structure. Believing in the "inner light," he maintained that God's word could be experienced "without the help of any man, book or writing."[1] A rebel in his time, Fox defended women's and poor people's rights and the "liberty for any to speak." He soon got into trouble for his refusal to follow traditional beliefs and to take legal oaths. (Having to take an oath, Fox believed, implied that one was not obliged to tell the truth otherwise.) Like many Quakers after him, he was jailed and tortured.[2]

The Quakers were committed to the abolition of slavery, to prison reform, and to the education of freed slaves. The first modern mental institutions in Great Britain and in the United States were established by Quakers. Because they opposed violence, many Quakers refused to go to war and to pay war taxes—which again made them subject to imprisonment. In 1947 the Nobel Peace Prize was awarded to the American Friends Service Committee and the British Friends Service Council.

Although relatively small in numbers—there are thought to be about 350,000 in the world—the Quakers' impact on society has been remarkable. The first women's rights convention, the Don't Make a Wave Committee (the predecessor to Greenpeace), Oxfam, and Amnesty International were organized by Quakers. Believing in the ongoing transformation of humanity, Quakers have always run active prison ministries, in which they welcome not only Christians but also Jews, Muslims, and Buddhists. They forgive people and don't judge them based on their past. It is the present that counts to them—a notion that must have suited Angel.

Two Quakers to whom Angel had gotten particularly close were Sarah and Anne, who had run the Attica worship group for the past twenty years. I had met Sarah during her visit to the Quaker meeting at Harlem's Riverside Church. She and her family had come to see Angel, and we spent the afternoon together. Sarah and Anne insisted on putting me up.

I arrived at Sarah's house in the early afternoon, giving me enough time to enjoy a cup of tea in a dark blue souvenir tea mug adorned with the golden silhouette of what looked like a castle. The mug, which was given to volunteers by the prison, read "Attica Correctional Facility" in thick gold letters. It presented the infamous prison as a landmark one would want to visit while in the area, not the place of terror and isolation I envisioned.

Sarah's children had hung a welcome sign for me: "Peace, Love, Wisdom." The house's walls were plastered with family photos, dragonflies, nature paintings, peace signs, doves, and hearts. A quick slice of pizza, a rebriefing of the puzzling rules for visitors—no wire bra, no talking in the hallway, no shirt with zippers or metal buttons, no miniskirt, no shoes with open heel or toes—and it was time to go.

Powdery white drifts obscured the road as we approached the "Buffalo Snow Belt." Pine trees gleamed in rainbow colors, and armies of snowmen and inflatable Disney characters stood guard in neat front yards. Deer lingered by the side of the road. When I marveled at how cozy and neat everything looked, Sarah informed me that the white "sugar coating" only covered up poverty and decay.

A snowfield lit in bright orange heralded Wyoming Correctional Facility. Then we reached our destination: "Welcome to the town of Attica." At the foot of the "castle," the prison's powerful lights turned the snow an aggressive blue. We pulled into the parking lot and got out of the car. Pointing at a man with a rifle case, Sarah laughed. "That isn't a violin case, if you know what I mean."

In the corner of the waiting area stood a decrepit little Christmas tree. NOBODY GETS IN TO SEE THE WIZARD NOT NOBODY NOT NO HOW read the sign above the reception desk.

Martin, another Quaker volunteer, greeted me with great exuberance, as if he had been waiting for my arrival for years. Anne, a former schoolteacher and current long-distance runner, arrived and kindly offered to smuggle my notebook and pencil through the checkpoint. "Nobody searches an old lady," she said. Later she told me that she used to smuggle tea bags in her bra for the prisoners, but now her self-assigned prison duty on Friday evenings between six and nine o'clock was limited to two words: "Show up!"

We took off our shoes and jackets and passed through the metal detector. Our hands were stamped with invisible ink. We waited in front of ornate black gates hung with big red signs that screamed, HANDS OFF! Then we put our hands under black light to reveal our stamps to the guard. A display case in one of the hallways featured a selection of confiscated shivs. We walked through endless corridors and stopped before a group of prisoners clad in dark-green uniforms. The men were waiting for their medication, and we had to wait for them to pass. The prisoners were assembled in two neat, parallel lines like a group of grade-schoolers. They stared quietly. The intense glare of a young man with a ponytail particularly pained me. I averted my eyes, but when I looked back his eyes were still on me. We continued our journey to the school building where the meeting was to take place. Windows looked out onto yards where, in the dark blue of the night, black silhouettes lingered like forgotten ghosts. Guards, their faces painted a sickly white by fluorescent hallway lights, sat at desks eating fries and drinking Kool-Aid. Then another sign: HANDS OFF! And another gate. We reached the central guard post, where the sign read TIMES SQUARE 42ND STREET.

This was ironic. We had moved so deeply into the institution's bowels that I would have never found my way back. It was my first prison visit, and I began to feel cold and isolated. A ten-minute walk and I was gone, gone from the world that I knew. "Don't stop to look at things and people," the Quakers had told me. I felt like I would disappear altogether if my eyes focused on this strange, inverted world.

The Quaker worship group was assigned a room painted with murals of idyllic mountain scenes: an alpine glacier, a forest in autumn colors, and a life-size deer. The men trickled in as Anne, Sarah, and I arranged chairs in a circle. Most of the men were murderers. Some had murdered several people.

Zachary, a former white supremacist who stalked and killed a black stripper, was cloaked in a cloud of eau de cologne.

After forty-two years in prison, Richard Robles was almost unrecognizable as the handsome young "Career Girls Murderer," whose sexual assault and gruesome stabbings of two young women in their Upper East Side apartment had dominated the news for weeks in the mid-1960s. Richard was overweight, and thick gray bags underlined his sad eyes.

Matt was a depressed, lumbering man with only a few remaining crooked teeth. Vincent looked wise, calm, and old, with an air of Morgan Freeman about him.

Then Miguel strutted in. His bright childlike features made it hard to believe that he had been in prison for twenty years.

So these were the men who liked to dance the Dance of Universal Peace? Once in a while the Quakers brought in a meditative dancer with whom the prisoners explored their spiritual and bodily awareness. The prisoners held hands; chanted sacred Arabic, Hebrew, and Persian phrases; and danced in circles to the rhythms of Native American and Turkish drums. The guards viewed the dances and their participants with suspicion, but Angel used to love participating.

We all sat down in a circle, and Miguel excitedly volunteered to speak about his week. He had applied for a job loading packages into a van. He thought it sounded almost too good to be true. "I'm just afraid that someone is going to snatch me out of here," he said, referring to the common prison practice of transferring inmates with only a few hours notice. Matt, who had only recently been transferred to Attica, said, "I just don't like it here. I'm not accustomed to this kind of treatment." He didn't yet have a job or any money. Martin, the Quaker hugger, shared a story of his recent trip to Peru and the Galapagos Islands. Within minutes he went from Darwin to altitude sickness and intestinal ills. He talked and talked and talked. "The Lord has been good to us," he said, finally ending his harangue. Anne reminisced about washing the feet of homeless people and about her neighbor who was picked up by an ambulance. "There is a question mark," she said. "Here I am washing feet, but I don't know about my neighbor."

Then it was my turn, and Anne said, almost reproachfully, "We want to hear more from you than just your last week." She seemed to mistrust me.

I explained that I was there because I was writing a book about Angel, Bruce, and Adam, all of whom had served time at Attica. The men questioned my credibility. With how many ex-prisoners had I spoken? "Fifty," I said. "Maybe more." Anne was visibly appeased. Martin interrupted to ask whether this was part of my spiritual journey. I said no. He seemed disappointed, so I told the men and women about my work and about what happens when I sit at the computer, alone with my thoughts and feelings; about how this focus, when it hits the right point, may feel like what they describe as "the inner light." I would never use this term to describe my feelings, but the Quakers appreciated silence, and so did I. Apparently satisfied, the men nodded.

Then Richard shared his struggles with drawing a portrait of a friend's fourteen-year-old daughter playing the cello. "I'm my own worst critic," he said. Coming from a double murderer, this comment struck me as odd. If trying to draw a fourteen-year-old with a cello caused Richard to criticize himself, how bad must he feel about having murdered two young women?

After my prison visit Richard Robles and I became pen pals. Richard let me know that he would not answer any questions regarding his crime. But he proved to be a reliable source when it came to describing Attica's alternate world. "Often the things prisoners worry about aren't the problems they actually have upon their release," he wrote me in one of his many letters. "Prison distorts reality. Expect the unexpected." But it turned out that Richard himself wasn't immune to this distortion. In one letter he asked me to describe my job at the publishing house where I was working at the time as an image processor and copywriter. Richard had worked as a sign maker at Attica and was proficient in Photoshop. "It sounds like something I could do and thus is a possible option I could have upon release that is 'REALISTIC,'" Richard wrote. "Therefore I would greatly appreciate if you could describe the work in detail, so I can ascertain what else in Photoshop I will have to study."

When I read Richard's letters and his imaginings about freedom and about our outside world, I doubted that, given the circumstances, rehabilitation could even be possible in prison. It was through his letters and my visit to Attica that I understood how far removed the men were from our world. Real rehabilitation could not be accomplished in prison.

Sarah talked about her two daughters, ballerinas-cum-gingerbread-cookies, and their excitement about their upcoming performance in *The Nutcracker*. Zachary added that the holidays were a difficult time. His medication for bipolar disorder kept him from sleeping. He had thought that doing time would eventually get easier, but it hadn't. He was depressed because he would never again have dinner with his family or a snowball fight with his niece. "You have no idea how devastating that is for me," he said, his eyes sinking deep into mine.

"You are going through a phase," Richard suggested empathetically. "It can knock you on your tail."

"I wish it would make me sleep," Zachary responded.

"Just don't think so much," Miguel said lightly. The conversation trailed off into relaxation techniques, and Vincent read Matthew 5:44-45: "But I say unto you, Love your enemies, bless them that curse you, do good to them that hate you, and pray for them which despitefully use you, and persecute you; That ye may be the children of your Father which is in heaven: for he maketh his sun to rise on the evil and on the good, and sendeth rain on the just and on the unjust."

Was Vincent asking for forgiveness? Did he want me to bless him, pray for him, love him? But again, there wasn't time or space for such questions. It was now time for silence. We closed our eyes. One of the men wheezed and the clock ticked loudly as if to remind us that the passing of time never ends.

Silence had been an important method of rehabilitation at America's first penitentiary. Philadelphia's Walnut Street Jail was built in 1790 under the pressure of the Quakers' Philadelphia Society for Alleviating the Miseries of Public Prisons. The society's goal was to bring humane treatment to the penal system.[3] As part of this treatment Walnut Street Jail had tried to rehabilitate prisoners through enforced silence, or solitary confinement, as it is called today. The cells were constructed so as to prevent the men from talking to each other, and their windows were so high up that the prisoners were unable to look out onto the street. The only person a prisoner would see during the whole of his confinement was the guard. Locked up with no work to do and rarely a book to read, such absolute isolation was intended to foster a reflection on the crime committed, resulting in true remorse and repentance. Instead, it drove prisoners to suicide and mental illness. Over the years the Quakers have distanced themselves from their history by transforming a measure of punishment, torture really, into a reward. Prisoners are always exposed to noise—constant catcalls and arguments, the sounds of stereos and TVs, the jingling of the officers' key chains, the opening and closing of iron gates. In light of this cacophony the period of silence during the Friday night Quaker meetings was like a mini vacation.

Following our period of silence, I was told that it was up to me to run "the program." I explained earlier that it made me uncomfortable to be put on the spot, that I would prefer to observe, but Sarah said simply that this was how they always did it when a guest visited the group. It quickly became clear that debate was not invited. I was told to come up with two or three questions to pose to the men.

I asked if they could share some memories of Angel.

All those who knew Angel concurred. "Angel—he's for real," Martin said, praising a poem he had written about the wind. "He can't help himself. He *is* a spiritual person." Sarah also had told me that she remembered Angel's ability to recognize beauty in the small things: a bird on the cell's windowsill, a bouquet of flowers. "Angel is full of force, and people recognize that in him," Richard said. The others nodded. Zachary, who knew Angel only in passing, said he used to work on Wall Street and would like to donate his used ties to Angel.

Hoping that my next question would lead to more substantial results, I said, "I'm curious to find out how Quakerism transformed you."

Richard said that while working in a mental hospital inside prison he realized that he harbored a genuine concern for people. "I realized that I have principles in my soul that are the same ones the Quakers believe in. I just fit in and they fit in me."

Like Angel, Miguel was raised in Spanish Harlem by a mother who practiced Santería. When he went to prison twenty years earlier, he studied several religions, but none of them seemed to fit. His attraction to the Quakers echoed that of the other men. "They just let you be," he said. "You are cared for. You are loved, [and] you don't have to worry about being judged." He added, "It shows me that there is much more to life. I'm a giver. I like to help people—like Richard."

Zachary found it hard to forgive himself for the crimes he had committed. But with the Quakers he felt comfortable talking. "It's good to know that people care about you," he said, despite the fact that other inmates had frequently made fun of him. "Are you still wearing the Quaker hat?" they teased. "Are you still with the Quaker oats?" To me he said admonishingly, "There is no reason to make jokes like that." He went on to list a number of issues he shared with the Quakers. They included the idea of shopping close to home and the problems associated with fossil fuels and green building techniques.

Environmental concerns were on Richard Robles's mind as well. He wrote me that once released he planned to get in touch with some "progressive Natives" about the "non-polluting concept" he had developed. "I intend to share my concept with them in an attempt to help them develop an industrial base." He added, "I do fear the American Government will attempt to steal the technology from them."

It's interesting how the unknown, outside world inspires prisoners to invent a possible future. As I write this, Richard is still in prison. Having been denied parole more than a dozen times, he has served close to fifty years of his twenty-years-to-life sentence. Yet he never gives up hope. He continues to invent things, and he still paints.

At last it was Matt's turn to speak. Overweight and unkempt, his clothes covered with stains, he stared at the ground while talking. He reminded me of the lifers Adam told me about—men who sat in a corner in the prison yard, not having showered for months, men who had given up and whom he tried to reach with his lifer program.

Like many others, Matt learned about Quakerism through AVP, the Alternative to Violence Project the Quakers had developed together with inmates in the mid-1970s. After completing his last sentence in 1997, Matt continued going to Quaker services on the outside. "[But] I got sidetracked; I got trapped between a rock and a hard place," he mumbled. "It's like a dog being caged up. When you let him out he gets wild."

I would have liked to ask some follow-up questions, but there was neither time nor opportunity. Sarah had made it clear that the meetings did not invite discussion. The objective was to share, to listen, and to accept.

A gong, sounding with the urgency of a fire alarm, signaled a sudden end to our meeting. The men quickly prepared to leave. There was hardly time to say good-bye.

My prison visit had left a large gap. Hoping to find some answers to my remaining questions, I accepted Martin's offer to visit him and his wife, Brooke. Brooke, Martin said, was eager to meet me and tell me about Angel.

The next day I stopped by their house.

We sat down at the kitchen table, where a cactus that seemed determined to die was propped up on sticks and supported by strings. Brooke wore pink jogging pants. Her suburban house was flawless. Although Brooke had known Angel through the Attica Friends Worship Group and the forgiveness workshops, she had never met him outside of the framework of these groups. Brooke required no input from me. Like her husband the evening before, she talked nonstop, endlessly explaining her system of forgiveness: *Step one, pick a burden the size of a pebble, then tackle the stones in the pocket and finally the boulder on the shoulder. Forgiveness doesn't mean forgetting. Anything can be forgiven by a higher power. It is more important to forgive yourself than being forgiven by the victim. If the victim is not ready to forgive, it may compound the problem. You can apologize in absentia. Forgiving doesn't mean condoning behavior. We are all victim, perpetrator, and bystander. We go through all of these rules in any one day.*

Brooke and Martin were sweet. They adored Angel. When I asked Brooke whether she knew what Angel had asked forgiveness for, she said that it was not important. "The individuals are choosing to shift their energy." I began to understand that for the Quakers, it was forgiveness for the sake of forgiveness. Nothing more and nothing less.

Brooke remembered how one day at the worship group, Angel's face "lit up." He said, "I'm looking at everybody as if they were Jesus. Then I think how much love I'd have if he was Jesus." Angel said he even looked at prison guards that way. Love for the sake of love.

Brooke handed me a couple of his poems and a piece of prose that had left a lasting impression on her. She said that other prisoners created collages based on Angel's writing:

I Will Not Judge You

I will not judge you, that is not my fate.
Mine is to love and wait.
For God to open up my soul,
So that the Light from me, to you may flow.
I could not judge you, that would not be fair.
Because my duty is to see what's there.
Not your flaws or your misdeeds,
But to see that place where lives your Seed.
So I will not judge you, that is up to God.
I can only smile and nod.
And reach out a helping hand,
To do for you what I can.

In the couple of hours I spent at Brooke's house I accumulated quite a folder, filled with documents, photos, and pamphlets—anything Brooke could find that proved, in her eyes, Angel's successful rehabilitation.

No one I met in Angel's Quaker community wanted to talk about murder. Angel said that Tanya, the Quaker woman he had recently started seeing, knew the basics but wasn't interested in it either. No one I spoke to knew any details of his crimes. They only spoke about forgiveness. I remember Angel saying his relationship with Tanya was "comfortable, like an old shoe." To bring his crime into play certainly stood to add some discomfort to their relationship. The more you know about people, the more complicated your relationship with them gets. Ignorance imparts protection. Learning about the crime Angel committed may complicate or inhibit the Quakers' love for him. It could make it considerably harder to forgive him. But unconditional forgiveness may also serve an additional purpose: it restrains anger and alleviates fear.

The Quakers repeatedly told me that a person was not defined by his or her past. Only the present counted. Love counted. I was told that Quakers believe in a person's ability to change, in second chances, and in God's forgiveness. Although I agreed with them on the first two counts, I remained skeptical of the dissociation between past and present and of the assignation of an outside force to forgive us for our sins. How could the present exist disconnected from the past? And who was this God who forgave us? This void had become a familiar motif in my life. I was unable to fill it with any generalizations. I try to accept the void, however uncomfortable it makes me feel. So the Quaker meetings mainly reminded me of my own wariness of religion. Although belief systems generally promise moral guidelines and a social support system, in me they spark the old fear that life—and murder—is far more complex and indecipherable than religion would have us believe.

On my drive back to New York I thought of Adam and Bruce. They, too, had served some time at Attica. Adam found a way of dealing with his life sentence by turning to politics, converting to Islam, and helping others who, as he had, were serving indeterminate sentences. Islam's discipline and structure helped him to survive days, months, and years behind bars. But however hard he worked on improving the lives of his fellow inmates, his incessant feelings of guilt didn't abate. Forgiveness for having planned a robbery that cost two men their lives was hard to come by. Adam often wondered what God, if he existed, could or would do to make him pay for his crime. And he wondered what *he* would have to do so he could forgive himself.

Then I remembered Bruce's words about the guilt and shame he experienced every day. "You take a life, you can't bring that back," he told me. "That's something you got to live with, man. You go to bed with it, you get up with it, you carry it. It's something you'll carry with you for the rest of your life." He added, "You gotta learn how to carry it."

CHAPTER SEVENTEEN

Lies and Good Luck

"That's a great dog." Bruce pointed to a German shepherd being walked as we stepped out from the Castle one late afternoon in spring 2008, roughly one year after his release from prison. Bruce began talking about the job interview he had gone to earlier in the day.

"I lied," he said matter-of-factly as we walked down Broadway. "When they asked what I was convicted for, I said 'robbery.' They are going to find out anyway," he said sadly.

The interesting part to me was not that Bruce had lied. He didn't go to the interview planning to lie. An opportunity had presented itself, and he lied, thinking it might spare him an uncomfortable situation. Bruce thought that *not* lying would never get him the job and that lying stood a slight chance of getting him the job.

The woman, pleasant, cordial, and in her mid-forties, had asked Bruce if he had ever been convicted of a felony. When he said yes, she asked what for.

"Bank robbery," Bruce said.

"Isn't that a federal offense?"

"The feds didn't pick it up. They passed it over to the state."

Bruce laughed his deep, raspy laugh as he told me the story. "The guy in front of me?" He glanced down at me. "I heard him, when they asked him. I had time to prepare myself for it. When they interviewed him, I was sitting there. It gave me enough time to think. I tried. I got to try something. When they hear that I was convicted for murder, they are not going to hire me."

Bruce and I walked down a tree-lined street and finally found a café, but a child outside told us the place was closed. We continued walking back toward Broadway. It was windy, and the trees rustled. We crossed a playground. Kids were screaming and laughing and crying. Bruce bent down to pick something up.

"What did you find?" I asked him

"A penny," he said. "Maybe good luck."

Good luck didn't present itself, so Bruce just licked his wounds and kept going. For months he prowled like an injured lion, one small but proud step at a time. The supervisor at the now-defunct nonprofit ACORN was looking for canvassers to go from door to door inquiring about voting ballots, said that he believed in second chances, that he was an ex-offender himself, and that someone once gave him a second chance. Bruce's application, though, had to go through another supervisor. Bruce thought that it was all a load of garbage. He was to come back on Monday; his shift would be from 1:00 p.m. to 7:00 p.m. But when he returned, there was yet another orientation. "What's your name?" a woman asked. "Jones," he said. A man came in and led him into another room. "My supervisor wants to do a background check on you."

"No problem," Bruce said, assuming that, having worked with Fortune before, ACORN knew what it was getting into. The man gave Bruce his business card and said that he would be hearing from him in a couple of days. He never called, and Bruce didn't call him either. But Angel and Adam, who had gone through the same procedure, did call. The man told Angel there was a hiring freeze and Adam that his background check hadn't been completed. In the end Adam never heard back from ACORN either.

For a few days Bruce worked in the warehouse of a jewelry company on 39th Street. Then he was told not to come back. "Poor productivity" was the reason they gave him. But Bruce thought that it just took Human Resources a while until they got around to the background check. He believed he worked as hard as he possibly could and "poor productivity" was an excuse to avoid talking about the proverbial elephant in the room.

"With this conviction thing," Bruce said to Angel one night, "do you think that we should see a psych?"

"I don't need to see a psych," Angel huffed. "You might need a psych; I don't need one."

"Angel got really uptight," Bruce said, remembering the conversation. "I was, like, 'Angel, we experience a form of rejection, maybe it's best we go talk to somebody about it. I'm starting to feel that we've got a problem.'"

Angel started seeing a therapist a few weeks later. Bruce didn't.

Mitch Brown, an instructor in Fortune's career development program, had told Bruce that his conviction "don't mean nothing." But Bruce didn't believe Brown ("the bozo"). He thought that the level of his conviction made a very real difference. After all, who wants to hire a murderer?

In the United States it is illegal to discriminate against people based on their criminal history, yet no one—or almost no one—will admit that they don't hire murderers. Statistics tell us that murderers are among the ex-offenders with the lowest recidivism rate. According to a 1994 study by the Bureau of Justice Statistics—the most current data available—roughly three-fourths of all burglars, larcenists, and car thieves are rearrested within three years of their release, but only 1.2 percent of murderers are rearrested for another homicide.[1] But who wants to take a one-in-a-hundred chance with a murderer? An employer could trust his instincts, but that might be a lot to ask for a job position that could easily be filled by someone else.

Murderers are, of course, only the tip of the iceberg. According to New York's National Employment Law Project, one in four American adults have arrest and conviction records.[2] Thousands of background-check companies make these records easily and inexpensively available online to employers, and a majority of employers take advantage of their accessibility.[3]

But even without a criminal record, African American males often find that employment opportunities look bleak. Devah Pager and Bruce Western, sociologists from Princeton and Harvard Universities, have conducted an audit study in New York to find out what role a job applicant's race and criminal record play for employers. They sent college students posing as low-wage work seekers to twenty-five hundred individual job interviews. The results of Pager and Western's study were alarming: in New York in 2004, a young white man with a criminal record has a better chance of finding employment than a young African American man *without* a criminal record.[4]

In light of these studies and statistics, Bruce's attempts at rehabilitation and his job search seemed ironic. He could reform himself all he wanted, but if the job opportunities in the mainstream world were virtually nonexistent, his options were narrow. He could either return to a life of crime or try his luck within the reentry scene, an arena that tries to rehabilitate and emancipate its clients yet keeps them caught within the same old system.

The Center for Employment Opportunities is one of several agencies in New York that try to ease the path into the labor market for ex-cons. A spokesperson at CEO told me that employers didn't like to hire murderers, arsonists, or sex offenders but claimed the organization decided on a case-by-case basis whether to accept an individual into its program. The agency was more outspoken when Angel told his interviewers about his conviction. He admitted to having killed someone, and the woman apologized and said that CEO didn't provide services to murderers.

Bruce had asked me before, "Do you think I should resort to lying?" I didn't know how to respond. On one hand, I understood that, given the obvious obstacles, lying seemed tempting, but I doubted that an employer who got his applicant pool from the Fortune Society would fail to do a background check. On the other hand, maybe he wouldn't *because* he got his applicants from the Fortune Society? I was not categorically opposed to Bruce's lying. After all, a murderer might know that he will never murder again while an employer could never know for certain. Or could he?

Apart from the questions that can be answered via studies and statistics, there are a number of important philosophical—and highly personal—questions. Does a murderer deserve a second chance? And if so, who is responsible for providing that second chance? Should an employer be saddled with the time, energy, and responsibility of keeping an eye on someone who may snap again? What would make a murderer a better candidate than someone battling a drug addiction? And even if we could be certain that he or she will never offend again, can a murderer's character really be reformed to equal the character of a person who has always lived a law-abiding life?

Of course, there are other issues besides the burden of trust and the background check. A job applicant is expected to produce a coherent job history. It was not that ex-prisoners had never worked, that they lacked skills, or that their former employers were all dissatisfied. In fact, most of the men I met had large folders brimming with training certificates and letters of recommendation. But a reference letter from the Corcraft factory at a maximum-security prison, for example, might alert a potential employer to something that may otherwise have gone unnoticed.

In Angel's, Adam's, and Bruce's cases there is a *but* for every positive assumption. Even if an employer takes the best possible route to accommodate an applicant with a homicide record—he knows the statistics, believes in second chances, relies on his character judgment, and is willing to get a hold of a former supervisor—his phone call to Corcraft might lead him to a dead end. The supervisor might not remember everyone who ever worked for him, because prisoners are transferred frequently and are often replaced overnight.

Even in the best-case scenario, with Bruce telling the truth, his references holding up, and a willing employer with a progressive outlook, one could always fall back on the fact that thousands of children grow up in even worse conditions and do not resort to murder.

"Everyone says you should tell the truth," Bruce said, trying to reason with himself. This is something that job-training programs for ex-offenders always emphasize to their clients: *always tell the truth.* You may embellish it, but you may never lie. But how can you embellish a homicide? A murder is the ultimate sign of bad judgment. Murder denotes a total inability to consider the consequences of one's own actions, which, of course, is one of the most important traits for any job applicant.

Having found no better recourse, Bruce decided to get a driver's license. He thought that a car would open the way to employment. He'd had a car before he went to prison, but his license had long since expired. Bruce knew from the start that he would spend his first available fifty dollars on the written test at the Department of Motor Vehicles.

Once Bruce passed the written test, his nephew picked him up to practice driving, and slowly things started coming back. "The only side you can pass [on] is the left side. How far you stand behind a school bus, how far you stand away from the curb, how far you park from the fire hydrant . . . ," he rattled. "At first I forgot it, but as I'm reading the manual, things come back."

"I spoke with a guy who makes thirteen dollars an hour and all he does is drive around and deliver flyers," Bruce said, his voice rife with excitement. "Thirteen dollars an hour and you just drive around all day? That's an opportunity." In fact, it seemed so good an opportunity that Bruce passed on a job in Mount Vernon. Four ten-hour days a week with a two-hour commute each way seemed like a stretch to him. "For $7.50 an hour? Three hundred a week. That would be a hard day," he said.

A car would allow Bruce to move fast and independently, which would put him in a good mood. A car would allow him to set his own rules, to take the roads he liked. It would make the routine of menial work more bearable. Bruce would have been able to work within a strictly defined structure, but also to make his own choices and to be in charge of a powerful machine.

A few weeks later Bruce passed his driving test and was waiting for a driver position at Fortune to become available. In the meantime he worked a bit at Fortune, which had since moved one of its offices to Long Island City in Queens. At first he did some demolition work, and later he ran errands and moved boxes.

It was Thursday afternoon, within a week of our walk through West Harlem, when I got off the subway in Long Island City. I was to meet with Bruce at a diner. If I had to select the most unattractive urban planning in New York, hands-down my choice would be Queensborough Plaza. The stormy spring weather didn't help, but no amount of sunshine could improve the intersection of Jackson Avenue and Northern Boulevard. Emerging from below, one enters a bubble of noise and exhaust. This is where the Q101 bus picks up the women and children on their way to visit the men in Rikers Island. This is where convicts become ex-convicts, as the shuttle buses from Rikers drop them off at all times of the day.

Above, the elevated train tracks' green mesh of steel is suspended like the web of a giant insect ready to pounce. I tried to recall something nice about this area, and one of Angel's ever-positive associations came to mind. The green of the tracks and their iron columns reminded him of forests, of evergreens and spruces, the brown rust resembling the trees' bark and the pine-needle-covered ground where they put down their roots. It was the color that made him forget that after an hour-long commute he was still in the city. And although the forest green matched that of the prison uniform he wore for almost thirty years, the association with nature proved stronger.

I called Bruce from outside the diner. He said he was delayed and would send Adam to "entertain" me.

I watched Adam fight his way through sheets of rain. He zigzagged across eight treacherous lanes of traffic, wearing a dark-green coat and, appropriately, carrying a dark-green umbrella. But the umbrella fit only in terms of color; it was much too big for just one person. As if reading my thoughts, Adam immediately shepherded me under it.

We decided to head back to Fortune and wait there for Bruce. Phone calls flitted back and forth.

"Where you at?"

"Hurry up!"

Adam and I found out that Bruce had been sent to Staples to run some last-minute errands. While we hung out in Fortune's nondescript waiting room, Angel came around. Looking dapper as always, he announced that Bruce had a problem with time management. He also reported that Bruce was still waiting to be approved for a job driving busloads of released inmates from Rikers Island into the city, but it was unclear when or whether the Division of Parole would approve it because normally parolees were not allowed to reenter jails and prisons.

I started to wonder whether Bruce would join us at all. The last time I called he said he'd be there in three minutes, but it had been an hour. Adam, Angel, and I decided to go to the little restaurant down the block. Angel ordered rice and pork. As always, Adam asked me what I was having, and when I chose a Greek salad, he ordered the same.

As we were leaving the restaurant, I saw Bruce walking toward us. I could see from afar that he was mad. His large, angry frame reminded me of a rolling tank. I instinctively made some space on the sidewalk. As soon as Angel, Adam, and I were near enough, Bruce started screaming his Staples story as if the relentless rain made it hard for us to hear him. He was wearing only a thin sweatshirt and his tiny blue baseball cap. He said he was sent to buy paper at Staples at five to one. His booming voice sounded hoarse, suggesting that he had been talking at that volume for hours. When he returned from Staples, he unloaded the many boxes of paper, carried them up the stairs, and placed them next to the copy machine. Just as he was done and thought he could leave for lunch, his boss told him that she wanted the paper somewhere else. No heavy rain or calming words could cool Bruce's anger.

Angel and Adam, seemingly unfazed by Bruce's eruption, started talking to Caz, one of Fortune's poster boys, who had just come out of Fortune to get lunch. In an attempt to exude professionalism and media savvy, Caz insisted on shaking my hand.

Here were four men of color with criminal records whose only job opportunities appeared to be within the reentry system. With few exceptions, no one employs ex-cons except the agencies that promise to help them.

Caz and Angel started talking about how many emails they had in their inbox. When Caz named a number in the thousands, Angel trumped him with how many *unread* emails he had in his inbox. His job as an intake worker was taxing, and time, or the lack thereof, had become an issue.

In the past, time was plentiful and meagerly paid. In prison, time was useless and dull. Time never seemed to end, and it was nothing to brag about. It was mostly *doing* time, not *spending* time. Time didn't mean money or recreation; time meant boredom. Now, suddenly, there was never enough time. The best years of their lives had been lost.

The concept of time had always been perplexing for these men, but in the last few months it had been turned upside down. Now twenty-four hours weren't enough. You tried to hold on to time by ignoring your emails or by getting up an hour earlier, but it always managed to slip away. The more time passed since his release, the more Angel tried not to think about his past. He was proud of his yearly wage of $27,000 before taxes, although by New York standards this sum was hardly enough to live on. But unlike Bruce and Adam, whose goal it was to move out of the Castle into an apartment by themselves, Angel didn't mind that Tanya introduced him to a lifestyle he wouldn't be able to afford without her.

Adam withered whenever Angel began bragging about his new achieve-ments and his lack of time. He didn't like to talk about time or the lack of it. Bruce briefly put his boiling anger on hold but started to vent again as he escorted me to the bus. He told me that Fortune called him in for day labor. He never knew which day they would call. He got ten dollars an hour.

Bruce rarely visited his friend in Albany. When I asked why, he countered with, "For what?" I didn't know for what either. He never shared much about the relationship he had with the woman, and I never prodded. The little bit of money from welfare didn't get him anywhere, he said. Besides, he added, "I have other things to focus on." A car splashed us as we waited for the traffic light to change, leaving us soaking wet.

CHAPTER EIGHTEEN

Sex, Love, and Race

Adam sat in his small, windowless office at the reentry organization where he had begun to work part-time in the summer of 2008. His main job was to connect prisoners with outside services but generally he tried to help where he could. His door was always open. He enthusiastically waved me in and suggested I sit down. He was almost done. Next to him sat a client.

Adam's computer mouse flitted back and forth across a torn-out piece of carpet whose pattern matched the one on the floor. He painstakingly typed something for his client, mouthing each word, then misspelling every other one.

I introduced myself to the client.

Scott had misplaced his certificate of relief, which removed certain legal bars and restored various rights, "somewhere around the house," and Adam was helping him to write a request to the Division of Parole to have the cer-tificate reissued.

Scott was a flirt. In his mid-thirties, he wore a smile that made even his braces look sexy. He was inquisitive and coquettish yet almost painfully polite.

"Where are you from, miss?" he asked when Adam left the room to print his letter.

"Germany."

Scott's face lit up even more. He had always been fascinated by German engineering and wanted to drive on the Autobahn. Visiting Germany was high on his to-do list.

"And they have a lot of war babies in Germany," he added.

Scott had met and chatted with women on Blackplanet.com who told him that they were war babies, the children of American soldiers and German women conceived during and after World War II.

I was trying to do the math. Unless Scott preferred women twice his age, he must have chatted with the children of war babies. Either way, Scott made sure to let me know that he had a way with women.

After his release from a California prison, he would sleep here and there, and occasionally moved in "with females." The women would get sick of him after a while and kick him out. Then he would move in "with another female" and so on, until the Division of Parole finally transferred him to New York, where his family offered him a place to stay.

"How did you meet all those—females?" I asked. The word *females* always reminded me of TV programs about the mating habits of animals. I thought that one had to be somewhat detached from a woman to call her "a female."

"I guess they all want to be with a guy from New York," he said brazenly. He sank back into his chair, smirking, relaxing, and apparently waiting for me to respond.

Adam finally came back from his printing enterprise, and Scott asked him for another business card. Adam seemed confused and distracted. He obviously had other things on his mind.

"Didn't I already give you one?" he asked Scott.

"Yeah, but I must have misplaced it somewhere in my house," Scott said. "I will call later. I don't want to make this lady wait." This was another thing. When addressed directly women were "ladies," but in the abstract they were "females."

Adam was eager to get out and talk about what nobody else wanted to talk about. The few times he tried to share his secret with Bruce, Bruce just got up and left. Other halfway house residents had been equally unsympathetic.

Adam had recently met a new woman. Leslie had managed to push Minnie out of the picture at last. Adam had finally invited Minnie out on a date, but she cancelled last minute. "Minnie is white," he said as he related the story to me. He couldn't help but think that it was their difference in skin color that kept Minnie from getting involved with him.

Leslie was white as well, but she was—different. Adam liked Leslie more each day. Yet there was something he didn't know how to tell her. It was hard to confront her with his bad news so early into their relationship.

The penile cancer had come back. Adam was scheduled for a partial penis amputation at Memorial Sloan-Kettering Cancer Center in January 2009. It came at the worst time possible. Adam told people, Leslie included, that he was going to the hospital for prostate treatment. He was frightened, and his fear was apparent in the way the words flooded out of his mouth. A race against time suddenly seemed like not such a bad analogy after all. One of his doctors told him that sex wouldn't be possible after the operation and that he had better have all the sex he could in the next couple of days. (Had his doctors really said that, I wondered?)

But there was only one woman Adam wanted to have sex with—Leslie—and he didn't want to rush into things. He didn't want to screw things up by pushing himself on her.

Leslie had invited him over for dinner that night, and Adam didn't know what that meant. "This could mean several things," he said. Adam always had to consider every possibility before he acted. The mutual attraction was apparent, but the question was whether or not tonight was the night Leslie wanted to go all the way. If not, and it really was just a dinner, what if he told Leslie? Would she have sex with him out of sympathy? This was a difficult issue.

Adam had met Leslie once before in one of the Quaker groups in Green Haven Prison. It must have been in the 1980s. Back then Leslie was married. Adam lost touch with her but couldn't get her out of his mind. She was one of the fantasies he nurtured when he was alone in his cell. Adam's mental image of Leslie competed with memories of former love affairs and possibly pictures of women in magazines next to his cot. When Adam accompanied Angel to a Quaker meeting upstate, he immediately recognized Leslie. When he found out that her husband had died, he showed his interest in establishing a relationship. Adam and Leslie started to go out.

According to Adam, Leslie had something that only a few white women possess. She reminded him of an African Venus.

"She has a small protruding tummy that dovetails down into the delta of Venus," Adam said. "You find that most often in African American women. Very rarely you see it in white women. But when you do—oh, maaaan! It attracts men to no end." He laughed. He continued to tell me that in white culture a tummy was a "no-no" and that white men demanded "outstanding beauty." He believed the white man felt he was lowering his standards when he got involved with someone who didn't meet his ideals of beauty. Black men, on the other hand, were more flexible. They could find beauty in all different types of bodies, movements, and facial features. Adam returned to Leslie. "She's not a beautiful woman. She's not an ugly woman either. In our culture I can understand her not having a great appeal among white men."

But then again, what did Adam know about sex? He wasn't even sure what white people called a woman's vagina. He seemed certain that white people considered the term *pussy* an insult. He complained that the sexes knew so little about each other. The same held true for the different races. What did white people know about black people, and what did black people know about white people? What did women know about men, and what did men know about women? Adam found himself in a perplexing predicament.

He remembered having conversations with prostitutes and other "loose women" before he went to prison. Or he would sometimes use the ladies' restroom in a bar and overhear the women's conversations. Black women called their vaginas pussies. They would brag about what their pussies could do. They were proud of their pussies. "I got a commanding pussy. My pussy will get 'im. My pussy will hold him," Adam remembered women bragging. He had seen women exercise their pussies and train them to pick up quarters from a table. "They use their pussies as a form of getting things," he told me. "I read stories about how women talk about being gold diggers."

To take on a demanding and self-confident pussy—or vagina?—seemed like quite an undertaking. It seemed an impossible task tackling a resolute pussy without a penis or with only part of a penis left.

I thought that maybe a walk through Sunnyside Gardens, a lush, land-marked neighborhood in Queens, might take Adam's mind off his problems. I showed him the wooded courts surrounded by little brick houses.

Adam had heard about Sunnyside, and he had told me that he had always wanted to go there. When he was young, he would listen to the live radio transmissions of the boxing matches at the Sunnyside Garden Arena. But he never made it there, and the arena had long ago ceased to exist.

As I had expected, Adam marveled at the gardens. "Do people play ball games here in the summer?" he asked. "Do they picnic? Does it look like that in Europe?" When I was with Adam, I sometimes felt like I was with a child. Before I could finish answering one question, the next one had been asked.

I was always surprised by how Adam managed to maintain his sense of curiosity, his ability to marvel at the world, and his candor. Adam always seemed to be going somewhere—to concerts, museums, lectures, supermarkets, thrift stores, on walks—yet he often lamented his lack of exposure. He could never get enough of the new, the unexplored, the unexpected. Perhaps more important, he often mentioned that he would like to be with a woman who could take the lead and show him more places. A woman who could give him advice on how to behave among intellectuals and what to pick from a buffet—that would be ideal. If she could also help him understand how women feel and what they expect from a man his age—that would be even better.

At the gardens we had to brush the twigs of bushes and trees out of our way and climb over piles of leaves and thick branches that were left on the narrow path to rot. Suddenly a cat jumped out of a dense hedge. We both jumped. Adam almost fell over. "She scared me!" he said, holding his chest while bending down to pet the cat. He cooed, and the cat started to purr. "You scared me!" he said again, laughing.

As we sat down for lunch at a Turkish restaurant in Sunnyside, Adam wondered whether his penis cancer was a punishment from God.

"I told you my crime never sat well with me," he said. "It cost two people their lives! There has got to be a payback for what I did. Maybe this is the payback."

"Why?" I asked. "Isn't the time you served payback enough?"

"Maybe for one life. But not for two," he shook his head sadly. "Doing time in itself is not really suffering. It is not the equivalent of two lives being taken. They had wives and children! If this is the payback for it, I'd feel a lot better about myself."

"But it wasn't you who actually shot them," I said.

"But all the planning was me," he countered.

Adam never gave himself an easy way out. Even in his most burdened moments he desperately searched for a valve that would allow him to release his guilt and remorse.

In the end Adam found love. Upon returning to the Castle after lunch, Adam decided to write Leslie an email, explaining that he was going to the hospital for penis surgery. She immediately asked him to come over to her house so they could talk. As it turned out, sex wasn't even that important to Leslie. The desired intimacy could be reached by other means. One of his doctors had already told him that for older women sex might be secondary, but Adam, whose interest in sex had never faded, found this hard to believe. To have Leslie reaffirm his doctor's statement was a huge relief.

A few weeks after his surgery, when we were walking from the Castle to the Italian restaurant down in the valley on 12th Avenue, Adam excitedly told me about his sex therapist, his psychotherapist, his psychiatrist, and the other doctors who cared for him. He had just gotten a prescription for Viagra, and the sex therapist encouraged him to take a pill and find out whether he could get an erection with what was left of his penis. He immediately went to the pharmacy but was stunned to learn that six pills of Viagra cost $100. He laughed his most characteristic Adam laugh. "One hundred dollars!" He couldn't stop laughing. Then suddenly he turned serious. "I got to sit down and talk to Leslie about this. Because there is no doubt in my mind that she has already made mental arrangements."

Leslie seemed to enjoy helping Adam out with his daily tasks and whenever else he was at a loss. And Adam seemed to enjoy having someone step up in his times of struggle. One time Adam, Leslie, and I had lunch at Cove, the Italian restaurant that had become one of his favorite places. Adam insisted on paying. When the waiter brought back his ATM card and receipt, Adam got nervous. How much tip should he add and where? And where should he sign the receipt? Leslie calmed him down. She went to great lengths to clarify the procedure for him.

I was surprised mainly because Adam and I had had the same discussion at the same restaurant a few weeks earlier. Initially, I thought he might have forgotten or that my explanation hadn't made any sense. But watching him and Leslie interact, I could see that he enjoyed Leslie's extra attention, the care with which she led him through the process, her slow and soothing voice. And Leslie seemed to enjoy her role as well. They made a lovely couple.

Adam was very frank about what Leslie could give him. He was thankful when Leslie told him not to rent a small studio apartment in Harlem and to instead wait for the apartments in the new Castle to be finished. He praised Leslie for opening up conversations with strangers and drawing him in. She cut out articles from magazines for Adam to discuss because Adam was always

Sex, Love, and Race

afraid that he would run out of topics to talk about when he was among people who didn't share his background. "Prison can't be the only thing you talk to people about," he told me.

Although Adam's face always lit up when he talked about Leslie, he once admitted that sometimes Leslie made him sad. With all the good things she brought to his life, she was also a reminder of what he had missed.

Over lunch Leslie voiced her regret over the loss of his scrapbooks. She could have accompanied him to the sites he yearned to visit. Leslie enjoyed taking charge, but their relationship did not seem one-sided. They both shared a strong interest in criminal justice issues, and here it was often Adam who took the lead and broadened Leslie's horizons. Adam had become a strong advocate for evidence-based rehabilitation programs in prisons. He found it odd that the Quakers received funding for their Alternative to Violence Project, a respected rehabilitation program in the prison system, without having to provide evidence that the program actually reduced recidivism. At a Quaker meeting he caught people's attention when he criticized the Quakers for not testing their program's efficiency.

Adam was a strong advocate for Alternative to Incarceration (ATI) programs that treat offenders in the community as opposed to locking them up, and at advocacy meetings (or whenever the topic arose) he spread what he had learned about crime risk factors and the avoidance of recidivism.[1] But on a personal level Adam did not seem too concerned with recidivism. Whether in prison or on the outside, he was tortured by the loss of two lives. He needed to "purge," to confide. In that spirit Adam helped to establish a "transformative healing" group, in which ex-prisoners and others were encouraged to talk about their crimes and about the pain they had inflicted on others and on themselves. A strong believer in exchange and analysis, Adam thought it necessary not only to talk about guilt but to take apart his actions, their consequences, and his feelings of guilt. Leslie even accompanied him to one of his Transformative Healing sessions. But even without the program, Adam could talk with Leslie about his crimes and his feelings of guilt whenever he felt like it. This seemed to help somewhat.

Adam "dug" Leslie, and Bruce's question—*What the fuck do you want with a white woman?* (in Adam's words)—seemed easy to answer.

"One of the reasons I dig her is that she gives me exposure," Adam said. "She can open doors for me, man; she can broaden my horizon."

It wasn't that race was not on Adam's mind. Race was always on his mind—not because it mattered so much to him but because he knew how much it mattered to other people.

The first public display of their love was timid. Leslie and Adam were walking to the bus on the Upper West Side when Leslie suddenly grabbed his hand. Adam's heart almost stopped. In prison it had never entered his mind that this would be possible. Walking around the Upper West Side, holding hands with the woman he loved? With a white woman? His heart leapt, and he felt years, if not decades, younger. Adam thought about the hand-holding all night as he lay by himself in his bed in the Castle. He tried to remember the last time he had held hands with someone. But he couldn't. It wasn't the custom in the black neighborhoods he frequented as a young man.

Adam liked walking hand in hand with Leslie, but he was always wary of the looks of others. One time Adam and Leslie were riding the subway. They sat quietly next to each other in the crowded subway car when Adam turned to look Leslie in the eye. Leslie took the opportunity to kiss him. Adam was surprised. He looked at the two elderly white women across from him who offered cold, angry stares. "OUTRAGE!" he yelled as he related the story. "OUTRAGE!"

CHAPTER NINETEEN

From Attica to Broadway

While Bruce and Adam plodded on, one step at a time, Angel's new life zoomed to lightning speed. Angel had moved in with Tanya at the beginning of 2008. By April he had secured himself a job at the Fortune Society and become a small media star.

"From Attica to Broadway!" he shouted on the phone one evening as I headed home from my day job. He had come up with a title for my book. "We are going to Broadway!" he continued. "Er . . . Off-Broadway." He could hardly contain himself.

Angel had begun starring in a stage play called *The Castle*, for which David Rothenberg had edited the life stories of four ex-cons and Fortune clients into a script. He had then found a producer and an Off-Broadway venue: the New World Stages on 50th Street between 8th and 9th Avenues. Revenues from the play, which featured Casimiro "Caz" Torres, Kenneth Harrigan, Vilma Ortiz Donovan, and Angel, would help offset construction expenses for Castle number 2.

A postcard advertised *The Castle* as follows: "Four formerly imprisoned New Yorkers, with a total of 60 years of incarceration, relate their journeys of crime, privation, and redemption. A breathtaking drama you will never forget!"

When I closed my eyes, I could hear the copy recited in a movie trailer announcer's commanding voice. Suitably, the text and a photo of the Castle appeared on a black background framed with barbed wire. Rothenberg's four protégés were ready for the bright lights.

If Rothenberg told Angel to step over the Castle's ledge, he would do it. "I'm not gonna question why he'd ask me to step over the ledge," Angel gushed. "He's not gonna harm me. So I step over the ledge in faith. Of course, the building is burning and that's why he asked me to step over the ledge. I'll survive the fall."

Rothenberg didn't ask Angel to step over any ledges. Following his mission and longtime vocation as a PR professional, Rothenberg had, however, encouraged Angel repeatedly to promote himself and Fortune through various media outlets.

Angel appeared with Rothenberg on NY1, the city's popular news channel, when Rothenberg had been named "New Yorker of the Week." He was there as living proof of Rothenberg's good deeds and Fortune's successes. Angel also appeared on NPR's *Talk of the Nation*, where he spoke about the challenges facing ex-offenders and the Fortune Society. Other media contributions followed, and Angel enjoyed his public persona and all the attention it attracted. Suddenly, I found myself one of many journalists who wanted to find out about Angel's life.

One day Angel took me on a tightly choreographed tour through El Barrio, the neighborhood where he grew up. The tour was a logical extension of his sudden elevation to media personality. It began in gray, drizzly weather. Blackened snow piled up on the sidewalk. When I complained, Angel told me that he found the weather quite wonderful. This didn't surprise me. Whenever I complained about anything, Angel would counter that the world was wonderful.

As always, Angel volunteered to hold my tape recorder. His left hand held it to his lips like a microphone while his right hand held a burning cigarette. His voice seemed particularly resonant today. He pronounced each syllable with the intensity and clarity of an old-fashioned newscaster. In measured steps he led me from the place where one of his childhood homes used to stand to the schools he attended and the former factory his aunt Jesusa had allegedly asked him to set on fire after losing her job there. Here his public persona briefly slipped. "And guess what I found?" Angel concluded, chuckling. "It was all concrete and steel! How are you gonna burn that down?"

Angel pointed to the empty Jefferson Park pool, remembering how his brother Junior pushed him into the water. Angel, seven years old and unable to swim, almost drowned. It was this event that began his lifelong fear of water.

About midway through the tour Angel's brother Frankie called. "What's up?" Angel huffed into the phone. "I'm in an interview right now," he said and hung up.

We had approached the tour's culmination, the house where Angel had killed Olga Agostini. The house had been tastefully renovated, and the street was altogether quiet, uneventful, unassuming.

"The crime was necessary for me to be who I am," I remembered Angel telling me a couple of months ago. Now, approaching the murder house, he added, "If somebody would have grabbed me and given me a job, I think it would have changed my life. But then again I wouldn't be living the fantastic life I'm living now."

I was stunned by Angel's comments. But recalling that he had been deprived of love, attention, and freedom for most of his life, I also felt sorry for him. Angel had always been confined—by poverty, violence, fear, shame, anger, and barbed wire. No wonder that I came to consider his need for attention and love—and not his remorse—as two of his most authentic characteristics. No wonder he always tried to focus on the beauty of things. It was a coping mechanism that allowed him to survive.

At the end of the tour I mentioned that I needed to use the bathroom before making my way back home. But public restrooms are virtually nonexistent in East Harlem. The intimidating McDonald's "bouncer" on 125th Street forbade me to use the bathroom without first purchasing something. Angel snapped at him, saying we would take our business elsewhere. Concerned, he then asked whether I would be okay until I got home.

This was the Angel I had gotten to know: a man who within seconds oscillated between anger and sweetness, between selfishness and generosity, between clichés and originality, aloofness and insecurity. In this whirlpool of conflicting forces the media provided the controlled and structured environment he had been seeking so desperately.

To incorporate Angel's story into a play seemed like a logical conclusion. Angel was charming and media savvy, and Rothenberg recognized his potential as a marketing tool. Interspersed with factual information about the Fortune Society, the play never lost track of its didactic message and fundraising objective: regardless of their criminal past, under Fortune's supervision ex-cons could be trusted and constituted a worthy investment. The play provided enough harrowing details about the performers' childhoods and upbringing to put their transgressions into perspective. There was plenty of sad and shocking material that tugged at the listeners' heartstrings.

The night I visited New World Stages, I saw Angel from afar, nervously chatting into his cell phone while smoking a Newport. There was a microphone attached to his tie. When I came closer he turned to me. "I am not supposed to mingle," he said sternly before vanishing backstage.

I was seated. The curtain opened. Accompanied by the sound of organ music, Caz, Kenny, Vilma, and Angel solemnly stood in front of a photographic projection of the Castle. Reading from the script, the four actors explained the history and purpose of the Castle.

Angel provided the transition to the performers' personal stories. "We are typical of those who arrive at the Castle. We enter with a lot of baggage, and it isn't made by Samsonite." The audience laughed. The projection was replaced by a spooky, black velvet curtain. The actors then took turns reading from the script. They sat on barstools and shared their stories in chronological order: childhood, youth, criminal life, prison, transformation, clean living, taxpayers. All their pain and confusion were distilled into a simple story line one could make sense of. I understood why this would appeal to Angel. The sustained narrative provided safety and built-in redemption.

The man on the chair in front of me looked a mess. I first noticed him because he would underline each of the cast's sentences by mumbling, "Have mercy!" He reminded me of the thousands of men and women who fall through the gaps, who aren't transformable and lack Angel's, Kenny's, Caz's, and Vilma's sustained narrative—and, possibly, a support system.

When Kenny shared the disturbing childhood story about seeing a dead black woman hung from a telephone pole near his home, the disturbed man laughed. Each time Vilma mentioned that she was Hispanic, he yelled, "God bless you!" After Caz told his traumatic childhood stories he called out, "Amen!"

Vilma had become legendary for her "glow"—an expression used at the Castle to describe residents who may have made the same mistakes several times but who really wanted to get it right this time. I have seen "the glow" fade on some people after a few trying months on the outside, but I had never seen it disappear from Vilma. Now, as she related her story, Vilma wept openly. In fact, for the next year, as *The Castle* toured various prisons and institutions, Vilma would at some point or another begin to cry during her performance. Her story was not the most heartbreaking one. She described herself as the child of caring parents raised on Long Island who somehow had gotten on the wrong path. In the play she explained that her low self-esteem drove her to marry a drug dealer and become an addict and dealer herself.

As Vilma released her sorrow, as she relived her trauma, the audience readily cried along. This was what they had come for. The play was advertised as a drama, after all. Subconsciously, Vilma seemed to respond to the audience's expectations.

Caz said he didn't cry because he was afraid that once he started, he would never be able to stop. And it made sense. With the looks of an Italian street gang member, buff and tattooed, Caz's life seemed to consist almost exclusively of death, drugs, prison, sadness, and violence. He came across as the play's most ambivalent character. His presence and the sixty-seven arrests on his record made him seem intimidating, yet his story about how he and his brother were made to fight as children while adult onlookers placed bets was gut-wrenching.

Kenny said he was offered a basketball scholarship as a teenager, but his friends, who taught him how to roll joints and cut coke, won him over. The ghetto he grew up in did the rest. He eventually ended up serving twelve years for burglary. He now claimed to have been transformed by his love for Jesus. Kenny's was a familiar narrative as well: hanging out with the wrong crowd in a segregated environment, drugs, crime, finding God, redemption. Sitting in the Castle's cafeteria, I had heard this narrative again and again.

Angel's feet didn't reach the footrest on his barstool. He was, as always, dressed in a suit. His story almost came across as comic relief. He mentioned his upbringing in "a crazy house," his mother's addiction and her beatings, but, at the same time, seemed removed from the events that shaped his life. "My business philosophy was 'Good weed, great quality at a low price,'" he said about his teenage drug-selling business. The audience roared. Angel's narrative focused on the good things that had come out of his crime. He spoke of learning to read and write, getting a college degree, and becoming a Quaker. The main crime he mentioned almost in passing.

"When I was eighteen, I got into an argument with a friend. That argument ended with my friend dead and my life forever changed." Although Angel had changed his statement from a previous draft in which he said that he had killed a man, he was still not able to admit that he had killed a young girl. He was not even able to say, "I killed my friend." Instead he chose an impersonal construct—"That argument ended with my friend dead"— quickly followed by the consequences his crime had for *him*. He also limited the tale to one of the three crimes he was convicted for. His atmospheric voice seemed to tell someone else's story. He would throw in a joke here and there to put the audience at ease. He didn't want to spook people. He managed to be, even as he related his childhood horrors, a charmer.

"I am finally, *finally* a taxpayer," he triumphantly declared at the end of the play, eliciting fervent applause.

The play made the audience feel good. It fostered unity among those who had been to prison, their families, and the reentry scene. It offered viewers an opportunity to wipe away tears in unison. At this point we all knew that the problem was pressing and needed to be addressed. In reality, though, we were powerless. What else could we do but listen? Hire Vilma, Kenny, Angel, and Caz? Invite them into our homes? Seeing the criminals onstage—rehabilitated, successful, and charming—was reassuring. One thing less to worry about. Good had prevailed. Never mind that there were millions of ex-cons out there—many of them suffering from serious mental illness—and that two-thirds of them would land back in jail.

I had problems with the play because it gave the illusion of easy answers. And there were other aspects that didn't sit well with me. Rothenberg had told Angel to stop defining himself by his crime. "It's just one bad incident," Angel had said, paraphrasing him. "If that was the stand where we would get judged, we'd all be criminals. Because we have all committed crimes. We cheated on our taxes, crossed the street in the wrong place . . . "

Despite the director's enlightened stance, the play did define the performers by their pasts. By making them repeat their sad and violent stories week after week, it shackled them to their traditional roles. Vilma, Caz, Angel, and Kenny were—and always would be—ex-cons.

After the play Angel and I went to a little Thai restaurant around the corner. A couple across from us recognized Angel from the play. He waved them over to our table.

"Now you are a famous man; you have to get used to it," the woman said. "Now that *she*'s with a famous interviewee," she continued, pointing at me, "*she* has to get used to it." The woman apparently mistook me for Angel's girlfriend.

Angel was pleased with the attention.

"You know, I was just saying to Michael," the woman continued, "I wonder what it's like when Angel tastes his first Thai food because probably, before you went to prison, you didn't have a chance. Is this your first time?"

"Literally!" Angel said. "This is my first time. This is wonderful!"

"We are witnessing history!" the woman screeched.

The play's reviews followed Angel's and Rothenberg's lead. They further developed the mitigating circumstances of Angel's crime, which the play had accentuated. Most notably, in an article published in July 2008 the *New York Times* chopped a year off of Angel's age at the time of the murder; according to the paper he had been seventeen years old, a juvenile.[1] His prison sentence, to which Angel and most publications added another year to make it a rounded-off thirty, appeared now crueler, particularly when the *New York Times* described Angel as having served "a 30-year stretch for a violent altercation."[2]

The media loved the play: "A powerful testament to the resiliency and determination of the human spirit" *(Curtain Up)*[3]; "a visceral, almost disconcerting immediacy" and "a banner ad waving in the wind as the savior of lost souls" *(New York Press).*[4]

The *New York Times* gently chided, "This is theater nearing a public service announcement."[5] This was as critical as the media coverage of the production got. No one dared scrutinize a charitable cause. Here were four ex-cons who, from what we could tell, had been rehabilitated by education, love, and religion. And then there were the Fortune Society and the Castle, which continue to provide education and a safe haven while openly reveling in the dependents' transformation. More important, perhaps, they needed the money for their new construction project.

The Castle received its most extensive and celebratory coverage when Angel and David Rothenberg appeared as guests on New York senator Tom Duane's public access TV show, *Tom Duane in the Neighborhood.*[6]

At the beginning of the twenty-eight-minute show, Duane, baby-faced and with a chronically furrowed forehead, asked Angel how old he was when he committed his crime. "I was a child," Angel says. "I had just turned eighteen. I became an adult and didn't get the chance to vote or anything else."

After Angel retold his usual childhood narrative, Duane praised his outfit. "You present as, you know, a very accomplished, professional, you know, intelligent guy on the go. Why?" Duane asked.

"My friend Mae," Angel responded, going on to credit her as his savior. He began to explain how he first met her after his escape from Rikers Island. As soon as Angel mentioned his attempted escape, Duane interrupted. "Which means you are pretty smart." They shared a laugh. The thought that crossed my mind when I heard Angel and Duane share a laugh was that had he managed to escape, he may have killed another human being.

Angel repeated his favorite memoir title, "From Attica to Broadway," and Duane concluded, "I wept. A space has to be left for tissues. I could have wept all the way through."

CHAPTER TWENTY

The New Home

One Saturday afternoon in late February of 2009, Bruce invited Adam and me to visit him. Bruce had recently moved out of the Castle. The Fortune Society had helped him find an apartment in the Bedford Park section of the Bronx. His new home was roughly twenty-five blocks north of where he had committed his crime.

Bruce was afraid I might get lost and suggested I call him once I got off the subway. My instinct told me to take the staircase on my right up from the subway. There were no signs indicating that the staircase had collapsed, and I suddenly found myself in a dark corner, surrounded by piles of human feces and plywood sheets boarding up what was left of the staircase.

Bruce considered Bedford Park, the area around the second-to-last subway stop on the D train, to be central and an okay part of town. To him it hadn't changed much since he committed his crime. He'd noticed a few new buildings here and there, more Chinese and Indian residents, but most of all, more female bus drivers and subway conductors. Bruce measured distances in relation to the Castle, where he now worked part-time in the kitchen, and in terms of what he was familiar with. He once remarked that I lived far out because it was an area he had never been to. To him it didn't matter whether I was a fifteen-minute subway ride away from Grand Central. What mattered was that he didn't know Queens well and that I had to change trains to get to the Castle.

Aboveground, Grand Concourse cuts across town like a fast gray river. Its side streets spread into a delta of concrete and asphalt. As I began walking the shores of 203rd Street, I noticed a ghostly house. A blackened tree leaned over its fence as if frozen in the act of walking away. Next to the house was Bruce's building. I dialed his number. Bruce, it seemed, had his thumb on the button of his cell phone. He picked up on the first ring.

"Cross Grand Concourse!" he yelled, as if encouraging me to traverse battle lines.

I told him I had already crossed Grand Concourse and that I was right in front of his building. "I'll come down. Wait for me. I'll be right down."

Bruce didn't have the patience to wait for the elevator so we took the stairs. Adam was still making his way from the Castle. Bruce smiled his broadest smile as he opened the door to his apartment, his eyes hungry for approval. We walked down a long, dark hallway that led to the kitchen, a large bedroom and an even larger living room.

"It's huge!" I said.

"Is it?" Bruce asked, his face beaming. I told him that most people I know lived in much more crowded conditions. This was New York, after all. He seemed satisfied. He remarked that he didn't like studio apartments because they reminded him of a cell.

"What you got in your bags?" he then asked. I pulled out a cake.

"And . . . I bought you a home-warming gift."

"Housewarming gift!" he corrected me. "What you got?"

"A cake pan and a fancy measuring cup—for your cheesecake."

"I almost made a cheesecake today," he said, briefly spinning the measuring cup, then putting it to the side.

I had secretly hoped there would be cheesecake.

As if to welcome me Bruce turned on the TV. "News 12 The Bronx" blasted from his big flat-screen TV. All the windows were covered with blinds and curtains, and we sat in the dim artificial light oozing from two table lamps with plastic-covered shades. "There's no view," Bruce explained about his windows. "I should have doubled up the curtains, so it looks more fuller." The walls were caked with beige paint. Facing the TV was a big table situated right next to a black velvety couch. "You learn from your mistakes," he commented. He bought the table for the kitchen only to realize it didn't fit. There were two pictures in Bruce's living room. A landscape in a golden frame hung by the door. I wondered if it covered up one of the walls' many blemishes. On the table stood a framed photograph, a paper bag with the logo of the Ritz Carlton hotel and a Valentine's card that read, "My heart belongs to you." A friend—"we are just friends, you know. We ain't putting no claims on each other"—gave Bruce the card and a bottle of eau de cologne. She worked at the Ritz Carlton.

I got up to look at the photo. It was a blurry, black-and-white computer printout, crookedly attached to its frame, featuring Bruce's grandmother and her nine sons. The grandmother and seven of her sons were fairly light-skinned. Bruce's father and one of his brothers were so dark-skinned that it looked like someone had erased their features. I was reminded of a photo Angel once shared with me. The picture showed Bruce and Adam hugging in the Castle's computer room. I told him that it was hard to recognize his friends. "You can't take pictures of black people down there," he said.

Adam arrived, and Bruce gave us an official tour. His bed was complete with paisley-covered shams. Adam admired the dark-wood kitchen cabinets. I pointed out the good luck spray on top of the fridge.

"Where you know that kinda stuff from?" Bruce asked, surprised.

"They have it at the botánicas in my neighborhood."

Bruce just stared at me. I was still a mystery to him.

The bathroom needed some work, he said. The bathtub faucet was dripping and the super had yet to come and fix it. We had a look. The faucet actually resembled a miniature waterfall. The toilet wouldn't stop flowing either. Someone had painted over the tiles, and the paint was chipping off. Bruce's sister and his niece had furnished the bathroom with contoured beige rugs and a matching toilet lid cover. A set of red scented candles stood next to the toilet.

We sat down on the couch and ate cake from paper plates. The blaring television competed with the deafening hisses of the radiators. To adjust the temperature Bruce opened the windows. The traffic sounds from Grand Concourse now blended into the cacophony. We faced the TV set, which Bruce had bought for $388 on Black Friday, in awkward silence. *Hillary Clinton in Asia, jewelry infomercials, golf, basketball.*

Adam started talking about the deteriorating atmosphere at the Castle. Tamara was pregnant by one of the residents; two kids went out to smoke and then broke into a car; and "that dude" was always borrowing from him. "What kind of shit is that?" Adam asked without taking his eyes from the TV. Then he fell asleep. The side effects of his chemotherapy included nausea and sudden bouts of fatigue. *Senator Kerry in Syria, a charred body with missing limbs found on top of an apartment building, a fire on Eagle Avenue.*

At first I was surprised to find an entire news channel dedicated to the Bronx, but with each segment it began to make sense. *An empty lot on Westchester Avenue attracted mice and roaches and was a hazard for children exploring. A New York Post cartoon compared Barack Obama to a chimpanzee.* At this point Adam awakened and voiced his outrage. As Adam pulled himself up and out of the depths of the cushiony black velvet, Bruce's phone rang.

"Yo, listen," he said to Pedro, who worked in the Castle kitchen on the weekends. "I've got him gagged up, man. If you want him back, it's gonna cost you. It's gonna cost you big time. I mean, if you don't want him back, I'll just knock him off in the river. I mean, are you gonna pay or what? He's in the bathroom tied up." Bruce chuckled. "I mean, you're not gonna pay? This is what I want you to do. I want you to go to your bank, withdraw all the cash you got on hand, put it in a bag . . . put it in a bag. Look, just shut up and listen. Take the D train to 203 and Bedford Park. You come up, there's a garbage can right there. Put the bag in the garbage can. Don't worry about the FBI, just go to Citibank. So you don't want him back? Yeah, he made it. He made it, Battista. What do you want? You wanna talk to him? Hey, Adam, Pedro Battista wanna talk to you. I'll tell him you won't even pay for him. That's fucked up, that's your friend, too. Yo, you told me to go ahead and kill him. Yeah, Battista won't even pay a ransom for you."

"You got him on the phone?" Adam asked sleepily.

"Yeah. I tell him, go to Citibank," Bruce continued. "I got Adam in the bathroom, and if you want him back go to Citibank, throw all the cash you got on hand, and then take the D train to Bedford Park and dump the cash in there. . . . Don't make me fire you. You'll be on the unemployment line when I fire you. From eleven o'clock to three o'clock. Yeah, I been trying to fix it up the way they want it. You know, I'm even getting help when I need it. Tables around and stuff. Yeah, I gotta let you go. What you cooking for dinner?" Bruce listened for a moment and then hung up.

"What did he cook?" Adam yawned.

"He's making franks and salad," Bruce replied.

Then Bruce and Adam discovered a connection when they began exchanging memories of North Carolina. Adam's son lived in North Carolina, and his late wife, Marietta, was raised there.

Here's how Adam and Marietta had met: While driving down an endless country road with a friend, he saw a girl walking. She appeared like a vision, a hallucination. With nothing around but miles of tobacco, suddenly the beautiful girl appeared by the side of the road. As he got closer he saw that she carried a six-pack of Dr. Pepper. Adam asked his friend to stop.

"What a pretty car you got," said the girl. She must have been around seventeen years old, which made her ten years his junior.

"It's a Cadillac. You live here?"

She got in the car and said, "Drive down near Pete's. Slow down, stop right here." There was a road cutting right through the fields. "I live back up there, three miles."

"Damn," Adam said. "You walk three miles down that way?"

"I had to go a mile to the store!" Bruce interrupted Adam's story.

"I said, 'Three miles to get to the store,'" Adam continued. "Oh, lady!"

Adam and Marietta fell in love, and she moved to New York to be with him. The first time Adam went to North Carolina was for a visit; the next time he went to North Carolina was for a stickup.

Marietta told him that her father worked at a motel and that he saw his boss stashing large amounts of money in his safe.

"I thought, Ohhhhh-oh-oh-oh!" Adam laughed as he remembered.

"Whatever you do, don't hurt my father," Marietta said.

"I'm not gonna hurt nobody," Adam assured her. Marietta's father ran and hid in the closet in fear while Adam stole $17,000 out of the motel safe.

Adam and Marietta returned to New York. They had a son, Adam went to prison, and Marietta left him.

Our visit was nearing its end, and Bruce insisted on walking us to the subway. He carried his keys on a long, blue strap, as if needing to reach locks that were far away. The strap indicated power. Bruce looked like a super.

We decided to take the elevator. When it finally arrived, the doors wouldn't open. Bruce kept pulling and pulling and finally ushered us inside. The smell of urine was overwhelming. "Someone uses this as a bathroom," Adam remarked. I noticed the drawing of a penis on the wall. Bruce saw me looking and said that every time someone defaced the elevator the super painted it over. Always in yellow. Our laughter overpowered the smell.

Grand Concourse had turned from gray to black. The headlights of cars waiting for the traffic light to change shone like little boats in the far distance. We hurried to cross.

On the subway Adam admitted that he wasn't very impressed by Bruce's apartment. He would prefer a smaller space in a nicer area. A nice little studio would do. This brought the sorrow that he held back all afternoon to the surface. Moving in with Leslie wasn't an option, he lamented. Leslie's son-in-law was a "real Muslim" and certainly wouldn't approve of it. Even if Shelter Plus paid 70 percent of his rent, the $700 from Social Security—the survivor benefits he received thanks to Marietta—wasn't enough to cover the remaining 30 percent, to buy food and clothes and pay for electricity, gas, and other necessities. "I am on the cusp," he said. "Right now I'm on the cusp."

Yet again Adam mimicked his inner guardian, who continued to scrutinize every thought he had and every step he took. "Let's go over the limits. What *won't* you do?" he told me. "Drinking muddy waters and sleeping in a hollow log. I won't do that. It would put that gun back into my hand. I'm not going to sleep in a subway. I'm not going to sleep in the gutter. I'm not going to be homeless and be smelling and stinking."

Although Adam was now always aware of his age and knew that he was not as strong and flexible as he used to be, it sometimes crossed his mind to plan another stickup. The money and carelessness of others provided, theoretically at least, opportunities for him.

"What opportunities come to mind?" I asked.

It was hard to hear Adam's faint voice through the train's rattling. I was surprised at how far his plan had progressed and how concrete it sounded. Several times a week a white, unmarked truck came by his work to pick up the money from a candy vending machine. He had recently recognized the truck in a quiet residential street and saw the drivers unloading containers into an inconspicuous garage. The subway was right nearby, so he wouldn't even need a car. Besides, he was an old man, and who would suspect an old man of robbing a garage? Any witnesses might be more likely to help him carry his loot down the subway stairs. To execute his plan without a partner had the added advantage of ensuring that no one could snap and turn the robbery into a bloody nightmare. Adam himself would never kill. He wouldn't even carry a gun, let alone pull the trigger.

Clearly, Adam could *imagine* committing another crime, but I asked myself whether his imagination had any connection to reality. Fantasies were as much a part of his life as were practical demands. I couldn't help but wonder whether they served as a release valve when the potential reality of being down and out became too painful to endure. There was always this very last way out. I remembered him saying, "If I had to do life, I could do it." Having faced freedom, prison was no longer a threat.

Adam always had to take everything into consideration. He had to play through every possible scenario. How could he not at least reserve some space in his imagination for the life of crime he had left behind? Adam knew that he could never shed his past, but it didn't mean that he would actually act on his thoughts.

CHAPTER TWENTY-ONE

On Guard

Bruce now worked two jobs. On weekdays, for seven hours a day, he worked as an aide in the kitchen of the original Castle, where he cleaned appliances, served hot food, and prepared sixty bologna and turkey sandwiches for the residents. On Fridays and Saturdays between 11:00 p.m. and 7:00 a.m., Bruce sat on a plastic chair by the side of the road wearing an orange security vest, guarding the construction site of "the new Castle." Altogether he worked fifty-one hours a week. At ten dollars an hour he made a little over $2,000 per month before taxes. Needless to say, he did not receive any benefits. What remained after taxes could barely cover the bills. At least for the time being, a car, one of Bruce's dreams, was out of the question.

Yet Bruce was officially "rehabilitated." He had a home and a job and had managed to stay out of prison. As I approached him half an hour before midnight on July 3, 2009, Bruce looked hopelessly sleepy. He was talking on his cell phone. It was a balmy night, two years and one month after his release from prison. Small groups of men hung out on the corner of Broadway and 140th Street. Women sat on stoops rocking infants in strollers and on laps, while young children threw firecrackers in anticipation of the Fourth of July.

"Gotta go now," Bruce abruptly said into the phone and hung up.

"A friend," he said to me, secretive as always. "Just a friend."

Bruce's social life was now limited to his cell phone. When he got home at night or early in the morning, he ate, watched TV, went to sleep, ate, and then watched more TV until it was time to go back to work. He always emphasized how much he enjoyed arriving back at his apartment, closing the door and being by himself.

I, too, worked at least fifty hours a week, but my time and his were entirely different. Decision making, which was required on the outside on a daily basis, still seemed to take a lot out of Bruce. He mentioned it as one of his primary struggles each time we met. He was still struck hard by certain aspects of freedom, such as the exorbitant electricity bill that accompanied his new air conditioner and the table he couldn't get into his kitchen.

Although he said a bad day outside topped a good day in prison, Bruce complained about how boring his new security job was. He also thought the construction company that hired him on Fortune's recommendation could at least have provided him with a trailer and a TV set. When it was raining he had to sit inside the ghostly, unfinished building. When he was cold, the only source of warmth was a jacket. On the other hand, he reasoned, these days you had to be grateful to have a job at all. Most people he knew from the Castle who had their own apartments worked at least two jobs to make a living. I remember Bruce telling me during his job readiness class at Fortune two years before how he would like to work as a janitor at night in an empty office building. With nobody there to look over his shoulder, he could be his own boss. But being his own boss had turned out very differently from what he had imagined.

On weekend nights Bruce sat between wooden barricades, a locked-up trailer reserved for construction workers in front of him, a porta-potty behind him, 140th Street on his left, and the new Fortune Academy complex on his right. A tattered newspaper and a couple of empty coffee cups lay at his feet. Whenever he began nodding off, he would read the paper and pace around. Every hour or so he walked along the plywood wall that protected the construction site. Each day he could see the building growing like bamboo. The residents frequently commented on the speed at which construction progressed and eagerly talked about the prospective rooftop garden but rarely mentioned the building's green features. With 114 living units spread out over 110,000 square feet and 11 floors, the building would provide housing for low-income residents in the community and ex-convicts. Its green elements—including solar shades above each window, energy-efficient appliances, low-flow plumbing fixtures, additional insulation, a green roof, and a rainwater harvesting system—set an example for urban apartment building.

I asked Bruce whether he would like to move into the new Castle once it was completed.

"I would like to, but no one said nothing to me, so I don't know," he said. "It would be nice, you know. I like this area over here with the park and everything. That whole riverside area is nice. We'll see what happens once it goes up." It didn't occur to him that he might have to secure a spot before the building was finished.

A loud bang startled me. Fireworks possibly. A rivulet from the construction site formed on the street. A hose leaking upstairs, Bruce reasoned.

I had brought some homemade food to share with him.

"What's that?" he asked, unwrapping his piece.

"Rhubarb cake."

"What's that?"

"I'm not sure if it's a fruit or a vegetable. It's tart."

"A vegetable? Is it Jewish?"

"Jewish? No, why?"

"'Cuz you said 'ruba.'"

"No, it's German."

"It looks like bread pudding."

"That's the whole wheat."

No comment. He took a bite. "It needs more sugar. It's not sweet." He chewed and took a second bite. "Nah," he said, shaking his head. "Nah." He flung the piece of cake onto the street and laughed.

"How come your husband lets you go out this late to do an interview?" he asked.

"He knows that it's part of my job."

"Yeah?" He laughed.

"Why? Does that surprise you?"

"Yeah." He laughed some more. "It surprises me he doesn't make you change your job. You are out this late doing an interview?" He paused. "With an ex-felon? I mean, you have no fear being out this time a night with a uh . . . uh . . . uh . . . an ex-felon?"

"No, not with you. Why? Should I?"

"I mean, you shouldn't be. But most people would be. I mean, at a construction site with a, you know, a felon."

"I could tell you about a couple of ex-felons from the Castle that I wouldn't visit at a construction site late at night."

He cracked up. He could hardly calm himself down. His whole body quivered.

"Why are you laughing?" I asked.

"I didn't know there's someone at the Castle that make you feel like that. Shady characters, huh?"

"What do you think? Do you think it's weird that I would be sitting here with you?"

"I mean, knowing my crime, you know, I thought that would create a barrier where you would keep it in certain areas where we could be monitored. You never know what's going on in a person's mind."

"No, you don't," I agreed. "But judging from your crime, I would imagine that you wouldn't harm a woman."

"No, I wouldn't." He frowned.

I told him about a situation I had recently found myself in that made me uncomfortable. Looking for a quiet public place to interview a man who responded to an ad I had posted for an audio feature, I chose a little recording studio at NYU. The place was a small, windowless, soundproof room. The man I was interviewing stank. He clearly hadn't washed or brushed his teeth for a long time. Despite being eloquent and apparently educated, he was cranky and fidgety. Without pausing for a breath, he went off on tangents about things that barely related to my questions. I could sense his aggression boiling under the surface. Then I realized that if he snapped, no one outside would be able to hear me scream. For the first time in my career I was scared. I mentioned to Bruce that the man was a white sound technician his age.

"Yeah?" Bruce seemed surprised.

Furthermore, the guy later emailed me to ask me out for a date.

"Did it ever occur to you to do something to a woman?" I asked Bruce.

"Nah. I don't have no kinds of thoughts. I just find it strange that you would trust me like this. Knowing my crime. Most people, once they find out my crime, before they even get to know me, they put up a barrier."

"Most people don't differentiate between murder and murder?" I asked.

"Yeah, murder is murder. I had a lady telling me one time, she don't care. 'If you killed somebody, it shows a mind-set.' I don't agree with that. She said it shows you are capable of killing because you are sick. I don't agree with that. You can get into certain situations, you get into an altercation. That don't show that this person has the ability to kill. I believe there is different levels of everything."

I agreed. Bruce and I went through a couple of examples. Was it worse to kill your own children by driving drunk? Or was it worse to kill after getting into a fight with an adult who had a chance to back off but continued provoking? One was considered manslaughter, the other one murder, and the latter could get you a considerably longer sentence.

What I found more interesting, though, was how Bruce had internalized the stigma of his status. Our society never allowed ex-convicts to truly "pay their debts." They always remained convicts. Society's judgment was so powerful that it had an ex-felon convinced he couldn't trust himself.

It was time for Bruce's hourly security walk along the plywood wall from trailer to porta-potty and back. Bruce yawned and moaned as he got up from his chair to stretch his boney legs. He still had another five hours ahead of him. We walked toward Broadway. Someone had scribbled "Remember Jesus" on the last plywood panel behind the toilet. "Remember Jesus," Bruce slowly read. He shook his head and made his way back to his plastic chair.

Epilogue

It is July 2011, roughly four years after Angel, Bruce, and Adam were released from prison, as I make my way up to the Castle. Adam now has a studio apartment at Castle Gardens, Fortune's new, green complex for housing ex-cons and other low-income people from the community. Castle Gardens was finished in the summer of 2010. Adam meets me downstairs in the slick, new reception area and whisks me upstairs to his studio. The apartment is "not much bigger than a cell," he notes, but it is bright and clean and looks out on a little rooftop garden where he is planning to grow some vegetables. Adam still loves plants. That's why I got him an orchid as a housewarming gift. He breaks out into excited laughter when I hand it to him. He thanks me profusely, carefully chooses a spot on his windowsill, and decides we should go to our old haunt, Cove, the restaurant down below Riverside Drive.

Adam is off parole. "I'm starting to lose my self-consciousness," he tells me. Now the victims of his crime "visit" him less often, and his inner guardian is beginning to withdraw. He was declared healthy after his most recent cancer checkup, and his relationship with Leslie is prospering. The couple doesn't want to live together because they consider themselves too set in their ways. But they go to events and keep each other company. Every week Adam "Googles up" all the free concerts in the city. Just yesterday he went to Shakespeare in the Park. Technically, Adam works part-time, but in reality he works *all* the time. He connects soon-to-be-released prisoners with outside services and lectures about alternatives to incarceration programs, about how to "treat" people in the streets instead of locking them up. His work and his apparent struggle garner Adam respect among other community advocates.

Once we sit down and order food, Adam's mood suddenly darkens.

"I am not truly happy out here," he says. Sometimes, at social gatherings, he suddenly has to leave. "You don't spend twenty-five years in prison and not lose things," he tells me. "[Outside] it is hard to do what is expected from you." Adam often gets lonely. "Everything I know was behind that door. There's times where I wish I was back."

Adam did go back to prison for a while to do advocacy work inside, but he was soon denied access because the authorities found out that he had an attempted escape on his record. (For the first time he tells me that he paid a correctional officer at Rikers Island to bring in a steel blade to cut the bars.)

Adam still sometimes feels like a stranger in this world. Not that it would be impossible to overcome this pain. "If I lived long enough to confront that whole thing about being happy, maybe it would change," he says. "All these dreams . . . ," he continues. "So much is missing. It ain't what it's supposed to be."

"Where you at?" Bruce shouts into the phone.

"I'm just two minutes away," I shout back.

"Good enough," Bruce screams and hangs up.

I said I would meet him at the Castle at 8:00 a.m., when he finishes his night shift.

Bruce lost his job as a security guard at the Castle construction site. The company fired all the security guards it had hired from Fortune, after one of the other guards went inside the building and fell asleep. But Bruce was lucky. He was soon picked up again by the Fortune Society and offered a job as a residential aide. He now makes fifteen dollars an hour. From midnight to early morning he sits at the reception desk, answering phones and assisting residents. Sometimes one of the residents has a seizure. Then Bruce needs to call an ambulance. If the man refuses to go to the hospital, Bruce has to put him on a cot near his workstation and watch over him. The phone rings all night. Homeless people call trying to find a place to sleep. Bruce has to explain to them that the Castle has a specific intake process, which involves a lengthy, face-to-face interview, among other things. It is still hard to get a bed at the Castle.

Bruce is not allowed to watch TV while he works, and there is little diversion aside from Adam's nightly visits. Each morning at two o'clock Adam embarks on his daily exercise walk. Often he stops at the reception desk to say hello to Bruce.

On our way to the coffee shop around the corner, Bruce and I pass a group of residents.

"We're getting married," Bruce chuckles, pointing at me. With his freshly shaved head, the smile on his face, and his checkered shirt he looks dapper and happy.

"But you told me I'm gonna be your best man," a toothless man jokes back.

At the new coffee shop on Broadway Bruce barks at the shy waitress.

"A roll with egg and bacon!" The waitress whispers that she has neither bacon nor rolls. Ciabatta, bagels, or baguette are Bruce's options.

"But what you gonna put on it?" he asks.

Eventually he settles for a bagel with egg.

"Shoot!" he says to me.

"Are you happy?"

Looking back to where he came from, Bruce thinks that he's doing okay. He didn't relapse and didn't get himself into "an altercation." It's a day-to-day struggle but he's making the best of his situation. He has an apartment, a job, and a car—"a treat to myself," he calls it. He lives from paycheck to paycheck. This summer he only turns on the air conditioner when the heat becomes unbearable. He still doesn't have a dog, because a dog, he says, is like a child, and he still has enough to work out with his two grown sons. While his one son has forgiven him for his crime, the other one still holds it against him. "You did nothing for me," Bruce quotes him saying.

In his spare time Bruce goes to a sports bar across from Yankee Stadium to meet friends—"no girlfriends, just friends," he says as always. He doesn't drink, he doesn't smoke, and he doesn't volunteer any information about his past. "I go in, have a good time, and leave for home."

Most important, perhaps, Bruce isn't afraid of himself anymore. "I don't jump the turnstile; I don't pick up nothing that doesn't belong to me; I keep a job. If I get into an altercation, I move on. A lesson learned. The first one could have been avoided. I used to think I could do it again, but I can't do it again."

"Do what again?" I ask.

"Kill someone."

Bruce says he hardly thinks about his crime anymore. The longer he stays out, the better it gets. At work he suddenly noticed people who were more mentally torn up than he was. He says it helps him to compare himself with others who are "more fucked up."

"I accumulated too much to lose it now," he explains.

"The more people accumulate through their own making the more they try to hold on to it," I say. "Was that why you committed crimes when you were young?"

"Yeah, I didn't have nothing. I was out trying to get something. [But] I had no sense of direction. I'd get it and spend it."

On our way out Bruce hits his head on the door. Hard. He rubs his head but barely flinches. This must have happened a hundred times before. As always he insists on seeing me off at the subway. I still need to use the bathroom, and Bruce suggests a McDonald's down the street. He guards the restroom because the door doesn't lock. Then he drops me off at the train station. "You a'ight?" He asks as always.

I am all right. I've changed much in the five years since I first met Bruce, Angel, and Adam. I have learned that judgment is one of the easiest but least interesting ways to look at another human being. The deeper I dug, the more complex the men's stories became, and the harder I found it to judge them. Of course I needed to look at their pasts and understand what propelled them to commit their crimes, but to understand who they have become— whether they are worthy of redemption and forgiveness—I had to focus on their present.

If it weren't for the mirrored cop shades, I wouldn't have recognized Angel. As he approaches the subway station in downtown Brooklyn, I see that he has exchanged his suit and tie for swimming trunks, tennis socks, sandals, a straw hat, and a T-shirt with an American flag on it. He grabs my tape recorder and immediately bursts into chatter. He speaks fast and without transitions. Maybe it is the stifling heat—almost one hundred degrees at ten o'clock in the morning—but I can hardly follow his train of thought. Here is what I gathered from the recording: Angel studies public administration at John Jay College for Criminal Justice, a college that doesn't hesitate to accept ex-offenders; he may work in Albany once he graduates; he is also in the process of creating his own business, a place called Breathing Space, for ex-cons and others who need time and space to work on their potential. (He later explains that Breathing Space already exists and that it only hired him as a consultant.) He says he got a real estate company to donate two acres of land ("an agreement among gentlemen"). Angel's voice is getting louder and louder, and he seems to have forgotten all about me. "Put them to work on a project that they want to [do]," he says about his future clients. "Whatever it is. You stick a key in them and then you watch them go. . . . If someone wants to start a business, a taxi business, we might buy them a medallion." He then trails off into green technology, which he also wants to implement at Breathing Space, and into hiking trails for tourists. When I show my confusion about his disparate plans, he adds a writers' residency. "I was thinking of you," he says. "That time you went to that, that, you know . . . " I try to finish his thought but can't get a word in. He asks about my husband. I tell him he just got a new job, but he interrupts me, saying that Breathing Space will soon have a much better job for him. He then starts on something about "converting a car alternator into a vertical solar system" and of "plastic bottles and bicycle wheels to catch wind and run the ceiling fan in the bathroom." He chuckles. "Nice engineering stuff to keep a boy busy."

On our way back to the subway Angel tells me, "I decided to become a Republican. I'm from the thinking faction of the Republican Party. Government money is enabling bad social behavior in some respect." I am surprised. After all, Angel, Bruce, and Adam all depended on government support when they were first released. The Fortune Society depends on government support. The Castle depends on government support. What happened to Angel's feelings about New York's former Republican governor, the "quite dangerous" Pataki? Then I remember that Adam told me that Angel had married Tanya, the hospice nurse who had given him the Digiwalker, credit card, and cell phone. She took him off of government care and pays for much, if not all, of his living expenses while he goes to school.

"But what about the crime?" I ask him. Angel stalls for the first time since we met.

"Live your life as a reflection of the life you've taken," he says.

"Like, make amends?" I try.

"Lessen the opportunity for that tragedy to happen to somebody else. I feel bad for both sides. I threw a big rock into a pot, and it echoed and a lot of rings came out of that. Now I'm calming the pool, throwing positive rings. . . . Those waves have the potential to reach more, to reach the ends of that pot."

I am reminded of Brooke, the Quaker woman in Rochester, and her impersonal forgiveness speech. *Pebbles in the pockets, a boulder on the shoulder.*

"Did you forgive yourself?"

"At some point you have to forgive yourself and move on in a direction that is worthy because I'm living for two people," Angel says. "My life has to honor [that of my victim]." I understand but don't see how this notion is reflected in Angel's life.

Things become a bit clearer when I ask Angel whether he has heard from Adam recently. Angel doesn't understand why Adam still suffers. "He could go to Florida," he says, "lay on the beach and fan his *cojones*." Instead he chooses to "shake the tree and see what falls out and talk about it. Let's look under the lawn and expose the worms to the light of the day."

I guess I'm more of a tree-shaker and worm-exposer like Adam. I like asking complex questions and am okay with ambiguous answers.

As I write this, I am reminded of what my friend Franzi said after the Castle's Halloween event: "The only one the murderer could really apologize to—and who could forgive him—is the victim. But the victim is dead." Her comment expressed the hopelessness of the situation. "There is a cycle in the aftermath of murder. It never concludes. One morning you wake up and *Boom!* it is back."

Can a murderer ever be rehabilitated? What does freedom *feel* like after two or three decades in prison? Can we forgive Bruce, Adam, and Angel and welcome them back into our world? Have they become better human beings? These were the questions that guided this book. They have served as the point of departure, an attempt to open up a much-needed dialogue.

I don't think that genuine rehabilitation is possible without a person's desire to change—and without the *capability* to transform. But I am also aware that not everybody possesses this capability. Rehabilitation at heart is an effort, an ongoing process. It revolves around the notion of true remorse, of being able to see, really see, what you have done.

"Are you remorseful?" I ask Richard Robles, the "Career Girl Murderer" and Quaker whom I met at Attica prison, in one of my letters.

"What is remorse?" he counters. Richard says he has thought about the issue quite a lot. Nightmares of the murders? Education, work, and therapy? Helping others? "Is that remorse?" he asks.

There are no instruments to measure true remorse the way criminologists measure a program's efficiency in terms of recidivism. This is what makes Richard's question tricky. "Everyone feels and expresses remorse in different ways. If they regret what they did and/or wouldn't do it again, if there was a rewind button they could push, if there was such a thing like a rewind button . . . " There is none.

But Richard is right. There are different ways of feeling remorse. Each person's path to (and understanding of) rehabilitation is unique. Adam faced up to his crime to an almost debilitating degree. He had internalized it. The victims *visited* him in his cell. They told him to devote his time to "acts of contrition," and Adam established the lifer programs. He helped other prisoners by passing on his knowledge about introspection, self-awareness, empathy, and the intricacies of human interaction.

Bruce said he will "carry" his crime for the rest of his life. He will always remember the victim's name and not "put it on God." To carry the burden was his responsibility. All Bruce wanted was a job (preferably during the day), a place for himself, and a car. "I accumulated too much to lose it now," he said. The tide had turned and the perks of freedom were outnumbering its detriments. Yet he continued to carry his crime. This made Bruce appear strong and honest.

Angel was determined to leave his past behind long before he was released. Fortune, the Quakers, and the media readily absorbed his sustained narrative of rehabilitation: "Brutal Childhood Turns Innocent Boy into Killer" and "Prisoner Turns Productive Member of Society." He had a job, went back to school, got married, found support among the Quakers, and has managed to stay out of prison. To Fortune and the Quakers he was a poster boy of successful rehabilitation. While this was certainly one way to read his story, it was important to me to show that his story was far more complex than that.

When we talk about remorse and rehabilitation, we need to remember the impact some individuals made on Bruce, Adam, and Angel—people who refused to judge the men based on their crimes, people who didn't give up on them. For more than a decade the Quakers have listened to Angel. They listen in a way that no one ever listened before. Angel's friend Mae said she *trusted* him. She might have been the first person ever to trust Angel. "He clearly had become a different person from the young, immature and impulsive kid I first met at the Brooklyn House of Detention," she said in an e-mail. "He had paid for his crime and deserved to be free. I felt he had a lot to offer to society, and that he must not be presenting himself adequately to the Parole Board or they would have granted him parole (naive perhaps in retrospect)."

Bruce had Ms. Bracy, the "older black lady with [the] good heart that really cared for black men." Ms. Bracy sat him down and talked to him. She, too, listened. She told him he should admit to his crime and to "go think" in his cell. Bruce did a lot of silent thinking in his cell. He cooked, worked out, and reflected on his crime. Over time he began to understand why he acted the way he did.

Adam made friends with reverends and group leaders from the outside. At night he conversed with his victims. "They had told me, 'Listen, when you are truly sorry, when you really make amends for what you did and your life is on the path of true forgiveness, when you feel more about helping other people than yourself, we don't come back no more,'" Adam remembers. Yet he painfully discovered that it is impossible to make up for the two lives his accomplice took. Adam finds relief from his burden while helping others, but at night, when he is by himself, the tormenting thoughts reappear.

Neither legislation nor society delivers cohesive guiding principles that define what a murderer could or should do to be forgiven and allowed back into the community. But this might be the reason behind America's tough-on-crime stance. We block people with criminal records from housing and employment to avoid facing their burden—emotionally and intellectually. We don't allow them to vote to keep them from having any say on the decisions that affect their lives. Behind those barriers hide complex moral questions: Have Angel, Bruce, and Adam become better human beings? Are we ready to welcome them back into society? What steps are we willing to take to help Adam, Angel, and Bruce in their endeavors?

Currently ex-offenders receive help primarily from other ex-offenders and from religious and reentry institutions. While the work of these institutions is certainly admirable, it is also inherently limited and flawed. Reentry organizations are instrumental but lack the "luxury" of dealing with a murderer's past. Their work is anchored in the here and now and tied to immediate constraints: time, space, patience, energy, human resources, and money. (The reality is that the phone at the Castle rings all night long. The reality is that between 30 and 50 percent of parolees are homeless.)[1]

The reality is also that these reentry organizations are having a hard time helping ex-offenders emancipate themselves from the institutional world. Many of their clients never cross over into the mainstream but remain caught within the hermetic cycle of the reentry scene.

Religious groups provide comfort. Although they may demand regret, they rarely deal with the causes of violent behavior. God is forgiving; no man is beyond redemption. This notion is as noble as it is naive—as if redemption could be achieved without facing the chain of events that led up to the crime. Scientific research has shown that criminal behavior originates from various factors; treatment has to be administered in accordance with them. It is only once we understand the individual cycle that we can try to break it.

In 2012 more than half a million prisoners were released back into our world. I hope that Adam's, Angel's, and Bruce's stories will make them more visible. I hope you will now see them as they ride the bus wearing clunky, outdated glasses and pants two sizes too big; sweep city streets wearing the blue "Ready, Willing and Able" uniform of the Doe Fund (another prominent reentry organization); get off the Q100 bus at Queens Plaza, looking jumpy and confused; cross the street erratically; bristle when bumped on the subway; struggle at the ATM machine . . .

INTRODUCTION

1. Heather C. West et al., "Prisoners in 2009," *Bureau of Justice Statistics*, Dec. 2010, 4, http://bjs.ojp.usdoj.gov/content/pub/pdf/p09.pdf.

2. Patrick A. Langan and David J. Levin, "Recidivism of Prisoners Released in 1994," *Bureau of Justice Statistics*, June 2, 2002, http://bjs.ojp.usdoj.gov/index.cfm?ty=pbdetail&iid=1134.

3. West et al., "Prisoners in 2009," 27.

4. Upon request, some of the names of the book's subjects have been changed.

5. See Ted Conover, *Newjack: Guarding Sing Sing* (New York: Random House, 2000); and Alex Kotlowitz, *There Are No Children Here: The Story of Two Boys Growing Up in the Other America* (New York: Doubleday, 1991).

6. Chris Mitchell, "The Killing of Murder," *New York Magazine*, Jan. 7, 2008, http://nymag.com/news/features/crime/2008/42603/index5.html.

7. For readers interested in the public-policy dimension that led to the mass incarceration and disenfranchisement of African American men over the last decades, see Michelle Alexander, *The New Jim Crow: Mass Incarceration in the Age of Colorblindness* (New York: New Press, 2010).

8. Francis T. Cullen and Cheryl Lero Jonson, *Correctional Theory: Context and Consequences* (Los Angeles: Sage, 2012), 148.

9. Ibid., 29.

10. David J. Rothman, *The Discovery of the Asylum: Social Order and Disorder in the New Republic* (Boston: Little, Brown, 1971).

11. Alexis M. Durham, *Crisis and Reform: Current Issues in American Punishment* (Boston: Little, Brown, 1993), 47-48.

12. Cullen and Jonson, *Correctional Theory*, 28, 29.

13. Ibid., 32.

14. Robert Martinson, "What Works? Questions and Answers about Prison Reform," *Public Interest* 35 (spring 1974): 25, www.nationalaffairs.com/public_interest/detail/what-worksquestions-and-answers-about-prison-reform.

15. Ted Palmer, "Martinson Revisited," *Journal on Research in Crime and Delinquency* 12 (1975): 133-52.

16. Edward Latessa and Alexander M. Holsinger, eds., *Correctional Contexts: Contemporary and Classical Readings*, 4th ed. (New York: Oxford University Press, 2011), 204.

17. Cullen and Jonson, *Correctional Theory*, 125, 126.

18. Patrick A. Langan et al., "Historical Statistics on Prisoners in State and Federal Institutions, Yearend 1925-86," *Bureau of Justice Statistics*, May 1988, 14, www.ncjrs.gov/pdffiles1/digitization/111098ncjrs.pdf.

19. Pew Center on the States, "One in 31: The Long Reach of American Corrections," March 2009, 4, www.pewstates.org/uploadedFiles/PCS_Assets/2009/PSPP_1in31_report_FINAL_WEB_3-26-09.pdf.

20. Christopher Glazek, "Raise the Crime Rate," *N+1*, Jan. 26, 2012, http://nplusonemag.com/raise-the-crime-rate. Glazek based many of his findings on Alexander's *The New Jim Crow*.

21. Cullen and Jonson, *Correctional Theory*, 11, 158.

22. Edward J. Latessa, Francis T. Cullen, and Paul Gendreau, "Beyond Correctional Quackery—Professionalism and the Possibility of Effective Treatment," *Federal Probation* 66, no. 2 (Sept. 2002): 43-49, http://tinyurl.com/79luut4.

23. Don A. Andrews, "The Principles of Effective Correctional Programs," in Latessa and Holsinger, *Correctional Contexts*, 228-37, 228.

24. Cullen and Jonson, *Correctional Theory*, 169, 120.

25. See David P. Farrington and Brandon C. Welsh, *Saving Children from a Life of Crime: Early Risk Factors and Effective Interventions* (New York: Oxford University Press, 2006).

26. See Sabine Heinlein, "Of Rehab and Reintegration," *City Limits*, April 23, 2007, www.citylimits.org/news/articles/3313/of-rehab-and-reintegration (which includes excerpts from interviews with Devah Pager, Jeremy Travis, Edward Latessa, Glenn Martin, and Ronald Mincy, five of the country's leading experts on ex-offender rehabilitation).

CHAPTER 1. FREEDOM DAY

1. Spatial Information Design Lab, "The Pattern: Million Dollar Blocks," Graduate School of Architecture Planning and Preservation, Columbia University, 2008, www.spatialinformationdesignlab.org/publications.php?id=84.

2. Pew Center on the States, "One in 31: The Long Reach of American Corrections," March 2009, 4, www.pewstates.org/uploadedFiles/PCS_Assets/2009/PSPP_1in31_report_FINAL_WEB_3-26-09.pdf.

3. AVP (the Alternative to Violence Project) is a program that was developed by prisoners and by the Quakers at Green Haven Prison in 1975; see www.avpusa.org/.

4. Washington State Institute for Public Policy, "Evidence-Based Juvenile Offender Programs: Program Description, Quality Assurance, and Cost," June 2007, 2, www.wsipp.wa.gov/rptfiles/07-06-1201.pdf.

5. Sean Kirst, "Doing Time on the License-Plate Line," *Syracuse Post-Standard*, July 18, 2010, www.syracuse.com/news/index.ssf/2010/07/doing_time_on_the_license-plat.html.

CHAPTER 3. STREET CODE

1. Corcraft, "Who We Are," www.corcraft.org/webapp/wcs/stores/servlet/WhoWeAreView?langId=-1&storeId=10001&catalogId=10051.

2. Carl P. Malmquist, *Homicide: A Psychiatric Perspective* (Washington, DC: American Psychiatric Press, 1996), 7–17.

3. Elijah Anderson, *Code of the Street: Decency, Violence, and the Moral Life of the Inner City* (New York: Norton, 2000), 33, 72.

4. Ibid., 33–34.

5. U.S. Department of Justice, "The Code of the Street and African-American Adolescent Violence," Feb. 2009, 4, www.ncjrs.gov/pdffiles1/nij/223509.pdf.

CHAPTER 4. TALKING MURDER

1. From Angel Ramos's unpublished poem "What Do I Owe You?"

2. John Lewis, "Nab Youth in Slaying," *Daily News*, March 15, 1978.

CHAPTER 7. JOB READINESS

1. FEGS Health & Human Services, "WeCARE," www.fegs.org/html/welfare_to_work/wecare.html.

2. Robert Martinson, "What Works? Questions and Answers about Prison Reform," *Public Interest* 35 (spring 1974): 25, www.nationalaffairs.com/public_interest/detail/what-worksquestions-and-answers-about-prison-reform.

3. In 1975 Ted Palmer refuted Martinson's study. See Ted Palmer, "Martinson Revisited," *Journal on Research in Crime and Delinquency* 12 (1975): 133–52. Cognitive-behavioral programs have been particularly successful in reducing recidivism rates. See Mark W. Lipsey and Nana A. Landenberger, "The Positive Effects of Cognitive-Behavioral Programs for Offenders: A Meta-analysis of Factors Associated with Effective Treatment," *Journal of Experimental Criminology* 1 (2005): 451–76.

4. See excerpts from interviews with Devah Pager, Jeremy Travis, Edward Latessa, Glenn Martin, and Ronald Mincy, five of the country's leading experts on ex-offender rehabilitation, in Sabine Heinlein, "Of Rehab and Reintegration," *City Limits*, April 23, 2007, www.citylimits.org/news/articles/3313/of-rehab-and-reintegration.

5. U.S. Department of Labor, "Workplace Violence," www.osha.gov/SLTC/workplaceviolence/.

CHAPTER 11. CAUSALITIES

1. J. D. Hawkins et al., "Predictors of Youth Violence," *Juvenile Justice Bulletin*, April 2000, 2, www.ncjrs.gov/pdffiles1/ojjdp/179065.pdf.

2. For more information on criminogenic risk factors, see Francis T. Cullen and Cheryl Lero Jonson, *Correctional Theory: Context and Consequences* (Los Angeles: Sage, 2012), 165–68; and Edward J. Latessa, Francis T. Cullen, and Paul Gendreau, "Beyond Correctional Quackery—Professionalism and the Possibility of Effective Treatment," *Federal Probation* 66, no. 2 (Sept. 2002): 43–49, http://tinyurl.com/79luut4.

3. One Cambridge study found that a child's (criminal) future depends on the number of risk factors he or she is exposed to. The percentage of youths convicted of violent crimes rose from only 3 percent for those with no risk factors to 31 percent for those with four risk factors (namely, low family income, large family size, low nonverbal IQ at ages eight through nineteen, and poor parental child-rearing behavior). See Hawkins et al., "Predictors of Youth Violence," 7; and David P. Farrington, "Early Prediction of Violent and Nonviolent Youthful Offending," *European Journal on Criminal Policy and Research* 5 (1997): 51–66.

4. Alfred Blumstein, "Youth Violence, Guns, and the Illicit-Drug Industry," *Journal of Criminal Law and Criminology* 86, no. 1 (1995): 15–18, www.saf.org/lawreviews/blumstein1.htm.

5. "Saving wayward children from a life of crime is really a policy that extends correctional rehabilitation to the earlier years in life. It is based on the sound criminological insight that we should not sit by and wait for troubled youths to commit illegal acts that place them behind bars" (Cullen and Jonson, *Correctional Theory*, 173).

CHAPTER 14. WAITING FOR NOTHING

1. William K. Rashbaum, "Fund-Raiser for Pataki Faces Charges," *New York Times*, Dec. 16, 1999, www.nytimes.com/1999/12/16/nyregion/fund-raiser-for-pataki-faces-charges.html.

CHAPTER 16. SILENT FORGIVENESS

1. George Fox and Jessamyn West, *The Quaker Reader* (New York: Viking, 1962), 47.

2. Thomas D. Hamm, *The Quakers in America* (New York: Columbia University Press, 2003).

3. See Larry J. Siegel, *Criminology*, 9th ed. (Toronto/Belmont: Thomson, 2006), 594.

CHAPTER 17. LIES AND GOOD LUCK

1. Patrick A. Langan and David J. Levin, "Recidivism of Prisoners Released in 1994," *Bureau of Justice Statistics*, June 2002, 1, http://bjs.ojp.usdoj.gov/content/pub/pdf/rpr94.pdf.

2. NELP (National Employment Law Project), "Criminal Records and Employment," www.nelp.org/site/issues/category/criminal_records_and_employment/.

3. Ibid.

4. Devah Pager and Bruce Western, "Discrimination in Low-Wage Labor Markets: Evidence from an Experimental Audit Study in New York City," http://paa2005.princeton.edu/download.aspx?submissionId=50874.

CHAPTER 18. SEX, LOVE, AND RACE

1. See New York State Division of Criminal Justice Services, "Alternative to Incarceration (ATI) Programs," www.criminaljustice.ny.gov/opca/ati_description .htm.

CHAPTER 19. FROM ATTICA TO BROADWAY

1. Jim Dwyer, "Four Ex-Convicts Tell of Lives Lost and Found," *New York Times*, July 19, 2008, www.nytimes.com/2008/07/19/nyregion/19about.html.

2. Andy Webster, "From Prison to Freedom, and Telling Their Tales," *New York Times*, April 28, 2008, http://theater.nytimes.com/2008/04/28/theater/reviews/28cast.html.

3. "The Castle," *Curtain Up*, 2008, www.curtainup.com/castle08.html.

4. Leonard Jacobs, "Theater: Passing the Prison Bar," *New York Press*, Sept. 3, 2008, http://nypress.com/article-18733-theater-passing-the-prison-bar.html.

5. Webster, "From Prison to Freedom, and Telling Their Tales."

6. " 'The Castle' Off Broadway & Promoting Successful Prisoner Re-entry," *Tom Duane in the Neighborhood*, July 25, 2008, http://blip.tv/mnn-community-affairs/the-castle-off-broadway-form-the-fortune-society-1120029.

EPILOGUE

1. Kendall Black and Richard Cho, "New Beginnings: The Need for Supportive Housing for Previously Incarcerated People," Common Ground Community/Corporation for Supportive Housing, May 2004, 6, http://documents.csh.org/documents/pubs/full_new_beginnings.pdf.

"Adjusting to Life beyond Bars." *Talk of the Nation*. National Public Radio. Feb. 26, 2008.

Agee, James, and Walker Evans. *Let Us Now Praise Famous Men: Three Tenant Families*. 1941. Boston: Houghton Mifflin, 2001.

Alexander, Michelle. *The New Jim Crow: Mass Incarceration in the Age of Colorblindness*. New York: New Press, 2010.

Anderson, Elijah. *Code of the Street: Decency, Violence, and the Moral Life of the Inner City*. New York: Norton, 2000.

Andrews, Don A. "The Principles of Effective Correctional Programs." In Latessa and Holsinger, *Correctional Contexts*, 228-37.

Black, Kendall, and Richard Cho. "New Beginnings: The Need for Supportive Housing for Previously Incarcerated People." Common Ground Community / Corporation for Supportive Housing. May 2004. http://documents.csh .org/documents/pubs/full_new_beginnings.pdf.

Blais, Madeleine. "Arithmetic of Need." *Washington Post Magazine*, June 7, 1992, 7-19.

Blumstein, Alfred. "Youth Violence, Guns, and the Illicit-Drug Industry." *Journal of Criminal Law and Criminology* 86, no. 1 (1995): 15-18. www.saf.org/ lawreviews/blumstein1.htm.

Bly, Nellie, et al. *Ten Days in a Mad-House*. New York: Munro, 1887. Kindle edition.

Boynton, Robert. *The New New Journalism: Conversations with America's Best Non-fiction Writers on Their Craft*. New York: Vintage, 2005.

Butterfield, Fox. *All God's Children: The Bosket Family and the American Tradition of Violence*. New York: Knopf, 1995.

Capote, Truman. *In Cold Blood*. New York: Random House, 1966.

Carrère, Emmanuel. *The Adversary: A True Story of Murder and Deception*. London: Bloomsbury, 2000.

"The Castle." *Curtain Up*, 2008. www.curtainup.com/castle08.html.

"'The Castle' Off Broadway & Promoting Successful Prisoner Re-entry." *Tom Duane in the Neighborhood*. July 25, 2008. http://blip.tv/mnn-community-affairs/the-castle-off-broadway-form-the-fortune-society-1120029.

Conover, Ted. *Newjack: Guarding Sing Sing*. New York: Random House, 2000.

Cooke, Marvel. "The Bronx Slave Market." 1950. In Kerrane and Yagoda, *The Art of Fact*, 252–58.

Corcraft. "Who We Are." www.corcraft.org/webapp/wcs/stores/servlet/WhoWeAreView?langId=-1&storeId=10001&catalogId=10051.

Cullen, Francis T., and Cheryl Lero Jonson. *Correctional Theory: Context and Consequences*. Los Angeles: Sage, 2012.

Dash, Leon. *Rosa Lee: A Mother and Her Family in Urban America*. New York: Plume, 1997.

Durham, Alexis M. *Crisis and Reform: Current Issues in American Punishment*. Boston: Little, Brown, 1993.

Dwyer, Jim. "Four Ex-Convicts Tell of Lives Lost and Found." *New York Times*, July 19, 2008. www.nytimes.com/2008/07/19/nyregion/19about.html.

Ehrenreich, Barbara. *Nickel and Dimed: On (Not) Getting by in America*. New York: Metropolitan, 2001.

Evans, Jeff. *Undoing Time: American Prisoners in Their Own Words*. Boston: Northeastern University Press, 2001.

Fadiman, Anne. *The Spirit Catches You and You Fall Down: A Hmong Child, Her American Doctors, and the Collision of Two Cultures*. New York: Noonday, 1998.

Farrington, David P. "Early Prediction of Violent and Nonviolent Youthful Offending." *European Journal on Criminal Policy and Research* 5 (1997): 51–66.

Farrington, David P., and Brandon C. Welsh. *Saving Children from a Life of Crime: Early Risk Factors and Effective Interventions*. New York: Oxford University Press, 2006.

Feldman, Adam. "Con Artist: Veteran Prisoners' Rights Activist David Rothenberg Opens the Doors to *The Castle*." *Time Out New York*, April 23–29, 2008.

Flynn, Jim. *Stranger to the System: Life Portraits of a New York City Homeless Community*. New York: Curbside, 2002.

Foucault, Michel. *Discipline and Punish: The Birth of the Prison*. New York: Vintage, 1977.

Fox, George, and Jessamyn West. *The Quaker Reader*. New York: Viking, 1962.

Frazier, Ian. *Great Plains*. New York: Farrar, Straus and Giroux, 1989.

Gates, Henry Louis. *Thirteen Ways of Looking at a Black Man*. New York: Random House, 1997.

Glazek, Christopher. "Raise the Crime Rate." *N+1*, Jan. 26, 2012. http://npluso nemag.com/raise-the-crime-rate.

Griffin, John Howard. *Black Like Me*. 1961. New York: Penguin, 1976.

Hamm, Thomas D. *The Quakers in America*. New York: Columbia University Press, 2003.

Hawkins, J. D., et al. "Predictors of Youth Violence." *Juvenile Justice Bulletin*, April 2000. www.ncjrs.gov/pdffiles1/ojjdp/179065.pdf.

Heinlein, Sabine. "Of Rehab and Reintegration." *City Limits*, April 23, 2007. www .citylimits.org/news/articles/3313/of-rehab-and-reintegration.

Jacobs, Leonard. "Theater: Passing the Prison Bar." *New York Press*, Sept. 3, 2008. http://nypress.com/article-18733-theater-passing-the-prison-bar.html.

Kapuściński, Ryszard. *The Emperor: Downfall of an Autocrat*. San Diego: Harcourt Brace Jovanovich, 1983.

Kerrane, Kevin, and Ben Yagoda, eds. *The Art of Fact: A Historical Anthology of Literary Journalism*. New York: Scribner, 1997.

Kidder, Tracy. *Strength in What Remains*. New York: Random House, 2009.

Kirst, Sean. "Doing Time on the License-Plate Line." *Syracuse Post-Standard*, July 18, 2010. www.syracuse.com/news/index.ssf/2010/07/doing_time_on_ the_license-plat.html.

Kotlowitz, Alex. *There Are No Children Here: The Story of Two Boys Growing Up in the Other America*. New York: Doubleday, 1991.

Krakauer, Jon. *Into the Wild*. New York: Anchor, 1997.

Kramer, Jane. *The Last Cowboy*. New York: Harper and Row, 1977.

Kramer, Mark, and Wendy Call. *Telling True Stories: A Nonfiction Writers' Guide from the Nieman Foundation at Harvard University*. New York: Plume, 2007.

Langan, Patrick A., and David J. Levin. "Recidivism of Prisoners Released in 1994." *Bureau of Justice Statistics*, June 2, 2002. http://bjs.ojp.usdoj.gov/content/pub/pdf/rpr94.pdf.

Langan, Patrick A., et al. "Historical Statistics on Prisoners in State and Federal Institutions, Yearend 1925–86." *Bureau of Justice Statistics*, May 1988. www.ncjrs.gov/pdffiles1/digitization/111098ncjrs.pdf.

Lareau, Annette. *Unequal Childhoods: Class, Race, and Family Life*. Berkeley: University of California Press, 2003.

Larson, Erik. *Lethal Passage: The Story of a Gun*. New York: Vintage, 1995.

Latessa, Edward J., Francis T. Cullen, and Paul Gendreau. "Beyond Correctional Quackery—Professionalism and the Possibility of Effective Treatment." *Federal Probation* 66, no. 2 (Sept. 2002): 43–49. http://tinyurl.com/79luut4.

Latessa, Edward J., and Alexander M. Holsinger, eds. *Correctional Contexts: Contemporary and Classical Readings*. 4th ed. New York: Oxford University Press, 2011.

LeBlanc, Adrian Nicole. *Random Family: Love, Drugs, Trouble, and Coming of Age in the Bronx*. New York: Scribner, 2003.

Lewis, John. "Nab Youth in Slaying." *Daily News*, March 15, 1978.

Lipsey, Mark W., and Nana A. Landenberger. "The Positive Effects of Cognitive-Behavioral Programs for Offenders: A Meta-analysis of Factors Associated with Effective Treatment." *Journal of Experimental Criminology* 1 (2005): 451–76.

Listwan, Shelley Johnson, et al. "How to Prevent Prisoner Re-entry Programs from Failing: Insights from Evidence-Based Corrections." *Federal Probation* 70, no. 3 (Dec. 2006): 19–25.

Mailer, Norman. *The Executioner's Song*. New York: Little, Brown, 1979.

Malcolm, Janet. *The Journalist and the Murderer*. Vintage, 1990.

Malmquist, Carl P. *Homicide: A Psychiatric Perspective*. Washington, DC: American Psychiatric Press, 1996.

Martinson, Robert. "What Works? Questions and Answers about Prison Reform." *Public Interest* 35 (spring 1974): 22–54. www.nationalaffairs.com/public_interest/detail/what-worksquestions-and-answers-about-prison-reform.

McGinniss, Joe. *Fatal Vision*. New York: G. P. Putnam Sons, 1983.

Mitchell, Chris. "The Killing of Murder." *New York Magazine*, Jan. 7, 2008. http://nymag.com/news/features/crime/2008/42603/index5.html.

Mitchell, Joseph. *Joe Gould's Secret*. 1965. New York: Modern Library, 1996.

Monkkonen, Eric H. *Murder in New York City*. Berkeley: University of California Press, 2001.

NELP (National Employment Law Project). "Criminal Records and Employment." www.nelp.org/site/issues/category/criminal_records_and_employment/.

New York State Division of Criminal Justice Services. "Alternative to Incarceration (ATI) Programs." www.criminaljustice.ny.gov/opca/ati_description.htm.

Orlean, Susan. *The Orchid Thief: A True Story of Beauty and Obsession*. New York: Random House, 1998.

Orwell, George. *Down and Out in Paris and London: A Novel*. New York: Harcourt Brace Jovanovich, 1961.

Pager, Devah, and Bruce Western. "Discrimination in Low-Wage Labor Markets: Evidence from an Experimental Audit Study in New York City." Princeton University. Submission to the Population Association of America Annual Meetings, 2005. http://paa2005.princeton.edu/download.aspx?submissionId=50874.

Palmer, Ted. "Martinson Revisited." *Journal on Research in Crime and Delinquency* 12 (1975): 133–52.

Pew Center on the States. "One in 31: The Long Reach of American Corrections." March 2009. www.pewstates.org/uploadedFiles/PCS_Assets/2009/PSPP_1in31_report_FINAL_WEB_3-26-09.pdf.

Price, Richard. *Clockers*. New York: Perennial, 1992.

Rashbaum, William K. "Fund-Raiser for Pataki Faces Charges." *New York Times*, Dec. 16, 1999. www.nytimes.com/1999/12/16/nyregion/fund-raiser-for-pataki-faces-charges.html.

Riis, Jacob A. *How the Other Half Lives: Studies among the Tenements of New York*. 1890. New York: Dover, 1971.

Rothman, David J. *The Discovery of the Asylum: Social Order and Disorder in the New Republic*. Boston: Little, Brown, 1971.

Sante, Luc. *Low Life: Lures and Snares of Old New York*. New York: Farrar, Straus and Giroux, 1991.

Sereny, Gitta. *Cries Unheard: The Story of Mary Bell*. London: Macmillan, 1998.

Sheehan, Susan. *Is There No Place on Earth for Me?* Boston: Houghton Mifflin, 1982.

———. *A Prison and a Prisoner*. Boston: Houghton Mifflin, 1978.

Shipler, David K. *The Working Poor: Invisible in America*. New York: Vintage, 2005.

Siegel, Larry J. *Criminology.* 9th ed. Toronto/Belmont: Thomson, 2006.

Simon, David. *Homicide: A Year on the Killing Streets.* New York: Ballantine, 1991.

Spalding, Linda. *Who Named the Knife: A Book of Murder and Memory.* New York: Pantheon, 2007.

Spatial Information Design Lab. "The Pattern: Million Dollar Blocks." Graduate School of Architecture Planning and Preservation, Columbia University, 2008. www.spatialinformationdesignlab.org/publications.php?id=84.

Stuntz, William J. *The Collapse of American Criminal Justice.* Cambridge, MA: Belknap of Harvard University Press, 2011.

Toupin, Laurie. "The Journalism of Empathy." Poynter.org. March 2, 2011. www.poynter.org/uncategorized/3679/the-journalism-of-empathy/.

U.S. Department of Justice. "The Code of the Street and African-American Adolescent Violence." Feb. 2009. www.ncjrs.gov/pdffiles1/nij/223509.pdf.

U.S. Department of Labor. "Workplace Violence." www.osha.gov/SLTC/workplaceviolence/.

Vollmann, William T. *Poor People.* New York: Harper Perennial, 2008.

Washington State Institute for Public Policy. "Evidence-Based Juvenile Offender Programs: Program Description, Quality Assurance, and Cost." June 2007. www.wsipp.wa.gov/rptfiles/07-06-1201.pdf.

Webster, Andy. "From Prison to Freedom, and Telling Their Tales." *New York Times,* April 28, 2008. http://theater.nytimes.com/2008/04/28/theater/reviews/28cast.html.

West, Heather C., et al. "Prisoners in 2009." *Bureau of Justice Statistics,* Dec. 2010. http://bjs.ojp.usdoj.gov/content/pub/pdf/p09.pdf.

Wideman, John Edgar. *Brothers and Keepers.* New York: Houghton Mifflin, 2005.

Williams, Terry M. *The Cocaine Kids: The Inside Story of a Teenage Drug Ring.* Reading, MA: Addison-Wesley, 1989.

Wolfe, Tom. *Radical Chic & Mau-Mauing the Flak Catchers.* New York: Bantam, 1970.

Wolfe, Tom, and E. W. Johnson. *The New Journalism.* New York: Harper and Row, 1973.